A *Kairos* Moment for Caribbean Theology

A *Kairos* Moment for Caribbean Theology

Ecumenical Voices in Dialogue

Edited by
GARNETT ROPER
and
J. RICHARD MIDDLETON

☙PICKWICK *Publications* · Eugene, Oregon

A *KAIROS* MOMENT FOR CARIBBEAN THEOLOGY
Ecumenical Voices in Dialogue

Copyright © 2013 Wipf and Stock Publishers. All rights reserved. Except for brief quotations in critical publications or reviews, no part of this book may be reproduced in any manner without prior written permission from the publisher. Write: Permissions. Wipf and Stock Publishers, 199 W. 8th Ave., Suite 3, Eugene, OR 97401.

Pickwick Publications
An Imprint of Wipf and Stock Publishers
199 W. 8th Ave., Suite 3
Eugene, OR 97401

www.wipfandstock.com

ISBN 13: 978-1-60899-999-6

Cataloguing-in-Publication Data

A kairos moment for Caribbean theology : ecumenical voices in dialogue / edited by Garnett Roper and J. Richard Middleton

xx + 222 p. ; 23 cm. Includes bibliographical references.

ISBN 13:: 978-1-60899-999-6

1. Theology—Caribbean area. 2. Christianity—Caribbean area. 3. Ecumenical movement. I. Title.

BR640 K25 2013

Manufactured in the U.S.A.

Scripture quotations marked NRSV are taken from the New Revised Standard Version Bible, copyright 1989, Division of Christian Education of the National Council of the Churches of Christ in the United States of America. Used by permission. All rights reserved.

Scripture quotations marked NIV are taken from the Holy Bible, New International Version®, NIV®. Copyright © 1973, 1978, 1984, 2011 by Biblica, Inc.™ Used by permission of Zondervan. All rights reserved worldwide. www.zondervan.com The "NIV" and "New International Version" are trademarks registered in the United States Patent and Trademark Office by Biblica, Inc.™

Scripture quotations marked GNT are taken from the Good News Translation® (Today's English Version, Second Edition) Copyright © 1992 American Bible Society. All rights reserved.

Scripture quotations marked NAB are taken from the *New American Bible, revised edition* © 2010, 1991, 1986, 1970 Confraternity of Christian Doctrine, Washington, D.C. and are used by permission of the copyright owner. All Rights Reserved.

For Jamaica Theological Seminary

and for Ashley Smith—

On half a century of serving the Caribbean Church

Contents

Foreword – Gosnell L. Yorke / ix
Preface – Garnett Roper and J. Richard Middleton / xiii
List of Contributors / xvii

PART 1: CONFIGURING CARIBBEAN THEOLOGY

1 The Caribbean as the City of God: Prophetic Possibilities for an Exilic People / 3
   —GARNETT ROPER

2 Language and Identity in Caribbean Theology / 20
   —ERICA CAMPBELL

3 The Significance of Forgiveness and Reconciliation for Personal and Corporate Relationships / 40
   —ASHLEY SMITH

4 Dingolayin': Theological Notes for a Caribbean Theology / 49
   —ERIC G. FLETT

PART 2: INTERPRETING THE BIBLE IN THE CARIBBEAN

5 Ashley Smith, Carnival, and Hermeneutics: Reflections on Caribbean Biblical Interpretation / 75
   —ORAL A. W. THOMAS

6 Islands in the Sun: Overtures to a Caribbean Creation Theology / 79
   —J. RICHARD MIDDLETON

7 Jesus' Healing of the Paralytic: Luke 5:17–26 and the Jamaican Church / 96
   —DAVID PEARSON

8 *Kairos* and Kingdom / 112
—STEPHEN M. CLARK

PART 3: THE CHURCH IN THE CARIBBEAN

9 Can Jamaica Be Restored? / 129
—LAS G. NEWMAN

10 Evangelicalism as a Sociological Phenomenon? A Movement in Search of a Caribbean Identity / 141
—DELANO V. PALMER

PART 4: CARIBBEAN THEOLOGY AND THE POLITICAL SPHERE

11 Constructing an Egalitarian Society: Women, Social Ethics, and the Policy Imperatives of Michael Manley's "Justice as Equality" / 165
—ANNA KASAFI PERKINS

12 Ideology, Religion, and Public Policy in Jamaica / 182
—RONALD G. THWAITES

PART 5: THE RELEVANCE OF CARIBBEAN THEOLOGY

13 Caribbean Theology: A Failed Project? / 191
—DEVON DICK

14 The Continuing Relevance of a Caribbean Theology / 200
—BURCHELL K. TAYLOR

Bibliography / 211

Foreword

IN 1985 A GROUP of concerned Christian theologians and pastors in South Africa produced a well-crafted statement called the *Kairos Document*. This document was a thoughtful Christian response to the prolonged and unconscionable contravention of the human rights of a majority of South Africans. The target of this document was apartheid, at that time the "Babylon" of oppression (or *down*pression, in Jamaican Rasta talk). The architects of apartheid felt it was biblically grounded and entirely in keeping with the divine will. For that reason, apartheid emerged in South Africa as a state-supported system buttressed by the legal, economic, academic, and political machinery of the privileged and the powerful. For the authors of the *Kairos Document*, however, apartheid was a heretical distortion of the gospel. In their judgment a turning point had come in the life of the nation; and the *Kairos Document* was testimony that such blatant and violent violation of human rights, in the name of both God and country, could no longer be countenanced.

As the Greek word *kairos* suggests, the 1985 document came at the right or proper time. This was not unlike what the apostle Paul was driven to declare to the Romans. Writing to Jew and Gentile alike, and pointing to those living in the shadow of the *Pax Romana* (the so-called Peace of Rome, the *down*pressor in his time), Paul wrote: "at just the right time [*kairos*], when we were still powerless, Christ died for the ungodly" (Rom 5:6; NIV).

As Rachel Baard explains: "The concept of *kairos* indicates an awareness that a particular moment in time is filled with revelatory meaning in which the church is called to reexamine its theology and praxis." She further affirms that a *kairos* theology is not abstract, but concrete, situational, or contextually grounded.[1]

The volume before us, with the key term *kairos* in its title, clearly alludes to the momentous time of democratic change or transformation in

---

1. Baard, "Responding to the *Kairos* of HIV/AIDS," 368–69.

apartheid South Africa. Unlike the South African situation, however, the call for emancipation in the contemporary Caribbean is now induced by the unrelenting hurricane-like winds of globalization and its attendant forces and structures. Such winds and forces are "huffing and puffing" throughout the region, seeking to deprive Caribbean peoples of that fullness of life that the gospel offers in Christ.

The liberation or emancipation the gospel brings goes beyond the private, psychological, and spiritual transaction between "savior and sinner" to one which is far more public in scale and scope. Such liberation or emancipation encompasses also the economic, academic, ethical, environmental, sociolinguistic, and political domains of life. Moreover, it is a liberation or emancipation that cannot be confined to the church as a confessing community, but that ought to reverberate throughout the public square represented by the Caribbean community as a whole. This is why the chapters that make up this excellent volume are so wide-ranging in their reach. The contributors grapple with issues that cannot be limited to a privately spiritual and/or psychological realm, but extend to the socio-political, economic, and environmental arenas.

The scope of the gospel also has another implication, beyond even the explicit focus of these essays. Although the majority of the chapters focus the reader's attention on the Anglophone sector of the Caribbean, with Jamaica and the Republic of Trinidad and Tobago foregrounded, the discussion cannot be limited to these lands. Indeed, similar issues are relevant to the Francophone, Hispanophone (Spanish-speaking), and Nederlanderphone (Dutch-speaking) Caribbean as well.

I propose that Jamaica, and Trinidad and Tobago—two island-nations in the sun, immersed in the sea, and surrounded by the sand—constitute a *pars pro toto* (part for the whole). They represent the much larger and richer multilingual and multicultural rainbow-like region we call the Caribbean.

Granted, the precise geographical borders and boundaries of the Caribbean continue to be matters of debate. For some, the region goes beyond the islands, and also takes in pieces of the Central and South American mainland, as in the case of Belize, Guyana, and Suriname. In terms of the demographic profile of the Caribbean, the region also covers a whole spectrum of skin shades or a veritable "multitude of skins."

In spite of the lack of consensus regarding the precise cartographical configuration of the region, and amidst the diversity characterizing Caribbean peoples—whether religious, denominational, ethnic, complexional, or cultural—it is the common socio-historical experiences of a Europe-driven West African slave trade that binds most of us together. This was a slave trade in which our ancestors were dragged "kicking and screaming" from

Foreword

the Motherland of Africa to the various sugar and cotton plantations of the Americas in order to contribute to the overdevelopment of Europe, and later America.

Further, the existential reality informed by colonialism and neo-colonialism in the case of all of us—whether we are descendants of slaves from Africa, indentured servants from Asia, or some other people group from elsewhere—place us "in the same boat" as a proud and independent Caribbean people. These shared experiences justify using the two relatively larger Anglophone island-nations of Jamaica, and Trinidad and Tobago, as a synecdochic representation of the region of some 16 million inhabitants or so.

Like latter-day heirs of the children of Issachar (the biblical character of 1 Chron 12:32), the contributors to this volume seek to read and interpret the times in light of the gospel as we find it encoded in the Bible, the church's book. They seek to articulate the desire and determination of Caribbean peoples to be free from all those sins and systems that function to keep them down. For these authors, the gospel is that which makes possible a meaningful encounter between Christ and the Caribbean such that a better quality of life can be lived in the here-and-now—in joyful anticipation of that much more abundant life which, in Christ, is yet to come.

For these reasons, I would encourage the reader to be engaged by each of the contributors in this volume. They write from both "at home" and in diaspora. In each case, they attempt to say the right thing at the right time (*kairos*) within the context of an emerging Caribbean Christian theology and within a postcolonial framework.

I heartily commit this volume to the reader's thoughtful and prayerful consideration. I do so with the ardent hope that it will help to spur all readers on to meaningful transformation, whether in thought, word, or deed, and in both the church and the Caribbean as a whole.

Gosnell L. Yorke

Preface

Lewin Williams, the late President of the United Theological College of the West Indies, called the 1980s the lost decade. Williams was lamenting the paucity of output by Caribbean theologians and their failure to continue the early impact of Caribbean theology on the process and agenda of Caribbean self-determination and self-definition.

It was partially to reflect on and remedy this situation that a Forum on Caribbean Theology was held at the Jamaica Theological Seminary (JTS) in Kingston, Jamaica in January 2010, a date that marked the fiftieth year of the Seminary's continuous engagement with theological education in Jamaica and the Caribbean.

Jamaica Theological Seminary is sponsored by the Missionary Church in Jamaica. It is an institution that, since 1960, has trained clergy for evangelical and Pentecostal churches throughout the Caribbean. It also trains guidance counselors and social workers. This volume of essays (and the Forum from which the essays stem) is significant because it signals a deliberate step toward greater ecumenism and also because, by it, JTS is taking a self-conscious step towards a deeper engagement in Caribbean theology. The evangelical tradition out of which JTS emerged has typically been wedded to the universal themes in the Bible, to the detriment of a more contextual orientation. Many JTS alumni and faculty, however, are outstanding contributors to the Caribbean theology movement, and some of them presented papers at the Forum, while others have contributed papers to this volume, along with friends of the Seminary.

Five contributors to this volume have a direct association with Jamaica Theological Seminary. Garnett Roper and J. Richard Middleton were students together at JTS in the 1970s. Roper, who has been a pastor and communicator (through various public media) on social and religious issues in the Caribbean, is now President of JTS; Middleton is an Old Testament scholar, currently serving as Professor of Biblical Worldview and Exegesis at

Preface

Northeastern Seminary in Rochester, NY. Delano Palmer is Deputy President, Erica Campbell is Head of the Department of Humanities, and David Pearson is Acting Academic Dean and Head of the Department of Biblical and Theological Studies—all at Jamaica Theological Seminary.

This *kairos* moment in Caribbean theology mentioned in the title of this volume is now being seized because of the urgent demand for a prophetic voice in, and theological impact on, the Caribbean development agenda. The problem of violence, which has reached proportions beyond levels associated with civil war, in places like Jamaica and Trinidad and Tobago (among others), demands clarity and compassion, and is an opportunity to give moral leadership in the region.

The Forum took place just a few days after a massive earthquake measuring seven on the Richter scale destroyed the Haitian capital of Port-au-Prince, killing hundreds of thousands of people and displacing one and a half million in total. Port-au-Prince suffered immense damage, leaving twenty-six million square feet of rubble on the ground. The catastrophe called attention to the developmental crisis in Haiti, as well as to the vulnerability of the Caribbean region to environmental disaster. Environmental shocks in the Caribbean merely complicate the vulnerability to economic shocks and the deep problems of Caribbean economies.

The Forum was conscious of the historical legacy bequeathed by our foremothers and forefathers who struggled against oppression and injustice, and overthrew slavery and colonialism. It was also impelled by reading strategies that appropriately engage reader response and that interpret the Bible from the Caribbean world in front of the text. This volume of essays is therefore in pledge of a future of consistent articulation from Caribbean voices in pursuit of building just and responsible societies in the region.

The Forum also celebrated the work of Caribbean theologian Ashley Smith on the occasion of his retirement, in the fifty-fifth year of his ordination. Ashley Smith was ordained a minister of the Presbyterian Church, now the United Church of Jamaica and the Cayman Islands, in May 1955. He has been a pastor, ecumenist, educator, and theologian of distinction. His contribution through his teaching, editing of the *Caribbean Journal of Religious Studies*, presidency of UTCWI, and books, *Real Roots and Potted Plants* and *Emerging from Innocence*, has been seminal. Ashley Smith has also been the spiritual advisor for former Jamaican Prime Minister Michael Manley. Themes covered in this *Festschrift* are some of those that Ashley Smith articulated and clarified over a lifetime.

In part 1 of this book, four essays lay out fundamental themes of Caribbean theology. Garnett Roper sets the table with a theological analysis of the nature of Caribbean socio-historical realities, leading to a

Preface

programmatic call for the contribution of Caribbean theology to building a just Caribbean society, while Erica Campbell explores the relationship of identity and language in the Caribbean, concluding with an articulate plea, rooted in the gospel, for the validity of Caribbean creoles. Ashley Smith draws on his immense pastoral experience to show the power of forgiveness and reconciliation in both personal and corporate relationships, while Eric Flett utilizes the Trinidadian concept of *dingolayin'* to sketch a vision for Caribbean reflection on the nature of God, creation, and humanity.

Part 2 consists of essays that address biblical interpretation in the Caribbean, beginning with Oral Thomas's reflections on Carnival as a model for how Caribbean Christians may interpret Scripture. J. Richard Middleton then suggests the value of biblical creation theology for Christian discipleship in the Caribbean, followed by David Pearson's exegesis of the healing of the paralytic in Luke 5 and its relevance to issues facing the Jamaican church. Finally, Stephen Clark aptly summarizes the nature of the kingdom of God in the Gospels and its application to the present *kairos*.

Part 3 directly addresses the church in the Caribbean. The first essay was originally a public address delivered by Las Newman at the 2010 Jamaican Prayer Breakfast, which confronts head-on the immense problems of Jamaican society and offers hope rooted in the God of Scripture. This is followed with a comprehensive analysis by Delano Palmer of the evangelical movement in the Caribbean, with reflections on a possible direction for evangelical Caribbean theology.

In part 4, the essays turn to the political sphere, first with Anna Perkins's analysis of the social vision and policies of Michael Manley, past prime minister of Jamaica, and their impact on women. Ronnie Thwaites then reflects on the role of ideology as it intersects with biblical faith and public policy in Jamaica.

The volume concludes with part 5, consisting of two essays addressing the continuing relevance of Caribbean theology, by Devon Dick and Burchell Taylor.

It is our hope that these essays are a just a foretaste of what is to come in the years ahead from committed Christian theologians addressing Caribbean realities with the power and relevance of the gospel of Jesus Christ.

Garnett Roper and J. Richard Middleton

Contributors

ERICA CAMPBELL is Head of the Department of Humanities and Lecturer in Humanities, Theology, and Biblical Studies at Jamaica Theological Seminary, Kingston, Jamaica.

STEPHEN M. CLARK is Senior Pastor, Old Cutler Presbyterian Church, Miami, FL, USA. He is the author of *As Good as It Gets: Love, Life, and Relationships: Fifty Days in the Song of Songs* (2010).

DEVON DICK is Pastor of Boulevard Baptist Church, Kingston, Jamaica. He is the author of *Rebellion to Riot: The Jamaican Church in Nation Building* (2002) and *The Cross and the Machete: Native Baptists in Jamaica: Identity, Ministry and Legacy* (2010).

ERIC G. FLETT is Chair of the Christian Studies Faculty and Associate Professor of Theology and Culture, Eastern University, St. Davids, PA, USA. He is the author of *Persons, Powers, and Pluralities: Toward A Trinitarian Theology of Culture* (2011).

J. RICHARD MIDDLETON, an Old Testament scholar, is Professor of Biblical Worldview and Exegesis, Northeastern Seminary at Roberts Wesleyan College, Rochester, NY, USA. He is the author of *A New Heaven and a New Earth: Reclaiming Biblical Eschatology* (2013) and *The Liberating Image: The Imago Dei in Genesis 1* (2005), and is coauthor (with Brian Walsh) of *The Transforming Vision: Shaping a Christian World View* (1984) and *Truth Is Stranger Than It Used to Be: Biblical Faith in a Postmodern Age* (1995).

LAS G. NEWMAN is a church historian and President of the Caribbean Graduate School of Theology (CGST), Kingston, Jamaica. Until his appointment at CGST, he was associate general secretary of the International Fellowship of Evangelical Students, a world evangelical student movement spanning 150 countries.

Contributors

DELANO V. PALMER is Deputy President and Lecturer in Biblical Studies, Jamaica Theological Seminary, Kingston, Jamaica. He is the author of *Messianic 'I' and Rastafari in New Testament Dialogue: BioNarratives, the Apocalypse, and Paul's Letter to the Romans* (2010) and *Romans in Context: A Theological Appreciation of Paul's Magnum Opus* (2011).

DAVID PEARSON is acting Academic Dean and Head of the Department of Biblical and Theological Studies, Jamaica Theological Seminary, Kingston, Jamaica.

ANNA KASAFI PERKINS is Senior Programme Officer, Quality Assurance Unit, University of the West Indies, Mona campus, Kingston, Jamaica. She is the author of *Justice as Equality: Michael Manley's Caribbean Vision of Justice* (2010).

GARNETT ROPER is President and Lecturer in Theology, Jamaica Theological Seminary, Kingston, Jamaica. He is an ordained pastor in the Missionary Church Association, Jamaica and is well-known throughout the Caribbean as a communicator on social, political, and religious issues. He is the author of *Caribbean Theology as Public Theology* (2013) and *This is the Year of Jubilee* (2012).

ASHLEY SMITH, an ordained minister in the United Church of Jamaica and the Cayman Islands, is retired from fifty-five years of service to the Caribbean church, as pastor, ecumenist, educator, and theologian. He has served as President of the United Theological College of the West Indies and editor of the *Caribbean Journal of Religious Studies* and is the author of *Real Roots and Potted Plants: Reflections on the Caribbean Church* (1984), *Emerging from Innocence: Religion, Theology and Development* (1991), and *Pentecostalism in Jamaica: A Challenge to the Established Churches and Society* (1993).

BURCHELL K. TAYLOR is Pastor, Bethel Baptist Church, Kingston, Jamaica, and vice-president of the Baptist World Alliance. His publications include *The Church Taking Sides* (1995), *Saying No to Babylon: A Reading of the Book of Daniel* (2005), and *In God's Presence: Reflections on the Twenty-Third Psalm* (2010). He is regarded as the doyen of Caribbean preachers and an eminent lecturer with special competence in the field of ethics and hermeneutics.

ORAL A. W. THOMAS is Methodist Tutor/Warden and Lecturer in Biblical Studies, Theologies in the Caribbean, and Contextual Theologies, at the United Theological College of the West Indies, Kingston, Jamaica. He is the author of *Biblical Resistance Hermeneutics within a Caribbean Context* (2010).

RONALD G. THWAITES, an Attorney at Law and Deacon of the Catholic Archdiocese of Kingston, Jamaica, has been among the most popular talk-show hosts on Jamaican radio. He is currently a Member of Parliament and the Minister of Education for Jamaica.

GOSNELL L. YORKE is Director of the E. G. White Research Center and Professor of Religion and Bible Translation at Northern Caribbean University, Mandeville, Jamaica. He is the author of *The Church as the Body of Christ in the Pauline Corpus* (1991).

PART 1

Configuring Caribbean Theology

1

The Caribbean as the City of God
Prophetic Possibilities for an Exilic People

GARNETT ROPER

WHAT IS *CARIBBEAN THEOLOGY*? To begin to answer this question we need to acknowledge that the contextual realities of the Caribbean are the starting point of our reflection upon God.[1] Acknowledging these contextual realities requires two fundamental changes from the way theology has been conceived in the Western European tradition. First, we no longer ask the questions that have typically been posed by Western theology; but, beyond that, the interlocutor (the one asking the questions) has changed.

Western theology typically raises questions about whether or not God exists. In some cases, theologians have gone as far as asserting that God is dead. Caribbean theology is not interested in an armchair discussion about metaphysics or ontology, but rather poses questions that are both ethical and existential. It wants to know *what kind of God* is the God that exists.

The interlocutors are not armchair secularists or academics, but are those from below and they are interested in questions of *justice*. The interlocutors are the poor and marginalized, along with the pastors and

---

1. The context for these reflections is Caribbean *Christian* theology.

intellectuals who share an organic connection with the marginalized or a commitment to and solidarity with them.[2] They want to know, therefore, if the God who exists is a just God, or is on the side of justice for those who have been denied justice. Issues of justice are of paramount importance to Caribbean theology.

While Western theology has been concerned to find ways of speaking about God in relation to non-belief, the issue for Caribbean theology is how to speak about God on behalf of, and in relationship with, those who are *non-persons*—that is, those whom the prevailing social order does not acknowledge as persons: the poor, the exploited, those systematically and lawfully stripped of their human status, those who hardly know what a human being is.[3]

Caribbean theology did not originate by the attempt to set out once and for all a system of theology that could be called *Caribbean*. Historically, there has been a tentativeness that, over time, sought to clarify what the project of Caribbean theology entails and requires. No one analysis of the nature of Caribbean theology is therefore right, to the exclusion of all others. Some are more complete than others, some earlier and others later. Caribbean theology is the combination of voices of Caribbean theologians who speak as they see it, as they attempt to come to terms both with the gospel of God in Jesus Christ and with the realities of the lived experience of the Caribbean.

IDENTITY AND SELF-DOUBT IN THE CARIBBEAN— THE CASE OF JAMAICA

Issues of identity arise in all postcolonial societies, and the Caribbean is no different. However, the circumstances of the Caribbean as a whole combine to make the issue of identity *the* central and most profound issue of development and selfhood. The problems of the Caribbean may be economic and political, but at their root is the problem of self-understanding and the difficulty of affirming Caribbean selfhood.

The problems of identity are bound up with the learned, entrenched, and reinforced self-doubt of people of African descent, who form the base of the social pyramid in the Caribbean and are the majority demographic

---

2. Gerald West points out that liberation theology (of which Caribbean theology has great affinity) explicitly addresses the question of the interlocutor. See G. West, "The Bible and the Poor," 130.

3. See the insightful discussion of this issue in Gutiérrez, *Power of the Poor in History*, 57.

grouping. In the case of Jamaica, more than 90 percent of the population is of African descent. Among the black-skinned masses, attitudes still exist that betray a self-contempt and a lack of self-confidence. Rex Nettleford is surely correct: "Herein lies the greatest danger to attempts at finding an identity in terms of race. For a people who do not believe in themselves cannot hope to have others believing in them. The insecurities of this important racial grouping persist with a vengeance."[4]

Nettleford notes that while "the black-skinned Jamaican senses that he must compete on the same ground as his brown (Chinese and Indian) and white compatriots, ... he does not possess such a strong racial memory of great cultural achievements as these European, Chinese and Indian compatriots."[5] Rather, as Nettleford explains, "The Africans, of all the groups which came to the New World, came as individuals and not as part of a group which maintained identity through great religion, or activity through age-old recognizable customs."[6] Instead, all that was original to their culture—the language and customs, the retention of the ancestral past—has been systematically demonized, delegitimized, and discouraged in the new world. Tragically, observes Nettleford, "The obvious answer for the African or black Jamaican is to sink his racial consciousness in the wider, greater aspirations to acquire education and other means of making himself economically viable."[7]

The learned inferiority and self-contempt of African-Jamaicans has been reinforced and entrenched by a complex of factors, including the role of the mass media and religion as agents of cultural penetration. This sense of inferiority was co-existent with and in direct contrast to the popular notion of Jamaica as a multi-racial, harmonious society. Jamaica's ideal of multi-racial nationalism met its fiercest and most positive antagonism from the black activist Rastafarian movement, especially in the 1950s and 60s. Rastafarianism, which combined millenarianism with a revolutionary impulse, arose from within the squatter settlements in West Kingston in the 1930s, building on the teachings of Marcus Garvey as the harbinger of black redemption. Every expression of Rastafari was in protest against the traditional values of what it deemed a Euro-esque society.

Since the 1960s there has been progress in mainstreaming black-skinned Jamaicans. Self-doubt persists, but progress has been made in

---

4. Nettleford, *Mirror, Mirror*, 33.
5. Ibid., 35.
6. Ibid.
7. Ibid.

PART 1: CONFIGURING CARIBBEAN THEOLOGY

deepening a self-understanding among the people at the base of the social pyramid.

IDENTITY AND CREOLIZATION IN THE CARIBBEAN

The second issue that complicates Caribbean identity is its creolization. This refers to the fact that the Caribbean is an immigrant society. The indigenous Taino, Ciboney, and Carib populations were decimated by the early encounters with the Europeans. Africans, who were transported to the Caribbean for slave labor on sugar cane plantations, are the overwhelming majority. White Europeans came as pirates and then as planters, along with elements from the Middle East, including Jews who became the merchant class, later to be succeeded by Chinese and Indians, who originally came as indentured laborers. All these groups, drawn from each major people group in the human family across the globe, have become the melting pot or perhaps better the *pelau* that is the Caribbean.[8] While the non-African population in the Caribbean formed the minority numerically, they have exercised franchise and dominion over the life of the Caribbean people.[9]

There are therefore multiple attractions towards the varied cultures from which the minority people groups in the Caribbean originated, and these cultural influences have tended to dominate Caribbean life. But by far European culture trumped all—at least up to the 1960s. Then, in the second half of the twentieth century, the popular culture of the Caribbean came also to be diluted by North American influences. However, the pull has not always been in one direction only. Carnival and Crop Over in the Eastern Caribbean, for example, are festivals that originated in the planter class seeking to indulge itself in the revelry of the underclass. In these, the unmitigated joy of the underclass was copied by the owning class, in a festival of the flesh. Ironically, then, Carnival and Crop Over are disguises of the overlords disguising themselves as the underclass disguised as the upper class![10]

---

8. *Pelau* is a Caribbean creole cooking tradition (originally from Africa) that involves caramelizing meat till it turns brown.

9. This is more the case of white Europeans, who have been at the top of the social pyramid. The African population is not the majority in Trinidad and Tobago or in Guyana; there the population is divided equally between Afro-Trinidadian and Indo-Trinidadian, and between Afro-Guyanese and Indo-Guyanese.

10. Carnival Costumes originated in the attempt to mimic the "negro gardener" who was disguised and mocking his employer, and flocking without demur or inhibition. At Carnival today, therefore, it is the employer imitating the gardener, imitating him. See CarnivalPower.com, last accessed January 12, 2010, http://www.carnivalpower.com/

The phenomenon of Caribbean migration, with its huge Diaspora in the United Kingdom and the Eastern seaboard of the United States, also provides another source of cultural influence, since Caribbean emigrants also influenced life back home. The Caribbean is, therefore, to a large extent the combination of all these influences. This has resulted in Caribbean art, rhythms, folk wisdom, foods, colors—and more generally patterns of life characteristic of these societies.

There is also a Caribbean historiography, and a Caribbean sociology. What is at issue in both is the telling of the story of the Caribbean from the point of view of the Caribbean. This, however, has only recently (since the 1980s) begun to percolate into Caribbean mass experience as legitimate expressions of our society, rather than being seen as aberrations and distortions.

Caribbean theology in this respect is late in the day. It is playing catch-up with a people that are already ahead of the church's reflection on the society. The church has so far remained tied to the apron strings of Europe and America. It hardly sings in its liturgy anything but the songs from the metropole and, in general, avoids using the vernacular and accent of the Caribbean in its liturgy. Both song and language are imports from the metropole. Caribbean theology therefore needs to rely on the new historiography and the sociology that seek to give account of the social contours that are crucial strands of Caribbean identity.

IDENTITY AND POVERTY IN THE CARIBBEAN

The issue of Caribbean identity is further distorted by the lived experience of persistent poverty in the region. It is the lot and experience of the majority of black-skinned members of Caribbean society that they have not been economically enfranchised—not since they were brought to the region by way of the Middle Passage. Neither have they been compensated for the unpaid labor of their forebears during the three hundred years of their enslavement. For example, they were not given access to land when King George IV signed the Emancipation Act in 1834, nor any time since. Instead, it was the planters who were compensated for the loss of *their* property (the enslaved) to the tune of fourteen million pounds sterling. Nothing that has happened since adult suffrage or political independence has sought to deal with this issue of reparation in any fundamental way.

The doctrine of African inferiority, which was engendered by the culture of enslavement, colonization, and European dominance, has been

history_of_carnival.htm.

PART 1: CONFIGURING CARIBBEAN THEOLOGY

reinforced by the economic circumstances and, in particular, the landlessness of the black-skinned masses. It is fair to say that the Afro-Caribbean people are still waiting, in economic terms, for their year of Jubilee.

Economic disempowerment and economic marginalization have a bearing on the understanding of Caribbean identity. The struggle for the ownership and control of the means of their subsistence is a perennial struggle of Caribbean people. It is fundamentally a struggle to become the masters of their own destiny. A black middle class and a black intelligentsia have emerged over time, but persistent poverty and economic marginalization (with their life-distorting and life-diminishing propensities), have delimited and detoured the struggle to break this glass ceiling. Economic independence and economic mobility among the underclass have so far been elusive dreams.

In this respect Caribbean theology is of necessity concerned with the persistence of domination and discrimination in subtle disguises. It is also concerned to honor and assert indigenous Caribbean cultural forms, and also the neglected and denigrated African cultural retentions. Rastafarianism, Marcus Garvey, and indigenous religious expressions like Myal represent early impulses that Caribbean theology seeks to deepen and explore. Caribbean theology thus locates itself in the intersection between the legacy of life-diminishing and life-distorting realities that are part of the lived experience of the Caribbean, on the one hand, and, on the other, the struggle to assert the new Caribbean person, who is aware of who he/she is and aware of what the world is like.[11]

The Michael Manley political regime of 1970s Jamaica sought to address this issue in a somewhat oblique way with Pioneer Farms and with the National Housing Trust. During the 1990s, the P. J. Patterson administration attempted the Emancipation land project. The first was misconceived and failed to make any substantial gain. The second has been far more effective, though it is rooted in economic gradualism rather than in any clear conception of economic justice. The Emancipation land project has never really got going, for the want of sufficient buy-in by the society. And nothing has happened to build on the early gains in Jamaica of the Baptist free village movement, where land was given to freed slaves by the church.

As Caribbean theology attempts to pursue economic justice for the people of the Caribbean as a whole, it needs the assistance of social analysis, including economists and economic theorists, in analyzing the concrete economic circumstances—and the responses to those circumstances—that obtain in the Caribbean. It needs to deal with the persistence of squatter

---

11. Russell, "Emergence of the 'Christian Black' Concept."

settlements, which have had such a deleterious effect on social life in places like Jamaica, and Trinidad and Tobago, especially in terms of high rates of homicides in both countries.

Ivan Petrella criticizes liberation theology for a lack of institutional imagination; what we need, he correctly explains, is the *historical project* of institutional building. Caribbean theology is necessarily focused on this historical project, which accepts in part Robert Unger's social theory: the historical project, whatever it turns out to be, must include the entrenchment of democracy, the mainstreaming of the masses, and improving the quality of justice and expansion of economic opportunities for the masses.[12]

IDENTITY IN THE SHADOW OF EMPIRE

Religion and the media, as agents of cultural penetration and cultural imposition, have made their fair share of contributions to the distortion of Caribbean identity. Both religion and the mass media have been the agents for the transmission and promotion of the values of the North Atlantic. The issue of identity arises from the fact that the Caribbean is a region in the periphery, or as Burchell Taylor puts it, "in the shadow of empire."[13] As a subject people, Taylor contends, they are reduced to being imitators, never initiators, of what is considered worthwhile. "Their worth and value, the extent to which they are considered worthy of praise and the point at which they will be placed on the scale of civilization and development, are invariably determined by their imitative capability and achievement as a result of it."[14] The general approach from the perspective of the academy or the media, or those who speak about progress and development, has treated people in the shadow of empire as having no real story of their own. It is not thought that they have any significant narrative of their own existence; rather, they are understood in terms of approximating and reflecting (in varying degrees) life at the center of empire. They are no more than clients, conformists, consumers, and imitators. Independent thinking, creative imagination, and cultural realities—with special and significant formative possibilities toward the fulfillment of their true human potential—are discounted, as a rule. What obtains at the periphery—by way of beauty, quality, morality, and value—is judged from the point of view of what obtains at the center.

12. Petrella, *Future of Liberation Theology*, 93–119, is an application of R. M. Unger, *Politics*, to the project of liberation theology.
13. Taylor, "Stepping Out of the Shadow of Empire."
14. Ibid.

PART 1: CONFIGURING CARIBBEAN THEOLOGY

Along with being valued only for their imitative capability, people living in the shadow of empire are often invisible. Their existence is not sharp or clear-cut and they do not have a properly defined identity. They have no real human face or substance. They are therefore open to being stamped with the stereotypical economic and ethnic images chosen by imperial interests. Matters of geographical size, ethnic/demographic composition, economic prosperity, and strategic location are attributed to whole nations and people as their only significance. Such peoples and nations can therefore be overlooked, bypassed, neglected, and disregarded in ways that are harmful to their welfare and well-being. They have no acknowledged identity, save that which is conveniently assigned to them; their importance or lack of importance is determined by their value in relation to imperial interests.

This is the case even in international forums that have a direct bearing on their existence and future; such forums are often conducted without giving them a voice at the table. The role of those living in the shadow of empire is typically to endorse the communiqués written by others who have a significant place at the table.

When people are valued only for their imitative capability, and when their existence is marked by this invisibility, they live with a perpetual identity crisis. This invariably forces them to rely on international experts, consultants, agencies, and media that make assumptions and express definitive opinions about them on the basis of an imposed stereotypical identity. In this regard, the project of a Caribbean theology is both in protest against, and in response to, this persistent identity crisis.

CARIBBEAN THEOLOGY AS EXILIC THEOLOGY

It is helpful to understand Caribbean theology as organized around the metaphor of exile. The sixth-century exile of Israel in Babylon was a defining period for what was to become of the nation of Israel in the post-exilic dispensation. A vigorous nationalism emerged out of the exile, as well as an impetus to develop and mature national conventions and institutions. Despite being a composite and admixture of uprooted peoples from Africa, indentured laborers from Asia, with a residue from Europe and the Middle East, the Caribbean has its own formative and distinctive consciousness. Caribbean theology accepts the metaphor and analogy of the exile as heuristic. The Caribbean is an exilic community.

Caribbean reality is, indeed, shaped in relation, reaction, and response to imperial hegemony and ideology. The metaphor of exile thus helps us recognize this hegemony as Babylon. But the metaphor of exile also suggests

Caribbean resistance to the hegemony and ideology to which the Caribbean has been subject.

The theme of *Babylon* runs through the Caribbean; it was central to the thought of Marcus Garvey, it is used by Rastafarianism, and now provides Caribbean theology with a symbolic deligitimization of those Western values and institutions that historically have exercised control over the masses of the African Diaspora. Referring to Western values and institutions as Babylon implies the view that the Caribbean has never been allowed to settle down and develop in its own interest. From the outset it was organized to sweeten the tables of Europe, to its own detriment. Indeed, Burchell Taylor has pointed out, in a presentation to mark the bi-centennial of the abolition of the slave trade in the Caribbean, slavery still persists in the contemporary world. He says: "This is so both in its grand old forms and also in newer and more modern correlates in varied forms of domination, oppression, exploitation and deprivation, all at the expense of human dignity, rights, destiny and hope. These continue in systemic ways, affecting critical sections of the human family at different times in different places, but for some, at all times and consistently so. This means that abolition of the trade and later forms of the practice do not mean destruction of the reality."[15]

Taylor contends, further, that "free trade," which is one of the modern developments, has been to the disadvantage of the Caribbean, whose forbears were traded as commodities. The power of the governments from the metropole to impose their wills upon the Caribbean peoples has been replaced by their surrogates in transnational corporations and multilateral lending and donor agencies. The terms of trade and the loan conditionality imposed by these surrogates are no less onerous, burdensome, or stringent than the decree and edicts from the British monarch and Parliament during Crown Colony Government. Caribbean theology, therefore, in its attempt to articulate the encounter with, and appropriation of, the redeeming presence of Christ, must not only account for old forms and old foes, but must equally and adroitly unmask their minions and confederates in modern and postmodern guises. In a word, Caribbean theology must account for and respond to domination as a matter of historical record, but must also expose the new configurations of power, with their no less oppressive intentions, since these are part of the new reality of the Caribbean experience.

It is significant that the Forum on Caribbean Theology, of which this essay was the opening presentation, took place on the eve of the signing of a mutual letter of intent that signaled the start of a new borrowing relationship with the International Monetary Fund in Jamaica. The conditionalities

---

15. Taylor, "Abolished but Not Destroyed."

being imposed included a 30 percent drop in earnings in passbook savings rate and pension funds, a 40 percent rise in bus fares, and the liquidation of the national airline of Jamaica. And the precursor to this letter of intent was the imposition of a tax package of J$40B on the Jamaican populace. Having ended the longest borrowing relationship that any nation has ever had with the IMF (lasting from 1979–1995), a mere fourteen years later Jamaica returned to the control of the politbureau that meets in Washington. Babylon thus represents not just the imperial forces (old and new) that have had their way with the peoples of the region; it also represents the force of globalization, and its values and ethos, which has captured the Christian church.

Beyond the *recognition* of Babylon, the symbol or metaphor of exile has been used for the *resistance* that has characterized and defined Caribbean. For the purposes of this essay, the concentration will be on the Caribbean as the "City of God." That is to say, the Caribbean is potentially the antithesis of Babylon. It is the best chance there is at a re-start, and at creating a community that facilitates the best of what makes us human beings.

Bill Watty is among the most enthusiastic, and also one of the earliest, to promote the Caribbean as a special place—the doings of God, which is marvelous in our eyes (Ps 118:23; Matt 21:42; Mark 12:11). He says, "I rejoice that I am Caribbean and have no antiquity. For our culture will be a culture of people and not of things. It will revolve around relationships and not so much around achievements. That's the difference and that's the glory."[16] Watty continues, "Remember your Creator, Caribbean man. Because what has happened to us over the centuries was no accident of history. The Caribbean is a modern miracle. Hardly one-tenth of our ancestors, captured and sold as slaves in Africa, reached these shores. Through those centuries they endured every form of brutality, humiliation, degradation and disorientation. And yet, we have survived to become a unique people."[17]

However, the historic opportunity and uniqueness of the Caribbean are no cause of self-congratulation. Rather, they present a challenge to Caribbean theology to develop a prophetic consciousness and take a prophetic stance towards the Caribbean's propensity to denigrate itself. Caribbean peoples must stand guard as stewards of the rich legacy of resistance, against any reversal. Caribbean theology must position itself in the public square and in the marketplace, to unmask the old foes in their new configurations and disguises, and it must continue the role of advocacy for a more just and

---

16. Watty, "Creator of the Young Culture," 65.
17. Ibid., 66–67.

more equal Caribbean society. It will find that the forces with which it now has to contend are more local than global.

PROPHETIC RESISTANCE TO INJUSTICE

The prophetic stance that is taken by Caribbean theology must first be directed against the legacy of inequality and the outstanding questions of justice that remain. A case in point is Haiti.

The January 12, 2010 earthquake in Haiti confronts us with challenge to our collective conscience as a people and region. How is it that Haiti seems to be able to mount so little defense against this act of nature? The monster earthquake in Haiti claimed 230,000 lives. It is therefore in total human casualties—and as a percentage of total population—one of the largest and most devastating catastrophes in the recent history of mankind. However, some have pointed out that an even greater 8.0 quake in Chile has taken fewer than two hundred lives. That Haiti has been able to mount so feeble a defense against Mother Nature has led some in the Religious Right to spout spurious arguments about a Haitian pact with the devil and the curse of Ham. While these arguments fly in the face of history and reason, they find resonance everywhere that real self-doubt dominates.

Yet this cannot obscure the historical record. Haiti won its freedom in a slave uprising against the formidable army of Napoleon Bonaparte that had conquered Europe. Under the leadership of the Haitian Tousaint L'Oveture and Bookman Dutty from Jamaica, Haitian slaves routed Napoleon's army in a ten-year war (1793–1804) that claimed the lives of 24,000 French soldiers. The result was the first black republic that emerged from the most brutal European colony. This victory was categorically rejected by France, Holland, England, and the USA (despite the revolutionary origins of the American people). The dominant powers in the region immediately blockaded Haiti from trade with the rest of the world, and this blockade lasted until 1825. In that year, broken by the North Atlantic Alliance and the trade blockade, Haiti sought re-admission to participate in international trade and in the international finance system. The North Atlantic alliance agreed, on the condition that Haiti would make reparation for its freedom and independence—the only time in the history of mankind the victor had been made to compensate the vanquished after a military defeat. Imagine if the United States had to make reparations to England for its independence!

A price was placed on very tree, head of cattle, building, and person in Haiti, for a total of one hundred and fifty miliion gold francs. The price was eventually reduced to ninety million gold francs. Today's equivalent is

PART 1: CONFIGURING CARIBBEAN THEOLOGY

US$21.7 billion. Haiti agreed to pay this in annual installments, which it did for the next ninety years, until 1922. The first year, in order to make the initial payment, Haiti had to close all public schools, and they have yet to be completely re-opened. Some years the total annual payment was 70 percent of Haiti's GDP. Talk about structural adjustments! But this systematic impoverishment of the Haitian people was not the whole story. When Haiti was unable to pay, it was invaded by the USA, who installed the brutal dictator Francios Duvalier (papa doc) in 1934; and this dynasty continued with the brutality of his son, Jean Claude (baby doc) Duvalier until 1986, when a popular uprising ousted the regime.

What is obscured by this summary of Haitian history is the role of the oligarchy (mulatoos and whites) that paid subsistent wages to black Haitians, and the role of the militia known as the Tonton Macoutes, who were the enforcers for the political classes and ruling elites. The increasing power of voodoo priests was also tied to the Duvalier dynasty, which gave them political clout.

One of the most savage reversals of progressive efforts was made when the twice democratically elected President Jean Betrand Aristide (a Catholic priest) was exiled to South Africa, right after he got France initially to agree to make restitution to Haiti for its systematic impoverishment. France agreed verbally to make restitution in 2004, and Astride was exiled in 2005. George W. Bush of the USA and his French counterpart shed no tears.

The Haiti whose pain is vividly pictured on the international media, with its depictions of the recent earthquake and its aftermath, began to fall apart long ago. It has crumbled under the weight of oppression by imperial forces, in tandem with internal misrule and exploitation.

Caribbean theology requires some new Moses to say to this Pharaoh, *Let my people go*; some Elijah to stand before another Ahab in this age of Baal and say, *As the Lord lives, before whom I stand*; some Amos to shout, *Let justice roll down like water and righteousness like an ever flowing stream.* Some Isaiah must declare, *Comfort, comfort my people, says our God, for Israel has suffered double for her sins, her long servitude has ended.*

The moment of sadness in the aftermath of the earthquake is therefore a moment of hope. It is a moment to claim the country for God. This is the opportunity to start over; this is the offer of a fresh start. This is the time to arise and build, and Caribbean Christians must play a pivotal role for the sake of our neighbor and our brother, in the name of our God.

We must be unequivocal in our insistence that there has been wrong done to this people. Further, we must acknowledge that it is the lack of resolution of those wrongs that continue to allow this people to be vulnerable to the ravages of nature. And we must reaffirm our brotherhood with them; we must not continue to distance ourselves from them and isolate them with negative criticisms about their culture as a place of backwardness and superstition. Although we should engage in every effort of charitable relief for Haiti after the tragedy of the recent earthquake, this is not a time just for pity and charity, but also for solidarity and fraternity. The words with which the French revolution cemented itself—Liberty, Equality, and Fraternity—must become the watchwords on which we should rebuild Haiti.

PROPHETIC PROTEST AGAINST MISRULE

The prophetic voice must also be raised against internal misrule in the Caribbean. Esther Tyson, a high school principal and regular newspaper contributor in Jamaica, has put the task of the church in the region succinctly and plainly. She says, "The Church in Jamaica is the most powerful non-governmental organization in this nation. There are more churches per square mile in this country than in any other. As a nation, we are in a state of crisis: economically, socially, morally and spiritually. The high levels of crime and violence have affected every aspect of our society. If we are to survive as a people, the Church needs to begin to take a more proactive approach in affecting what is happening in the nation."[18]

Her comments would hold true for the rest of the Caribbean also, and not just Jamaica. However, while she is correct in indicating the deficit in moral clarity in matters affecting the public life of the country, and in demanding greater moral leadership on the part of the church, her comments betray the perspective of Christendom. Great numbers do not equate to being powerful. What is required of the church is not the exploitation of the power of its numbers in order to exert greater influence on the society. What is required is greater truth-speaking to power in the society, at the risk of being marginalized in relation to privileges the church now enjoys. The church must unmask the realities of Caribbean life so that people may understand their context better.

Thirteen thousand persons were murdered in Jamaica in the first decade of the twenty-first century.[19] Why do we have such rampant apathy and cynicism in the face of the high rates of homicides? The answer is that we place so little value on the lives of those who are the majority victims of crime. It is, therefore, appropriate that the church should erect a memorial for these wasted lives and raise a voice of protest.

18. Tyson, "The Church and the Nation."

19. *The Sunday Herald Newspaper* (Jamaica), January 10, 2010, provided the statistics from police sources.

PART 1: CONFIGURING CARIBBEAN THEOLOGY

But prophetic consciousness within the church must do more to unmask the realities. As small emerging societies, the countries of the region do not have large middle classes, an independent intelligentsia, or mature societal institutions. Yet political parties have wielded enormous influence. Indeed, since the advent of adult suffrage, governments in the Caribbean have lost or gained power, with minor exceptions, through democratic elections. The will of the majority has been sustained over time. However, elections are blunt instruments in securing good governance. In between elections there are far greater forces that ought to be able to hold governments accountable. Churches in the region, which have a considerable following, have a unique opportunity to provide moral and ethical leadership. This is not to suggest a return to Christendom or the development of a new style of theocracy. It does not suggest that the church should muscle its way into exerting influence, based on its numbers or its resources. Rather, what is needed is a heightened prophetic consciousness against misrule.

In the fifty years just prior to the abolishing of slavery, and in the period immediately following emancipation, the church exerted enormous influence in defining the agenda of justice for the region. It did so not from official perches, but by a pressure from below. From within the Bible classes and prayer meetings, in the market places and parks, the demand for justice found resonance among the masses. The church did not act in isolation; there were other voices and other forces with which it found consonance. However, since adult suffrage, the church has simultaneously become more privileged and more peripherialized. It has largely narrowed its influence in the public domain to issues pertaining to its freedom to proclaim the gospel and keep Sunday a holy day, along with promoting issues deriving from the culture wars of the United States—such as anti-abortion lobbies and concerns about gambling. The church has largely failed to find its voice or give leadership on much of the life-distorting, life-diminishing, and life-destroying matters of the society.

The nature of the challenge to the contemporary Caribbean church can be illustrated from the situation of crime and violence facing Jamaica. As indicated above, Jamaica has a murder rate of greater than sixty per 100,000, which is six times the international average. In such circumstances the least that ought to be expected is a country united by its outrage at the murder of more than 1,500 persons each year and resolved in its insistence on the rule of law. Instead, there has been a history of the alliance between politics and crime. Examples abound of cynical disregard by political parties of international best practices and of public opinion; indeed, political parties are prepared to go to great lengths to safeguard this alliance between politics and crime, despite the seriousness of charges leveled against connected parties, and despite the fact that this alliance leads to intolerably high rates of crime and violence. There is no indication that if the church were to raise a collective voice of protest, this would make any difference. Nevertheless, faithfulness to what is right and good requires the church to speak up anyway. It is how the Old Testament prophets in the tradition of Deuteronomy regarded their mission.

Caribbean theology contends that there are to be prophetic voices seeking to hold the region and individual nation states to an ideal of justice and righteousness. The ideal is drawn from the Deuteronomic tradition in the Old Testament, nuanced by the Sermon on the Mount and the teachings of Jesus in the New Testament. Churches in local, denominational, and ecumenical manifestations have a duty to approximate this biblical ideal, where they have the opportunity to do so.

THE HISTORICAL PROJECT OF THE CARIBBEAN— SEEKING THE WELFARE OF THE CITY

Allusion may be made to the legitimate criticism advanced by Ivan Petrella that liberation theology has lost its distinctive mark because it has no historical projects to relate to God's reign.[20] This criticism cannot, however, be successfully launched at Caribbean theology, since Caribbean theology accepts as valid Petrella's citation of Claude Geffré's claim that liberation theology's special topic should be the "relations between an historical practice of liberation and eschatological salvation."[21] This focus is echoed by Enrique Dussel, when he notes, "that which is most specific to liberation theology is precisely the articulation of political projects of liberation and God's reign."[22] Petrella's claim also finds support in the observation by José Comblin that even "liberation" is being replaced by "life" as a theme.[23] While Petrella may be correct that present day liberation theology in its shift from a focus on the historical project to negative critique is closer to North Atlantic political theology than to its early manifestations,[24] this criticism does not hold for Caribbean theology. Going back to its antecedent form, when the enslaved rejected their enslavement and rebelled in protest against the denial of their

20. Petrella, *Future of Liberation Theology*, 111.

21. Ibid., 110, citing Geffré, *The Mystical and Political Dimensions of the Christian Faith*, 8.

22. Ibid., citing Dussel, *Teologia de la Liberacion*, 183.

23. Ibid., 111, citing Comblin, "La Iglesia Latinoamericana Desde Puebla a Santa Domingo," 40.

24. Ibid.

PART 1: CONFIGURING CARIBBEAN THEOLOGY

freedom, Caribbean theology has been wedded to the historical project. Its concern was not just liberation *from* oppression, but a commitment to the survival of a people. In this regard, Caribbean theology seeks to approximate the reign of God, the eschatological ideal of shalom, in the concrete situation of the Caribbean.

Historically and concretely, the institutional imagination we seek involves the following five components, which together constitute the historical project for a new Caribbean society and a new Caribbean person:

1. There is the need for an enhanced and enriched Caribbean selfhood, a clarified sense of self that allows its citizenry to relate to the Caribbean as the best place to live and work and raise their families.

2. The deepening and entrenching of democratic patterns and democratic institutions is necessary to procure public goods, good governance, openness and accountability in public life. This is intended to create a sense of stakeholder-ship among all the people who call the Caribbean home.

3. The enfranchisement and mainstreaming of the masses of the people is crucial. This means increased and enhanced access to land and housing, education, health care, and security. This is to enable the Caribbean to become a place of human flourishing.

4. The expansion of opportunities for quality employment that offer a livable wage is an important mandate.

5. Improvement in the quality of justice must be made available to ordinary citizens. This includes the protection of basic rights (including the right to life, the right to live in a well-ordered society governed by the rule of law, and the right to a physical environment supportive of an enriched quality of life), as well as increased and enhanced access to justice through the courts of law.

In the sixth century BC, the prophet Jeremiah wrote a letter to those taken into Babylonian exile. His advice was radical and well summarizes the prophetic agenda of Caribbean theology.

> Build houses and settle down; plant gardens and eat what they produce. Marry and have sons and daughters; find wives for your sons and give your daughters in marriage, so that they too may have sons and daughters. Increase in number there; do not decrease. Also, seek the peace and prosperity of the city to which I have carried you into exile. Pray to the LORD for it, because if it prospers, you too will prosper." Yes, this is what the LORD Almighty, the God of Israel, says: "Do not let the prophets and

diviners among you deceive you. Do not listen to the dreams you encourage them to have. They are prophesying lies to you in my name. I have not sent them," declares the LORD. (Jeremiah 29:5–9; NIV)

Seeking the welfare of the city is an inclusive way of speaking about accepting the full responsibility of citizenship. Caribbean people are not subjects; they are citizens. They must be prepared to work at building a society to the advantage and benefit of all its citizens. This will require at the minimum a strengthening of their sovereignty and the development of regional institutions that reflect the self-confidence and pride of Caribbean people. It will also mean the enfranchisement and the mainstreaming of those whose forebears were first treated as commodities rather than citizens. Caribbean theology has a significant role to play in facilitating the creation of just and responsible societies in the Caribbean, which constitutes the historical project of the Caribbean as the *City of God*, in the midst of an exile that is certainly not over.

2

Language and Identity in Caribbean Theology

ERICA CAMPBELL

"Who am I?" is a question that we all ask, consciously or subconsciously. Everyone has an identity, but not everyone has a clear *sense* of that identity or a sense of the worth of that identity. Caribbean people have their own unique challenges with acknowledging and accepting who they are. This, of course, inhibits any movement towards self-actualization, for self-actualization presupposes self-knowledge. And so, any attempt at redressing obvious economic and social imbalances in the Caribbean must include, as a matter of course and a matter of priority, the renewing of the mind (Rom 12:2).

Why has it been so difficult for the Caribbean person to seek, as April Bernard puts it, "an actualized self within an affirming and liberating environment"?[1] Perhaps the following story from Southeast Asia about Monkey and Fish can provide illumination:

> It seems Monkey and Fish got caught in a flood. As the waters rose higher and higher, Monkey found a tree and climbed to

---

1. Bernard, "Emancipating Spirit," 49.

safety. As he got above the water level, he looked down and saw his friend Fish still in the water. So, out of concern for his friend, he reached down, rescued Fish, and held him tight to his chest as he climbed higher in the tree.[2]

Caribbean people can identify with Fish since, for most, their ancestors were wrested from the place of their identity and, over time, there have been attempts to shape a new identity for them. Regardless of their status prior to arriving in the Caribbean, the majority of Caribbean peoples were ascribed, at the outset, the new identity of slaves and, later, of subjects of the Crown, a Crown whose interest was not in their development, but in the development of the colonizing power it represented. So, there is a clear point of divergence between the story of Monkey and Fish and the history of Caribbean peoples. It lies in the motive ascribed to the rescuer, for the motive of the colonizers was neither noble nor honorable. As Kortright Davis declares: "Europeans conquered these lands for their own mercantilist expansion,"[3] and it was in order to achieve that end that they "procure[d] African bodies and suppress[ed] African souls."[4]

But while the enslavement and subjugation of the body was never accepted, and the plantation slaves and Crown subjects fought for and eventually gained Emancipation and Independence, they found it a tremendous challenge to overcome the emasculation of selfhood inherent in slavery and subjugation.

The challenge remains. It has been easy to identify the injustice of physical enslavement. It has been easy to identify the injustice of economic exploitation. It has been easy to identify the injustice of social stratification and political victimization. But it has not been so easy for the oppressed to be conscious of the bonds of what we might call identity indoctrination and to recognize its relationship to the other forms of bondage. And so the fight for Emancipation, the fight for Independence still continues. It is a fight for freedom from "mental slavery" (as Marcus Garvey put it).[5]

---

2. Kraft, *Anthropology for Christian Witness*, 32.
3. Davis, *Emancipation Still Comin,'* 17.
4. Ibid., 50.
5. Although Bob Marley made this phrase famous in his "Redemption Song," he was quoting from a speech that Marcus Garvey gave in Sydney, Nova Scotia, Canada, in early October 1937. Garvey said: "We are going to emancipate ourselves from mental slavery because whilst others might free the body, none but ourselves can free the mind" (Garvey, "Speech of Marcus Garvey," 791).

PART 1: CONFIGURING CARIBBEAN THEOLOGY

LANGUAGE: A TOOL OF EXPLOITATION

Whereas the oppressed may not be cognizant of their mental enslavement, oppressors throughout history have used it to their material advantage. Alexander the Great, for example, understood the significance of indoctrination. He recognized that to truly conquer the world, he had to Hellenize it. And Greek culture did become the world's culture. Important in Alexander's battle on the cultural front were the philosophers, whose weapons were words—potent weapons indeed, as language is "a medium for projecting social identities."[6] Like Alexander the Great, our former "rescuers," the imperialists and colonialists of old, did not under-estimate the impact language could have. It was the major means by which they engaged in the identity indoctrination of the Caribbean people. They therefore used words to belittle, degrade, and suppress the colonized; and they made distinctions between their own languages and those of their subjects, which reinforced that sense of deficiency. Language was used as a tool of exploitation.

Language was an immediately obvious distinguishing mark between the European masters and the African slaves. With "some ten million Africans captured and deported to the Americas,"[7] there existed a considerable language barrier. It is a barrier that was bridged by the whip and other forceful methods. But the time did come when that barrier was also bridged by the development of Creole languages.

Imperialist Propaganda

With Creole narrowing the language gap, the imperative that the message of the colonialists be clearly understood led some to give instructions in it. Hubert Devonish points out that in the Danish Virgin Islands the desire to communicate was so great that a writing system for Dutch Creole was created.[8] The result was an unusually high literacy rate. Then in Aruba, Bonaire, and Curacao, Papiamento became the medium of religious instruction to the extent that there were translations of the Gospels of Matthew and Mark into that Spanish/Portuguese-based Creole. And in St. Domingue, now Haiti, French Creole was used to issue proclamations.[9] For example,

6. Devonish and Carpenter, "Towards Full Bilingualism in Education," 285.

7. Arends, "The Socio-Historical Background of Creoles," 17.

8. Now known as the U.S. Virgin Islands, the Danish Virgin Islands were populated mainly by Dutch colonists and African slaves. The Dutch Creole (also known as *Negerhollands*) that developed among the slave population began to die out in the nineteenth century, with the coming of the British.

9. Devonish, *Language and Liberation*, 49–51.

says Devonish, a "proclamation, written in Creole and dated 1801, was sent by the First Consul, Napoleon Bonaparte, to the rebellious blacks of St. Domingue, demanding their loyalty to the French Republic."[10]

The 1801 proclamation was most obviously a use of Creole to reinforce the socio-economic order that had been established by the plantocracy.[11] But this tactic was not limited to the political or economic powers that be. The institutions of the church and the school were by no means disinterested parties whose sole purpose was to enlighten through the gospel and through personal development those who had been dislocated by the enterprise of slavery. According to Devonish, they were instruments used by the state to produce "ideological acceptance of the status quo among the black population of the Caribbean."[12] For both church and school, the Bible was a sourcebook for this indoctrination.

The use of Creole by church and school was, like its use by the Consul, a demonstration of the language policy operating in the Caribbean. Creole was used to issue edicts to the so-called emancipated slaves. It was used to instill moral and ethical values that would benefit the plantation system. But it was not used in the writing of laws or for any other official purpose of communication. Devonish explains that, "in those colonies where English emerged as the dominant European language alongside an English-influenced Creole, the use of the Creole language in even as restricted an area as religious instruction was ignored. This was the experience of countries such as Jamaica, Barbados, Antigua, etc."[13]

There was an underlying message about the value of that which belonged to the colonialists in relation to that which belonged to the subjects. One *may* graciously condescend to communicate in the language of the people if one deems it beneficial, but certainly Creole is not to be ascribed equal or even comparable worth to the languages of Europe. This was true even for the northern state of independent Haiti, after the assassination of Dessalines in 1806. On the one hand, we have the following affirmation from Vastey, an official in the post-Dessalines administration, meant to distance Haitians from their colonial masters: "Next to the change of religion, a change of language is the most powerful method of altering the character and manner of a nation."[14] Yet the irony is that even then they did not accept

10. Ibid., 48.

11. It is interesting that just three years later Haitians declared their independence from France.

12. Ibid., 46.

13. Ibid., 51.

14 Vastey, *An Essay on the Causes of the Revolution and Civil Wars of Hayti*, 214; quoted in Devonish, *Language and Liberation*, 47.

Haitian Creole as their official language. Instead, "it was resolved in council . . . that instruction should be given in the English tongue, and after the English method."[15]

This is one example of a reality that consumed all plantation societies. As Patrick Bryan puts it:

> Habits of thought that had emerged out of the particular social relations of slavery continued to influence society well after slavery had been abolished, for hegemony during the slave period had involved not only the legal ownership of slaves but also a whole belief system that entrenched the white oligarchy as the economic, political and cultural leaders of colonial society.[16]

The result is that even when Caribbean people have been able to appreciate all other areas of cultural expression, and repudiate any suggestion of their inferiority, the legitimacy of their own language for use beyond everyday conversation and storytelling has been hard to accept.

Language and the Question of Development

There are many arguments against making the Creole of a given state its national language. These arguments are often founded in pragmatism. Why promote a localized, parochial mode of communication in this age of globalization? It must be a retrograde step. Why lessen the people's chance for progress and development just to make a nationalistic statement? Haiti has moved beyond its reticence to accept Creole, and so has made such a statement. Has it, therefore, blighted its prospects for economic recovery?

For some, this is a rhetorical question. The argument for the use of Creole seems to them to be an argument in favor of self-denigration and self-oppression. Thus, although Selden Rodman actually argues in favor of Creole use, his position in reference to Haiti, that, "Unquestionably Creole has played a part in keeping the peasant isolated on his acre,"[17] is for them a confirmation of their thesis. But Creole is not to blame for this, since until recently Haitian children were being educated in French, which Rodman contends is to them "a half-foreign language."[18] They could, therefore, hardly master the concepts they were supposedly being taught—concepts that would help them understand and gain access to the world beyond their

---

15. Devonish, *Language and Liberation*, 47.
16. Bryan, *The Jamaican People 1880–1902*, ix–x.
17. Rodman, *Haiti*, 33.
18. Ibid.

acre. So, although it can be made to appear that Creole itself is at fault, the problem is really systemic. It is a system created and sustained by elitism, both from without and from within.

The Haitian peasant has been isolated because the powers of this world isolated Haiti politically and economically. This isolation was a deliberate attempt to punish her for her "audacity of hope"; it was retribution for the Revolution.[19] She dared to think that she could govern herself at a time when white hegemony had thought itself well established. There was no way she would be allowed to succeed. She was to be "an example of black incapacity for self-government."[20] And Haiti's own, those who took charge after the Revolution, were not as concerned for the betterment of the masses as they were for personal status and prestige. This, they achieved, in part, through becoming more proficient in French.

> The continued official use of French in revolutionary St. Domingue and the spread of its use among the new elite, perfectly served the interests of this emergent ruling class. It served to ensure, as a French speaking elite, their access to and control of the various sections of the state apparatus. Simultaneously, it served to help dissipate any illusions among the Creole-speaking masses that they (the masses) were the true inheritors of the state and its economic base.[21]

Haiti's new leaders had become what their masters were. Haiti, therefore, experienced oligarchic rule for much of its history, both pre- and post-independence.

But the issue raised by Rodman concerning the Haitian's isolation goes beyond responsibility. If the continued use of Creole by the masses helps maintain a distinction between them and the ruling class, and leaves them unprepared for leadership, it is reasonable to say that the solution may be found in making the people literate in French. Then, it will no longer be a "half-foreign language." But Rodman, almost in rebuttal, points to a question asked by "advocates of a Creole education": "Is it more important to turn the peasant into a Frenchman with a consciousness of the problems of the outside world or to equip him to cope with the problems of his own environment by his own means?"[22]

19. The "audacity of hope" is an expression made popular by Barack Obama, the forty-fourth president of the United States of America, in his book of that name.
20. Bryan, *The Jamaican People*, ix–x.
21. Devonish, *Language and Liberation*, 46. The parenthetical insertion is Devonish's.
22. Rodman, *Haiti*, 33.

The options, however, are not mutually exclusive. To establish the credibility for any Creole language is not to undermine the significance of knowing other languages or other cultures. It is just to acknowledge a people's right to what is legitimately theirs, to what identifies them as distinct, but not inferior. Caribbean people cannot afford to accept the identity created for them by anyone else, except God their creator. Additionally, establishing the credibility of Creole is to defy a system that makes isolation and discrimination a reality for the masses, not only of Haiti, but of the Caribbean as a whole. By not accepting Creole, while accepting European languages, we are ceding ground to that system of discrimination.

This matter of Creole use in the context of a global economy is understandably of great concern. Both proponents and opponents of its use often argue from the standpoint of socio-economic development. But it is not only at the governmental level that the issue has currency. The church too has had to contemplate the issue.

The Church and the Question of Language

What would make it difficult for the church—in particular the church of the English-speaking Caribbean—to use Creole for instruction, and for worship in general? Ashley Smith contends that "the dominance of the culture of the plantation" has been one of "the enduring spiritual and psychological consequences of slavery."[23] Harold Sitahal points out one of these consequences: "In the Caribbean, the churches have been historically involved in the establishment of a white Eurocentric religio/cultural institution."[24] This state of affairs persists to the present day, with some exchanging *American* for *Eurocentric*.

Those who replaced the European church leaders propounded the missionary theology they had learnt. It was a theology that denied the reality or integrity of the Caribbean peoples. It denied the authenticity of their expressions; it denied the yearning of the human spirit for a form of worship that was related to the substance of its true identity; it denied the need for religion to be more than personal, the need for it to be communal, treating with issues of public policy as well as personal piety. It denied all these and more. It is little wonder, therefore, that many attempt to participate in both Christianity and some other form of (more indigenous) spirituality. Edward Seaga puts it this way:

---

23. Smith, *Emerging from Innocence*, 10.
24. Sitahal, "Caribbean Theology of the People/for the People," 7.

> Faith dwells both in Jehovah as well as in balm yard. Sunday morning is Jehovah's time; Sunday night many of the same observers 'jump revival.' There is no conflict: different spiritual powers are needed to deal with the problems of life and there is more than enough faith in our folk culture to embrace God, the Trinity, archangel and prophets, as well as the spirits of the dead.[25]

Seaga's point is well taken. The description is understood; the rationale has basis. But his assertion that there "there is no conflict" is without merit. Indeed, one is compelled to ask: *Why* do people engage in activity and practice that contradicts the dogma of the "other religion" to which they say they adhere? Should it not be a case of choosing one over the other? Is it that each meets a need that the other does not?

There may be what John Cole calls "a dualistic self-preservative existence of Christianity by day and African religion by night,"[26] but dualism extends well beyond the balm yard and the revival table. Even those who have accepted the admonition of the clergy and so do not mix "religions" may yet find great difficulty living an integrated life. Does this mean that Christianity is inadequate? Does it mean that the claims of Christ are not sufficiently relevant to the Caribbean person? Or does it mean that the message of the gospel has been poorly communicated, and therefore misunderstood? This final question goes beyond language. It speaks to attitude and to disposition, to presentation and to application. And yet, the issue of language has to be addressed as part of the larger equation.

Here are stanzas of three hymns that are still being sung in some Caribbean churches. A stanza from one hymn says:

> When careless of His rich repast
> We've sought, alas, to rove
> He has recalled His faithful guest
> And raised His banner—Love.[27]

How many persons in the average Caribbean congregation understand these words: "repast"; "alas"; "rove"?

Here is a second hymn sung in several Caribbean churches:

> Thy love we own, Lord Jesus,

---

25. Seaga, "Popular Religion," 88; quoted in Cole, "What can the Euro-Christian Churches in the Caribbean Learn from Indigenous Caribbean Religions?" 19.

26. Cole, "What can the Euro-Christian Churches in the Caribbean Learn from Indigenous Caribbean Religions?" 16 (see also 25).

27. Stanza 4 from "Our Tongues Must Spread the Saviour's Fame," author unknown.

PART 1: CONFIGURING CARIBBEAN THEOLOGY

> In service unremitting;
> Within the veil Thou dost prevail,
> Each soul for worship fitting:
> Encompassed here with failure,
> Each earthly refuge fails us;
> Without, within, at war with sin,
> Thy name alone avails us.[28]

Many persons have their understanding impeded not only by the unfamiliar vocabulary in these hymns, but also by their unfamiliar structure. Yet, congregations insist on singing them. To what end? For what purpose? Worship? Worship should come from the heart. How many can sing these songs from the heart? Can people sing from the heart that which they do not understand? Or, is worship so mystical that understanding is unnecessary? Some Christians criticize Muslims for proclaiming the mystical benefits of reading the Koran in Arabic even when they do not understand it, calling it absurd; yet they behave in similar fashion, using, in the worship of God, language that a great number of the congregation do not understand well.

Here is a third such hymn:

> The higher mysteries of Thy fame,
> The creature's grasp transcend;
> The Father only that blest name
> Of Son can comprehend.
> The sweetness of that name of love
> The Father gives us now to prove.[29]

It seems that there are those who want God to remain mysterious. The question is: Does God want to remain a mystery because of language barriers? Paradoxically, the God whose infinitude will always make him mysterious wants to be known, and actively seeks to reveal himself.

Let us consider another worship song, this one written in Jamaican Creole:[30]

> Faada Gad, Yu ina klaas bai Yuself
> [Father God, you're in a class by Yourself]
> And, abov Yu, mi se nobadi els
> [And, in my estimation, there is nobody greater than You]
> Onggl Yu aluon kyan mek mi fiil dis wie

---

28. Stanza 1 from "Thy Love We Own, Lord Jesus" by W. Yerbury (d. 1863).

29. Stanza 4 from "Thou Art the Everlasting Word," by Josiah Conder (1789–1855), adapted.

30. Translation given for non-native speakers.

[You and only You can make me feel this way]
Laad mi fiil Yu prezens roun mi die bai die
[Lord, I feel your presence around me day by day].[31]

Songs like these are sometimes discounted, and, certainly are not the regular repast; let us rephrase that: they certainly do not constitute a regular part of the worship experience. Yet, the words are understood, and the structure is familiar.[32]

What has been identified as a problem in the liturgy of worship in song is true also of preaching and teaching and general interaction around the Word of God. George Mulrain contends: "If all that a worshipper has heard . . . in church are incomprehensible technical terms [and] theological jargon, then how can [he or] she be expected to have a longing for worship?"[33] The resolute focus on "standard English" in the formal liturgy means that many have been robbed of a truly authentic worship experience. And so, language has been a tool of oppression even in the hands of Caribbean church leaders who, by continuing in the tradition of their former masters, may have inadvertently used it in that way. The Caribbean psyche has certainly been affected by centuries of indoctrination.

LANGUAGE: A TOOL OF LIBERATION

Another reason why language has been used inadvertently in an oppressive manner is ignorance about the nature of Creole and its use in relation to other languages. People are often afraid to encourage the use of Creole because they believe it is broken English or French or Spanish or Portuguese or Dutch. But is this really so?

Constructing a New Reality: A Linguistic Response

In the Caribbean, explains Dennis Craig, "the masses speak a vernacular that differs significantly in grammar and idiom from an official language with which it co-exists; but the vernacular and the official language nevertheless share the majority of a common vocabulary."[34] Yet, despite sharing

---

31. Patrick Douglas, "Class by Yuself."

32. They are very familiar when transmitted orally, but not so familiar when transmitted in written form, for many of us are not as *yet* used to the phonetically determined spelling system

33. Mulrain, "The Use of Senses in Worship," 34–35.

34. Craig, *Teaching Language and Literacy*, 1.

PART 1: CONFIGURING CARIBBEAN THEOLOGY

vocabulary with the official European languages, Caribbean vernaculars or Creoles are to be considered languages in their own right. They were formed in response to the new situation into which the Africans found themselves. Having been brought forcibly from diverse parts of West Africa, they faced the challenge of being able to communicate neither with the colonizers nor among themselves. Just as they were brought together by force, so did Creole languages develop "as a result of linguistic violence."[35] This was no "natural transference of a language over generations,"[36] but rather the development of a new language by a disparate group of Africans in order to meet an immediate and urgent need.

But why didn't the slaves simply learn the language of their masters? Not learning the European's language had nothing to do with their level of intelligence. It had, in great measure, to do with their level of exposure to these foreign languages whose grammatical structure was so different from their own. It is difficult enough for an adult to learn a foreign language, but this difficulty is considerably lessened through language immersion. The slaves did not have this opportunity. Even house slaves, though having access to the slave owner, were not sufficiently integrated into the owner's world to properly learn his or her language. Segregation, not integration, was the mantra of the plantation economy.

In any case, if the circumstances had been different, and there had been integration between Africans and Europeans, the result would likely have been an interchange between languages rather than the complete dominance of one language over the other, as will be seen from an examination of the origin and development of Koine Greek, French, and English. Indeed, the development of these languages illustrates clearly that no ancient or modern language springs fully formed from the head of Zeus; even these classical languages are basically hybrid in nature.

George Hadjiantoniou explains the origin of Koine Greek thus: From among the many Greek dialects, Attic had emerged as the "literary language of Greece." When Alexander the Great put together an army to conquer the world, since his recruits came from all over Greece, "a [new] dialect gradually formed, which, having the Attic as a basis, served as a common means of communication among all men of the army, and later among the merchants who followed the army into the conquered lands."[37] Although it is no wonder that Koine Greek became a universal language, since it was the language of the dominant imperial power, its use outlasted the Greek

---

35. Muysken and Smith, "The Study of Pidgin and Creole Languages," 4.
36. Ibid.
37. Hadjiantoniou, *Learning the Basics of New Testament Greek*, 3.

empire, as it gained the acceptance of the subsequent Roman empire. Indeed, Koine Greek eventually became the language in which the New Testament was written.

Like Greek, French emerged out of modifications of the language of invading forces (in this case the Roman invasion of what later was to become France). The spoken language of the invaders was called "vulgar speech" (today we know it as Vulgar Latin) because it was the language of the people—the average Roman citizen.[38] In France, however, Vulgar Latin was regarded as the language of the educated. According to Muysken and Smith, modern French developed from Old French, which developed in turn from Vulgar Latin and other linguistic influences.[39]

The development of English was also gradual. The Germanic tribes known as the Saxons, Angles, and Jutes occupied Britain in the fifth century. Their inter-related languages developed into Old English. Then with the invasion of the Normans and, thus, the introduction of Old French, further changes took shape in the language spoken in Britain. This new language has been called Middle English. This was the language of the masses. The elite spoke French. Over time, the language of the masses became the accepted language, but it still was not stable; it was continually changing. With the invention of the printing press came stability and standardization, and Early Modern English. Changes occurred thereafter, as is to be expected, because language is dynamic,

However, these changes were not as significant as had formerly been the case. And so, while a comparison of Chaucer's works with the King James Version (KJV) of the Bible will reveal very little similarity between Middle English and Early Modern English, a comparison of the KJV with more modern translations of the Bible will reveal noteworthy similarities between Early and Late Modern English.

It can be seen from the history recounted above that given languages developed from interaction with other language forms. Furthermore, there was a tendency to use language to cement a distinction between the masses and the so-called upper classes of a society. Despite this, the speech of the common person eventually became an esteemed language, in some cases even turning out to be the language of the elite and functioning as a distinguishing mark between them and the masses.

Like the languages examined above, Creole languages in the British colonies of the Caribbean developed from the interplay of language forms,

---

38. The literary language of Rome was Classical Latin.

39. Muysken and Smith, "The Study of Pidgin and Creole Languages," 4. They note that Vulgar Latin itself had developed from Classical Latin, which developed from Archaic Latin.

in this case the interaction of English and African languages. Yet within these former British colonies Creole languages have not yet become accepted, much less esteemed. Instead, Creole has functioned as an indicator or mark of low social and economic status. Those who are articulate in English are seen as educated and the well-to-do are expected to speak it.

An understanding of the history of Creoles and of other languages, however, could lead us to contend with firm resolve that "creole languages are not in the slightest qualitatively distinguishable from other spoken languages."[40] If this is acknowledged, communicating in Creole will not be seen as "talking down" to people. This perception has unfortunately caused individuals to believe that in speaking Creole they are either doing their listeners a favor (for which they should be grateful) or belittling them and reinforcing negative stereotypes. But neither is a necessary response. A Creole is as much a language as any other, and there is as much justification for its use in oral and written form as for any other.

In some territories, Creoles have become established written languages. In others, like Jamaica, there is a movement to standardize their use.[41] There is great hope among some scholars, especially Caribbean linguists, that the translation of the Bible into Jamaican will contribute greatly to this process. Then, instruction in Jamaican will be closer to becoming a reality, which could pave the way for such an initiative in other countries.

The earlier question we raised about development, however, is bound to resurface at this point of the discourse. Doesn't education in Creole inhibit the development of a people? Actually, teaching people to read and write *and think* in their own language, far from impeding national development, may prove to be its catalyst—all other variables considered.[42] People naturally think in the language with which they are most accustomed, the language they first learned at home. Teaching them to read and write first in a foreign language not spoken in the home (which these European languages are to most Caribbean people) inhibits their personal growth and development; this in turn inhibits national growth and development. It is best that one learns comprehension and critical thinking skills in the language in which one is most naturally at home. Of course, there are many who have achieved success in the current language environment. But they have done so in spite of, and not because of, how language education is done in schools.

---

40. Ibid., 4–5.

41 Standardization will not make local dialects obsolete.

42. Other variables include issues of political stability and political will, both national and international.

Soon after Haiti's declaration of independence, Etienne Gerin recommended that Creole should be made the national language. Gerin's goal was "to integrate the Creole speaking sectors of the population effectively into the education system."[43] He "proposed that only when the basic skills had been imparted that a transition to French should take place. In order to support his proposal, he wrote a Creole grammar intended for use in the infant classes within the schools."[44] His proposal was rejected.

Gerin's proposal is similar to that made by Caribbean linguists such as Hubert Devonish, that the particular Creole spoken by the majority should constitute that people's national language. These linguists believe that, since no language is innately superior to another, what we might call the *heart language* of a people should drive any conversation about national issues. An appeal to the limitations of Creole, though understandable, is not a legitimate reason to prevent it driving such a conversation. All languages have limitations in relation to others. Those limitations are linked to the limitations of the speakers. As people are exposed to new experiences and concepts, they create or adopt new words into their oral and written lexicon. The dynamism and adaptability of language must not be underestimated. Creole will, therefore, adapt to meet the new challenges imposed on it.

Additionally, the point must be reiterated that an endorsement of Creole is not a rejection of other languages. More and more people worldwide are recognizing the advantages of being multilingual. And we must too. We in the Caribbean cannot afford to thwart our development goals by being myopic. Therefore the argument for instruction in Creole is not an argument against instruction in English or any other European language. In fact, linguists believe that a firm foundation in one's own language leads to a better grasp of other languages. And so, as the Language Unit of the University of the West Indies engages in its Jamaican Bi-lingual Primary Education Project, in which it seeks to teach both Jamaican and English to primary school students, it "expect[s] that after 4 years, the pupils in this project, relative to their peers outside, would i) show superior self-concept in language and related areas, ii) demonstrate superior literacy skills in both languages, and iii) manifest superior control of the material taught in content subjects."[45]

These are all commendable, desirable, and even necessary objectives. But the primary argument for the use of Creole is that it facilitates a people's understanding of their reality, and of their reshaping that reality.

43. Devonish, *Language and Liberation*, 48.
44. Ibid.
45 Devonish and Carpenter, "Towards Full Bilingualism in Education," 288.

PART 1: CONFIGURING CARIBBEAN THEOLOGY

Constructing a New Reality: A Hermeneutical Task

According to James Spradley, "Language is more than a means of communication about reality; it is a tool for constructing reality. Different languages create and express different realities. They categorize experience in different ways. They provide alternative patterns for customizing ways of thinking and perceiving."[46] Caribbean reality needs reconstruction. It was constructed with language as a tool of oppression. This has led to a loss of identity—a loss of our true identity. It has led us historically to demean what is uniquely ours while we embrace what is not ours nor can be—the life and identity of our oppressors. This is part of the reality that we need to deconstruct before reconstruction can take place. The church has a critical role to play in this process.

There is no doubt the church in the Caribbean was in the past an instrument of an exploitive state. The Bible was used, in large measure, as a sourcebook to validate the condition in which we as Caribbean people had found ourselves. And for this reason, many reject the Bible today. But even in the days of colonialism there were elements within the church who brought a liberating message. The Bible as the Word from God is essentially a Word of liberation. And so, the church, into whose guardianship the Bible has been placed, needs to present the message that God intended and in the way that he intended. This will mean bridging the gap between the Word and its recipients.

Anthony Thiselton, one of the foremost contemporary thinkers on the subject of biblical hermeneutics, explains that: "Understanding takes place when two sets of horizons are brought into relation to each other, namely those of the text and those of the interpreter. . . . On this basis understanding presupposes a shared area of common perspectives, concepts, or even judgments . . . understanding as it were presupposes understanding.[47]

This goes well beyond just understanding the meaning of words. That is why Thiselton contends that "traditional approaches to language usually carry with them an inbuilt limitation."[48] When we "concentrate attention on the language of the ancient text and do not attempt to bring about a fusion of horizons between the world of the text and that of the interpreter,"[49] the result is that the Word is not made applicable and relevant to its audience. True understanding does not take place. It is important to establish the sig-

---

46. Spradley, *The Ethnographic Interview*, 17.
47. Thiselton, *The Two Horizons*, 103.
48. Ibid.
49. Ibid.

nificance of the words in *our* context because "any given symbol cannot be counted on to represent the same reality in more than one culture."[50]

For the average Caribbean interpreter, there are multiple barriers to understanding the biblical text. There is the barrier of the temporal, cultural, historical, and geographical distance of the text from his/her own context; there is the barrier of the original languages in which the text came to us; and there is the barrier of the language into which the text has been translated. The first will be true for all people today. The second is true for all, but obviously less problematic for those who have studied Biblical Hebrew and Greek. The third is not true for everyone. Those whose first language is one of the European languages do not have this challenge, for the Scriptures have been translated into these languages. For most of us in the Caribbean, however, these are our second languages, and while some do speak them with a great level of fluency, many are not at all proficient in them. And so, for those persons, the third impediment is even more of an obstacle.

If communicating meaning is critical, why not bridge the gap as much as possible by translating the Word into the language of the people and by speaking the language best understood by them? It is in an effort to bridge the gap for the Jamaican people that the Bible Society of the West Indies has undertaken the task of translating the Scriptures into Jamaican.[51]

But there are persons who have expressed reservations about this project. Some of the arguments relate to issues already discussed. But there are other lines of reasoning, such as the cost/benefit analysis that some proffer. But to argue that the Bible should not be translated into Jamaican because so few will benefit in relation to the monetary cost to be incurred is to devalue the individual, and to devalue the community for which it is being done. Why does smallness of number matter if the persons have worth? There is rejoicing in heaven over one sinner that repents because that one sinner is important. Once the goal of effective communication of meaning will be enhanced, the enterprise should be encouraged. It bears repetition: Meaning does not reside in the words by themselves. Meaning lies in what the speaker/writer wants to be understood and in what the audience actually understands.

Where the Bible is concerned, there are multiple speakers and writers and, therefore, different assignments of meaning. Hence, one cannot communicate a message with its original meaning only. Much transference of meaning takes place before it reaches the twenty-first century audience. The

---

50. Kraft, *Anthropology for Christian Witness*, 240.

51. The New Testament has been completed; there are plans to eventually translate the Old Testament.

original speakers/writers have their own meaning. The original recipients, who may in turn become speakers/writers, have theirs; the translators have theirs; the contemporary listeners/readers have theirs, and they in turn become "translators" for others. It is a never-ending saga. This is why (among other reasons) there need to be revisions in translations. As the matrix of understanding changes from one generation to another, or even within a generation, there is need to re-engage the biblical text so as to engage new readers.

To speak of reconstructing the meaning of the biblical text to reach a Caribbean audience is to speak of a radical shift in perception. In fact, Gosnell Yorke argues that since Bible translation plays a pivotal role in shaping culture and identity it should take place in Africa using an Afro-centric approach.[52] Such a suggestion at first glance seems heretical. It is easier to understand the concept of translating the Scriptures into the particular languages that African people groups speak, or, in the case of the Caribbean, into Creole languages; we can understand the need to apply the Scriptures bearing in mind the African or Caribbean context; we may even understand the creative reading of the Bible through the lens of African or Caribbean reality. But the approach proposed by Yorke seems to involve a distortion of the Word of God.

However, what Yorke is proposing is the redressing of decisions made by past and present translators. Citing Cain Hope Felder, an African-American New Testament scholar, he notes that: "European/Euro-American biblical scholars [and Bible translators] have asked questions that shaped answers within the framework of the racial, cultural, and gender presuppositions they held in common. This quiet consensus has undermined the self-understanding and place in history of other racial and ethnic groups."[53] Their intentions may not have been malicious but their presuppositions and biases "invariably impose limits on us—limits which no amount of formal education or life-experience seems able to eradicate entirely."[54] Yorke quotes New Testament scholar John Elliott: "All perception is selective and constrained psychologically and socially; *for no mortal enjoys the gift of 'immaculate perception.'*"[55]

Since these limits are not imposed by the text itself, but by the translator, it behoves those who do not have those particular biases to correct them through retranslation. Yorke gives a number of examples. Here is one where

---

52. Yorke argues this in, "Bible Translation in Africa," esp. 114.
53. Ibid., 116.
54. Ibid., 120–21.
55. Ibid., 115–16, emphasis original.

the rhetorical question in Jeremiah 13:23 is translated by the NIV in a way that could suggest that an Ethiopian may want to change the color of his skin:

> Can the Ethiopian change his skin
> or the leopard its spots?
> Neither can you do good
> who are accustomed to doing evil.

It would, however, be perfectly possible to translate the imperfect verb in the first line in terms of *desire* or *intent* to change, as opposed to the ability to do so. Thus we would render Jeremiah's question:

> *Would* the Ethiopian change his skin
> or the leopard its spots?

As Yorke puts it: "The unarticulated response is: of course not. Why would they want to do that? They are quite happy the way they are already! Jeremiah's point is that just as there is no desire on the part of either the Ethiopian or the leopard to change his skin or its spots, so there is no desire on Israel's part to change from her erring ways."[56]

The suggested retranslation of Jeremiah 13:23 projects a positive and affirming image of blackness in contrast to the negative one reinforced by a number of translations in circulation today. Retranslation has the potential of "valorizing" the vulnerable.[57]

The church community must contend with Yorke's challenge of the traditional understandings of Jeremiah 13:23. Even if his exegetical work in respect of this text is ultimately rejected, it does provide a basis for dialogue concerning the role of pre-understanding in the interpretive process. The European/Euro-American perspective does not have an exclusive place in biblical interpretation. The European/Euro-American scholar does not have primary right to communicate meaning. African-centered translations are potentially as legitimate as European or American ones are, and would benefit people of African descent all over the world.

Notwithstanding this benefit, Caribbean people must undertake for themselves their own translations. They must bring their own perspectives to bear on the text—not uncritically, and not without a basis which the text itself gives. And, they must determine to take an approach that, though limited in itself, removes inappropriate limits that were placed on them. One advantage that they definitely have as a people is their rich cultural heritage.

---

56. Ibid., 121.
57. Lipner, "Religion and Religious Thinking in the New Millennium," 94.

PART 1: CONFIGURING CARIBBEAN THEOLOGY

They are diverse in ethnicity, and if all contribute to the hermeneutical task, they will limit their limitations and so will play their part in the transformation of their societies.

CONCLUSION

"You change a society by changing the wind,"[58] says Jim Wallis, not simply by recognizing the direction in which the wind is blowing. Wind-changers are people who change the course of history. If the church as a whole were to accept Creole as a legitimate, appropriate way to communicate the message of the gospel and to develop the mental capacity and skill set of Caribbean people, could it be a wind-changer? Could it not impact people's self-understanding, leading to essential transformation? According to Burchell Taylor, we need to understand "what the Spirit [is] saying to the churches of the Caribbean context" so we might respond "to the call to act in obedience for new life and hope for the people of the region."[59] Analysis is good. Criticism is useful. But they are not ends in themselves. They serve as a call to action. It is time for the Caribbean church to act decisively. It must articulate its own theology and live it out. It must be bold enough to contend with the forces of discrimination in a given society. And, it must be radical enough to use the language of the people to communicate with the people.

Those who think that "breaking away from the Euro-American tradition is the watering down of Christianity"[60] need to be confronted in a way that challenges them to rethink their position. They must be helped to see the faultiness of the presuppositions that undergird their worldview, rooted as they are in the ideology of those whose agenda was to oppress. They need to see that people are not free simply because they have "mastered the masters' language."[61] They are not truly free until they accept their own.

Language has been, historically, a tool of exploitation. Now it is time to reclaim this gift from God by using it as a tool of liberation. We must, therefore, listen to the arguments of the linguists and acknowledge the worth of Creole languages.[62] And we must respond to the hermeneutical imperative and seek to construct a new reality. For if God's Word is translated into the

58. Wallis, *God's Politics*, 22.
59. Taylor, "Engendering Theological Relevance," 24.
60. Williams, "What, Why, and Wherefore of Caribbean Theology," 37.
61. Ibid.
62. It is not good enough to communicate in Creole. The colonialists were willing to do so for practical reasons, but still did not acknowledge its inherent value, even as they did not acknowledge the value of those whose language it was.

language of the people, and if it is repositioned through both retranslation and the contextual presentation of that Word to show that God does side with the oppressed, then the relevance of Christianity and the sufficiency of Christ will be more evident to Caribbean people. As Jean-Bertrand Aristide attests: "We are not looking for a God living off in the distance. God . . . has taken the close and immediate form of justice; Jesus was the king of justice . . . [therefore] fighting for justice means following the direction of our faith.[63]

Clive Abdullah concurs: Christ came "to liberate all men [and women] from the slavery to which sin has subjected them: hunger, oppression and ignorance, in a word, that injustice and hatred which have their origin in human selfishness."[64] These forms of slavery are overcome through liberation of the mind. Liberation *of* the mind makes liberation *beyond* the mind that much more possible. In any case, it certainly frees us from the most oppressive hold any human being can have over another.

---

63. Aristide, *Jean-Bertrand Aristide*, 165.
64. Abdullah, "Any Word from the Lord?" 16.

3

The Significance of Forgiveness and Reconciliation for Personal and Corporate Relationships

ASHLEY SMITH

ESTRANGEMENT, ENMITY, AND CONFLICT

ESTRANGEMENT, ENMITY, AND CONFLICT are common factors among the givens and constraints of relationships, globally. These factors are reinforced and perpetuated by other aspects of the human condition referred to in the English language as hubris, paranoia, vengefulness, and suspicion. There are always individuals in various categories and sectors of society who perceive themselves as having the right to subdue, command, and dominate those they have deemed to be either inferior or intimidating; these latter are, therefore, not only to be closely monitored but also rendered incapable of becoming competitive. War, conquest, colonial domination, military occupation, and even missionary activity, are all means that the dominant use to maintain the status quo.

Over against the dominant and their beneficiaries are the dominated and subdued, who may appear to be resigned to their status or even their fate, but who often remain hopeful of the day of deliverance or liberation. Further, among the dominated are always the conscious minorities who see the possibility of transforming or even reversing the status quo. Usually, in the course of all that is done to enable the dominant to retain often ill-gotten gains, many practices develop that are not conducive to human development and the enjoyment of the good life by all. As the aftermath of the U.S. invasion of Iraq has shown, persistent conflicts destroy much needed resources. Many are disinherited, made to starve, and are physically restrained daily, while vast resources are used for security, surveillance, repression, and propaganda or misinformation.

On the larger scene, and as is the experience of most Third World countries, much of what should be applied to the meeting of basic needs is put into the destabilization of small states, necessitating the continuous struggle of powerless minorities and suppressed numerical majorities to empower themselves in relation to the powerful states and giant corporations of the industrialized north. We have also seen in recent years the conflicts that occurred in places such as the two Koreas, Northern Ireland, Ethiopia, Somalia, South Africa, Central Africa, Sri Lanka, Guyana, Trinidad and Tobago, and in places like Jamaica and similar post-colonial outposts, where there is a mix of race, color, and class.

These conflicts are rooted in ethno-political or religio-political sentiments and the corresponding cleavages. What all of these conflict situations have in common are the elements of destructiveness, waste, and chronic retardation. It is against this scenario of waste, destructiveness, retardation, and suffering, that enlightened and concerned human beings call for forgiveness and reconciliation.

WHAT IS FORGIVENESS?

Contrary to what many think, forgiveness is not an intrinsic concern only of those who follow the Jewish and Christian faiths. Rather, it is a need of the human community everywhere. By the same token, forgiveness has reference not only to personal relationships, but also to corporate relationships at all levels, from the level of the local community to that of the community of nation states. Forgiveness is not a matter of mere politeness, but rather a comprehensive physio-psychological and social process that may entail much pain resulting from deep feelings of guilt, shame, anger, hostility, and remorse. Usually this process is expected to be initiated by the perpetrators of the offence or the guilty party, and granted on terms chosen or dictated by the victims or offended party. The outcome of the process is a new relationship between persons, parties, or factions that have been estranged from each other and whose relationship has been obstructed by feelings of anger, hostility, contempt, and shame.

The contempt of certain categories of offenders is a feature of some relationships in need of transformation. Some persons consider it beneath their dignity, first of all, to confess their indebtedness to someone (or a category of persons) deemed to be socially beneath them, and, secondly, to accept pardon from anyone. This is typified in colonial and postcolonial situations such as those in the Southern Pacific, Africa, the Caribbean, Latin America, and North America, and in personal situations involving persons at different positions on the social hierarchy. In such situations, it is possible for forgiveness to be offered but not accepted, because those to whom it is offered consider it infra dig to be at the receiving end in a situation in which their erstwhile subordinates are the donors. There have been cases in which personages with imperial powers have been made to stand barefooted, wearing their shirt as a gesture of penitence, but in such cases the person at the other end was the usual holder of superior power like the head of the church universal, the Pope. It is unthinkable that the chief executive officer of a transnational corporation would do similarly in respect of a lowly cleaner at one of the subsidiaries of a company under his/her jurisdiction. Similarly, a professor in a tertiary institution is hardly likely to do this in relation to a freshman. Yet, if forgiveness is to have the effect of transforming the guilt- and conflict-ridden relationships between persons in different categories in our world, there has to be, on the one hand, admission of guilt and indebtedness, with evidence of genuine sorrow, and, on the other hand, willingness on the part of the offended party to release unconditionally.

Geiko Müller-Fahrenholz explains that "Forgiveness is an exchange of pain resulting in deepened understanding of the other and one's self."[1] It is a process that entails profound turmoil of emotions, and a removal of deep-seated bitterness and shame, resulting in the discovery of a kind of joy never known before. Forgiveness as demonstrated in Jewish and Christian Scriptures, in cases such as those involving brothers (like Jacob and Esau, or Joseph and his half-brothers), goes beyond restitution of what the offended has been deprived of. It is the inauguration of new relationships, clearing the way for a new future, not just for those released from enmity but, indeed, for the entire community of which the formerly estranged parties are part. In the language and experience of Christians, none of this is possible without confession, submission, and openness to relationships that

---

1. Müller-Fahrenholz, *Art of Forgiveness*, 34.

are entirely new—relationships that cannot presently be envisaged, because they are known only when experienced.

Müller-Fahrenholz further explains:

> When the double bondage of shame and hurt blocks the mind, forgiveness releases new images of togetherness whilst anger and defensiveness cast the shadow of doubt over each fresh suggestion: the energy of ritual disclosure expresses itself in new avenues towards the future: such images of fresh beginnings are the fruit of liberation from the bondage of past hurts.[2]

FORGIVENESS AND RECONCILIATION AS "RE-MEMBERING"

Trust is an essential component of the relationship created by forgiveness. The increased capacity of the formerly estranged parties to trust each other and bear each other's burdens enables the community that had been dismembered through the ravages of enmity and conflict to become re-membered. Formally estranged parties no longer need to be on their guard against each other because they now live with the awareness of being members of the same household (*oikos*), and therefore have the common obligation to build the economy (*oikonomia*) in the interest of the entire household. In this new scenario, commitment to the sustaining of the economy comes naturally because, among other things, the features of self-centeredness and self-seeking are overcome, thereby reducing of the tendency to be competitive, deceptive, exploitive, and vindictive.

OTHER FEATURES OF RECONCILIATION

In all truly reconciled relationships, there are a number of crucial features. First, there is willingness on the part of erstwhile victims or offended parties to write off the debt owed by the offending parties in order that the ruptured relationship might be repaired. The parties involved are thus free to go on with their lives unfettered by guilt, fear, and rejection. Restoration may be offered but not demanded, and when offered it must be understood that it is not *in lieu* of genuine repentance on the part of the offending party or debtor.

---

2. Ibid., 35

PART 1: CONFIGURING CARIBBEAN THEOLOGY

Secondly, relationships after reconciliation are significantly different from what obtained prior to estrangement. The reconciled parties never return to the "innocence" of the pre-estrangement status. Yet, they are new, open, creative, and free of those traits that precipitate enmity—traits that are associated with arrogance, contempt, suspicion, greed, and insensitivity. Genuine reconciliation contributes to the maturation of persons and communities, as we have seen in the new South Africa through the magnanimity of Nelson Mandela and the ANC colleagues, and in the United States through the efforts of saints of peace and justice like Martin Luther King, Jr. and his many white and black fellow-martyrs, especially during the decade of the nineteen-sixties. The composition of the White House Administration under Barak Obama is only one of the many evidences of this in the United States of America.

Third, in the new reconciliatory situation, there are neither winners nor losers and none must end up feeling either victimized or demoralized, since those who feel demoralized today are likely to be just waiting for their opportunity to get even with today's victors. Maturity and magnanimity must characterize the behavior of erstwhile enemies.

Fourth, it must be understood that the benefits to the forgiver are even greater than to the forgiven. This aspect of forgiveness is sometimes not known even in the Christian community. The fact is that by clinging to resentment and insistence on retribution, the offended party remains chained to the object of his/her hatred, but on the release of the debtor, one becomes free to get on with life uninhabited by anger and ill will. Therefore, those who are victims of personal or corporate injustice need to be made aware of the danger to their own well-being when they retain resentment and hatred towards those by whom they have been injured.

Finally, reconciliation is not achievable in its most therapeutic form where those estranged from each other hold to the notion of their innocence, along with the unpardonable guilt of their offenders. In particular, when those who have suffered injustice think they cannot be held responsible for present injustices that they themselves are now inflicting upon others, this is not conducive to full reconciliation.

Release will not come until those who feel victimized find what it takes to affirm not only their own authentic humanity but also the humanity of the perpetrators of the injustices by which they are victimized. Only when this has been achieved, sometimes through the instrumentality of mediators, will victims become free to embrace offenders in the same manner as that in which Joseph, in the story of the Hebrew people, embraced his erstwhile unbrotherly brothers who sold him into slavery and reported that he was dead.

In doing what is required of us as victims, we not only take charge of the situation but also make space in ourselves to receive the forgiveness which God wants to bestow upon us, similar to the waiting father in the story on the Prodigal son (Luke 15), and as Isaiah meant in his injunction:

> Encourage the people of Jerusalem.
> Tell them they have suffered long enough
> and their sins are now forgiven.
> I have punished them in full for all their sins. (Isa 40:2; GNT)

In the final analysis, forgiveness is the work of grace and those who speak knowingly of grace as it is portrayed in the Hebrew and Christian Scriptures know that it is never earned or deserved. Further, it necessitates humiliation and submission on both sides of the divide. It entails what is referred to in the Beatitudes as *meekness* (Matt 5:5). We would do well to revisit and explore this term Jesus himself used. For our purpose, the most important thing about forgiveness is that it liberates persons and transforms not only personal relationships but communities and, ultimately, God's world. In the jargon of the World Council of Churches, it has the power of effecting the restoration of "the unity of humankind" and "the integrity of creation."

IN THE CONTEXT OF THE CARIBBEAN

The prevalence of degrees of self-hate, pessimism, and sloth in a number of types of persons in the region is a significant feature of the psycho-dynamics of Caribbean personality and relationships. These persons are identified as among the following:

- A person who is visibly black African, usually afflicted with a "victim" mentality, which predisposes him/her not only to be insecure and under-achieving, but also to be resentful of persons whose physical features are deemed to be more favorable.

- The "creole," whose physical features are similar to those of fellow inhabitants who are deemed to be well-favored in respect of economic and social life.

- The East Indians of darker hue, whose fore-parents were brought to the region as indentured servants and who therefore perceive themselves as being disadvantaged in the various spheres of life, not only by the earthly "powers that be," but also by the Supreme Being, as he is perceived by persons of their ethnic type and typical religious outlook.

PART 1: CONFIGURING CARIBBEAN THEOLOGY

- The Middle Eastern Semitic type who, despite their enviable achievements in the area of commerce and industry, are still comparatively disadvantaged in the spheres of politics, religious leadership, and the more prestigious professions.
- Persons born into broken family situations, who are victims of traditional religious, moral, and social stigma.

Students of social psychology and sociology of the Caribbean (like Errol Miller and Barry Chevannes) and exponents of feminism (like Christine Barrow, Patricia Mohammed, Elsa Leo-Rhynie) have written exhaustively on the marginalization, suppression, and oppression of women in the context of patriarchal religiosity and exclusivist Caribbean societies. Situations such as these in the Caribbean contribute to the evolution of psycho-social and socio-theological atmospheres in which persons remain hateful and suspicious of others, despite the apparently cordial relationships that obtain in formal situations such as are found in Christian churches. Despite the fervency of religious expressions, there is much in the personalities of persons of the various ethnic social categories who perceive themselves as victims in socio-economic situations that militates against the development of spiritually healthy or mature and joyful persons. Those who feel victimized and contained tend to be perennially angry and secretly hopeful of the arrival of the day when there will be a reversal in the actual or imagined order. Additionally, those who are now having the upper hand in terms of the exercise of power are equally suspicious of those who deem them to be the benefiting from an unjust situation. More than anything else, many feel that God is ultimately responsible for the entrenchment of systems of injustice, hence the deep-seated resentment of God by those who have ceased to be fatalistic about the structure of the cosmos. Many who speak for legitimized religious systems or institutions may, for many reasons, be fearful of articulating their feelings of anger towards God because of their ignorance about how God is portrayed in the person and teachings of Jesus the Christ.

In the light of the foregoing observations about the perception of socio-political systems and the nature of divine justice, it is safe to assume that there are many who, despite appearing to be horrified about the possibility of their being resentful of God, are indeed resentful of God. They are therefore in need of becoming free to relate without misgiving or fear to God so that they might become open, by the grace and power of God, to unfettered and meaningful relationships with both God and fellow humans from whom they are estranged by memories of injustices and other aspects of unhealthy, destructive relationships.

Genuine forgiveness is, in the final analysis, the only means by which persons estranged from God, neighbors, and therefore dimensions of themselves, can experience freedom. This comes from releasing their resentment towards those who obstruct their achievement so that they (the victimized) may become open to becoming reconciled to all those identified as foes, enemies, or antagonists. Until this happens, individuals remain trapped within themselves, without the freedom to be truly human in the light of the personality of the Christ whom Scripture describes as increasing in wisdom and stature and in favor with God and people (Luke 2:32). Human beings in all situations need to revisit the Truth and Reconciliation approach associated with the agents of the creation of the new South Africa under the leadership of Nelson Mandela and his black and white fellow South Africans. These architects of the new South Africa are indeed manifestations of both the invincibility of divine love and the necessity and power of hope, which is an integral dimension of the relationship between the faithfulness of a gracious God and the redeem-ability of humans; divine love and hope are needed since humans are by nature both rebellious and incapable by themselves of discerning the difference between what is in their best interest and what militates against it.

Those who have used their resources and skills to make us aware of the consequences of revenge and retaliation have done enough to enable us to see the wisdom of Jesus' injunction about love for enemy, and the tendency of revenge to destroy both the perpetrators of injustice and its victims. The story of the Good Samaritan illustrates the power of the magnanimous response to who are un-neighborly and antagonistic. Human societies, which over the years have been dismembered by enmity and vengefulness, can be re-membered by the willingness to forgive, in the hope of achieving reconciliation between those who have been estranged from each other. This is clearly illustrated in biblical stories like those of Jacob and Esau (Gen 32 and 33), and Joseph and his erstwhile treacherous brothers (Gen 42, 43, 44).

Common to all stories about reconciliation between enemies is that it is mostly the aggrieved person who takes the initiative in bringing an end to the enmity. In situations like those in the Caribbean, therefore, it is those ethnic and social types who have been excluded, deprived, and snubbed—even in church—that will have to make the first move towards restoring relationships that have been unhealthy and obstructive to personal or communal growth and development. Moreover, those who take the initiative need to have faith in the willingness of God to empower them to do what is in keeping with his will for humankind. The process is likely to be slow and painful, but, because it is desirable, by the grace of God it is not only possible but always achievable. It is in keeping with God's unswerving commitment to reconciliation between humans and the rest of creation that the Son of God came, taught, suffered, died, and was raised from the dead in triumph. This was all done in the course of the history of humankind in order to achieve reconciliation both to God and between estranged individuals and factions within the human family.

4

Dingolayin'
Theological Notes for a Contextual Caribbean Theology

ERIC G. FLETT

A GUIDING METAPHOR

In Trinidad and Tobago, to "dingolay" refers to any activity that is undertaken with spontaneous, joyful, and carefree abandon. It assumes a disposition of pride, a lack of calculated or cautious self-awareness, a desire to be provocative (but not offensively so), and results in a freedom conferred by an intent focus upon the inner-logic of the activity itself—whether dance or music. In all senses of the word, it requires one to give oneself fully to the activity, and in such a way where onlookers are either drawn into the activity themselves, or judge it as evidence of madness. Originating from the French colonial heritage of the twin islands, it refers most literally to that which is flung about in a crazy or carefree fashion.[1]

---

1. See Mendes, *Cote Ci Cote La* and Winer, ed., *Dictionary of the English/Creole of Trinidad and Tobago*. Though not fully responsible for the definition of "dingolay" developed here, I am indebted to both of these authors for their work in preserving the language and culture of Trinidad of which the term "dingolay" is a part.

PART 1: CONFIGURING CARIBBEAN THEOLOGY

This essay will draw upon the idea of "dingolay" to suggest a mode of theological reflection that results in a deeply contextualized theology that is distinctively Caribbean, while also having, in and through that contextuality, a universal reference. Drawing upon themes in the Christian theological tradition of the church, such as the created order as contingent, the human creature as a cultural being created in the image of God, and God as triune Creator, the essay will suggest that the development of a Caribbean theology is not only a contextual necessity, but a theological one.

Ashley Smith knows how to dingolay, and knows how to teach others to do the same. His life and ministry continue to witness to this fact. Though I only know Ashley Smith through his writings (and a brief lunch while attending a conference in his honor at Jamaica Theological Seminary in 2010) those alone are reason enough to make such an assertion, not to mention his many former, and deeply appreciative, students who now honor his legacy by dingolayin' themselves: in classrooms, churches, and through their research and writing.

Real Roots and Potted Plants: Reflections on the Caribbean Church, a book published by Ashley in 1984, was most frequently cited as a defining point in the lives and work of many I met at the conference.[2] At the time it was published, and even to this day, it stands as a provocative collection of essays addressed to the church in the Caribbean. It is no surprise that this provocation disturbed many, but had a magnetic effect on others (laypersons, church leaders, and educators) looking for a more biblically based, non-dualistic, theologically informed, and socially relevant faith that could put down deep roots in the unique soil of the Caribbean context while also transforming the sandscape of the islands, making them a place for human flourishing and, in the process, a witness to the grace of God in Christ. It is no doubt the work of someone who discovered, personally and intellectually, the deep logic of the gospel of Christ, and began to develop it in a confident and carefree fashion, regardless of the social taboos and theological boundaries others believed he was violating.

That confident abandon, characteristic of those who dingolay, can be seen from a simple survey of the Table of Contents, starting with "Christ, the Hope of the Caribbean," and continuing with subjects and categories, bound together in a provocative fashion, that many in church circles, both then and now, both in the Caribbean and around the world, would have perceived to be not only unfriendly to the gospel, but the antithesis of it. What has faith to do with economics, and the church with social justice? How can the gospel inform social development and how does it implicitly critique

---

2. A. Smith, *Real Roots and Potted Plants*.

political oppression? Who talks about the social responsibility of the church as if it were a gospel imperative on equal footing with the task of evangelization and witness? Ashley Smith does, and in so doing he draws together categories that are essential, not only for the development of a biblical theology, but a Caribbean theology. Provocative indeed! That provocation, and the reconciliation of categories formerly understood as enemies that gives rise to it, continues in another slim volume entitled *Emerging From Innocence: Religion, Theology and Development*, where he has the audacity to include gender equality, education, and health to the list of subjects that are a proper concern of the church and theological reflection.[3] To this reader it seems clear that for Ashley Smith gospel and context cannot be conceived apart from one another without severe damage to both.

If asked, Ashley Smith would no doubt say that these concerns arise from being a thinking, feeling, informed Christian person living in an environment where these issues impact every aspect of human life. Thus, they are impossible to ignore if one is to maintain any sense of the biblical witness or Christian integrity, not to mention human compassion. True enough. My suggestion in the remainder of this essay is that ultimately it is not context that forces upon us the need to dingolay a contextual theology, whether for the Caribbean or anywhere else. A contextual theology does not arise, nor can it be sustained, ultimately from a desire to be relevant or practical or compassionate, although these are important motivations. However, I think we can add an additional layer of justification for the kind of theological dingolayin' that has characterized Ashley Smith's work—a theological layer that underlies the explicit witness of the Bible and its imperatives to care for the poor, pursue justice, and embody mercy. These theological themes form a framework that ultimately makes a contextual theology not simply a practical concern, but a theological necessity.

Stephen Bevans, in his revised and expanded edition of *Models of Contextual Theology*, notes both external and internal factors that he believes make contextual theological reflection a necessity for the church.[4] The internal factors mentioned by Bevans are the most overtly theological, as they make explicit those dynamics that are central to the inner-logic of the Christian faith itself. Among those noted by Bevans are the incarnational nature of Christianity, the sacramental nature of reality, the personal nature of divine revelation, the inclusive catholicity of the church, and finally, the tri-unity of God. It is the final theological imperative mentioned by Bevans that I would like to develop at greater length in this essay, believing it to

---

3. A. Smith, *Emerging From Innocence*.
4. Bevans, *Models of Contextual Theology*, 9–15.

be the theological basis upon which the other imperatives mentioned by Bevans are based. I would also like to suggest that his assertion of the sacramental nature of reality is ultimately rooted in a doctrine of creation as contingent, and that an additional theological imperative for doing contextual theology may be found in the Christian doctrine of the human person as created in the image of God.

My argument will be that the tri-unity of God, the contingent character of creation, and the human person as a creature in the image of God form a network of relations that are both enabled by human cultures and contexts and stand as the basis for the continual transformation and production of culture. The cultural reality that emerges from this network of relations can be described as a deeply contextualized, embodied reflection on the identity of God, the purpose of creation, and the vocation of the human person in the midst of God's world that ought to foster human flourishing and divine shalom. Our reflection on God, and our action in the world in response to God, draws upon this network of relations producing, by necessity, a contextual theology, thus making contextual theology not a optional hobby for the theologically inclined, but the only kind of theology that honors this triune God. To avoid contextual factors in our reflection upon God is to somehow respond to a God that is not triune, who has not gifted to us a contingent creation, nor created us in his image. It is to absolve ourselves of our role in God's creative work in the world and for the world. If we make these theological affirmations (and most of the Christian church does) then we are also implicitly affirming that theologies that seek to describe and identify this God must do so critically aware that contextual factors are a necessity in this task. Removing them as factors of interest or concern endangers the identity of the God they seek to bear witness to. What is required then, is a *theology* that is explicitly aware that contextual factors are a positive necessity if it is to talk about God in a faithful manner. That requires the church to say not only some very detailed things about context, but also some very detailed things about the God who works within it. Context alone does not a contextual theology make.

IS CONTEXT ENOUGH?

In surveying the work done on the development of a Caribbean theology one is surprised to find much talk about the subjects of church, of context, of gospel, of liberation, but very little material reflection on God *per se*.[5]

---

5. There are legitimate reasons for this, particularly since in the early days of the development of a Caribbean theology church folk were struggling simply to legitimate

Could this be the Achilles heel that has thus far slowed the development of a truly Caribbean theology—that as eager as we are to develop a Caribbean theology, we have stepped back from actually saying some material things about the God who values context and comes to us in the midst of it? That context, while important, is not enough to sustain the creative theological reflection necessary for the development of a truly Caribbean theology.

Even Clifford Payne's essay in Idris Hamid's *Out of the Depths*, entitled, "What Will A Caribbean Christ Look Like," promises to move us from generic statements about God and God's concerns to more concrete statements about the Christ who comes to us clothed not only with the gospel, but also speaking with an identifiable accent. There is no doubt that this move from the general to the specific is a move in the right direction, but even when considering the particularities of Christ himself, Clifford Payne simply tells us that the Caribbean Christ will still be recognizably European, progressively Black (in terms of social experience, not simply skin pigmentation), will owe something to India, and will resist "ghettoization," in that Christ will not be content to be a tribal deity, of the Caribbean or anywhere else, even though coming to us in very particular forms.[6] Though each of these statements carries theological assumptions, those assumptions are not clarified. Context is left to carry the burden of telling us about God, of doing theology. One wonders if this is a sustainable position to be in as a Caribbean theologian who wants to ultimately talk about God, and not simply context.

Theo Witvliet, in his *A Place in the Sun*, notes that only marginal progress toward a distinctively Caribbean theology had been made at the 1985 publication of his survey of liberation theology in the Third World.[7] His observations occurred after Idris Hamid and others began "troubling the waters" with symposia dedicated to exploring the reasons behind the absence of a tradition of theological reflection that took the Caribbean context seriously. However, Witvliet observes that those who search the essays

---

the task itself, and articulate to others the uniqueness of their context and the necessity to address it. It seems that their work has succeeded, and that now the thick descriptions of the Caribbean context we do have (from anthropologists, sociologists, politicians, artists, and theologians) need to be allowed to feed back into the articulation of a theological vision for the Caribbean that has distinctive things to say about God and the Christian tradition, that in turn will enrich the global Christian community and nourish the work of the Christian community in the Caribbean. The reflections of Ashley Smith and Dieumeme Noëlliste are suggestive exceptions to this trend. See Ashley Smith's works already mentioned above, as well as Noëlliste, "Transcendent but Not Remote," 104–26.

    6. Payne, "What Will A Caribbean Christ Look Like," 1–8.

    7. Witvliet, *A Place in the Sun*.

produced for these symposia are "likely to be weighed down, willy-nilly, by the impact of the almost monotonous litany in which the charges against neo-colonial mission are constantly repeated. The negative element of criticism still predominates to such a degree that it is hardly possible to go on to the development of new forms."[8] The critique of colonialism is still present in more recent works, and rightly so, since colonialism continues to reach forward from the past to exert its presence in ever new forms. It continues to be a powerful force economically, politically, and culturally, in shaping the Caribbean context.

However, putting colonialism in its place does not a Caribbean theology make, and those interested in the development of a Caribbean theology know this. Their throats cleared of obstructions rooted in the past, Caribbean theologians have something to say, and something to contribute to the Christian theological tradition from the unique soil of the Caribbean. New forms have been explored, and the positive particularities of the Caribbean context articulated and appropriated. Some of these appropriations and explorations have been published,[9] but the majority have been explored through on-ground, praxis-based experiments that revolve more around the church than the academy, the true context for theological reflection and dingolayin' in the Caribbean, although also one of its main barriers. And yet, reflection upon, and articulation of, context, whether the historical context of the past, or the cultural context of the present, still seems to be the central preoccupation of many doing Caribbean theology today.

Perhaps the *kairos* moment facing the Caribbean church is to continue to keep the global Christian community aware of the negative powers of colonialism and the positive particularities of Caribbean culture, but also to contribute to the expansion of the theological tradition of the church through some theological dingolayin' that births metaphors, dynamics, and truths that could not be discovered or articulated anywhere else.[10] The Caribbean church need not piggy-back upon theologies crafted in other contexts, such as liberation theologies originating in Latin America or Black

---

8. Ibid., 105–6.

9. One thinks again of the work of Ashley Smith, as well as that of Kortright Davis, Noel Erskine, David and Aida Spencer, and George Mulrain, as well as the other contributors to this collection.

10. I am thinking here of my wife's home of Trinidad, where hybridity rules the day when it comes to race, religion, food, music, and language. For instance, what other environment could have given birth to the music of chutney, not to mention the broad varieties of calypso found throughout the Caribbean? If in music, food, language, and other areas, why shouldn't equally distinctive theological forms emerge from this region; forms that are as creative, vibrant, joyful, resistant, and as prophetic as the gospel itself?

theologies emigrating from America, as helpful as these reflections may be. But the Caribbean church does need to speak a little less of the particularities of context, and more about the particularities of the God who identifies himself through it.

In Kortright Davis' excellent and widely cited work, *Emancipation Still Comin'*, the author cites Burchell Taylor, who defines a Caribbean theology as one that is "both reflective on and responsive to the particularities of the Caribbean context in the light of the Word of God."[11] This is an accurate and concise definition, and if the past work of developing a Caribbean theology has been (rightly) concerned with articulating "the particularities of the Caribbean context" then it would seem the future of the project would need to spend an equal amount of time isolating and developing the "particularities" of the "Word of God,"[12] and what that Word affirms about the identity and action of God. From beginning to end it suggests that this God has designed contextuality into creation (and made creation the context for our relations with him), and placed human persons in the midst of creation to shape and direct its many potentialities in such a way that they bear witness to God and by so doing enable the flourishing of the created order God has graciously brought into being.

However, just as important as emphasizing the need to give proper attention to *both* particularities of context and particularities of divine identity and purpose, is the need to make sure that both are related in a healthy and mutually modifying dynamic. Without a dynamic of mutual modification, where gospel transforms context and context informs gospel, a truly Caribbean theology that enables human flourishing will not emerge, nor will there be a universal witness and reference for any context-specific embodiment of the gospel.

Now, with this as a goal, what theological resources are there in the Christian tradition to enable the church in the Caribbean to dingolay a distinctively Caribbean theology? There are, no doubt, many that could be drawn upon, but I would like to explore three theological notes in particular that together may help us sound an authentic Caribbean contextual theology.

---

11. Davis, *Emancipation Still Comin','* 94–95.

12. My understanding of the "Word of God" here is broad, and not limited to the Bible *per se*, although it most certainly includes it. Karl Barth referred to the "three-fold form of the Word," and it is in roughly that sense that I understand the phrase. The Word of God comes to us "incarnate" in Jesus of Nazareth, "written" in the pages of the Bible, and "preached" in the teaching, preaching, and liturgical witness of the Christian community.

PART 1: CONFIGURING CARIBBEAN THEOLOGY

NOTE #1: THE CREATIVITY OF THE TRIUNE CREATOR

A contextual theology is a theological necessity because the focus of our theological reflection is the triune God of Jesus Christ.

Affirming the particularity of the triune God is the first step in affirming and protecting the particularity of the human creature and the importance of the role of context in theological reflection. The particular God that we come to know through the biblical witness identifies himself contextually, and in terms of a very specific story, involving persons, plots, events, symbols, rituals, and problems that, while having universal reference, are very different from the contemporary stories, rituals, and symbols we use to organize and interpret our lives. Why is this so? Why does God employ the wanderings and musings of a collection of Near Eastern tribes, and, even more specifically, the life and words of a Palestinian Jewish male speaking with the accent of a Nazarene, to mediate to the world his identity and desires?

It certainly is not because God wants to reach the widest audience possible as quickly as possible, or that God was concerned with expediency and efficiency in carrying out his plans. That seems clear from the outset of the biblical story, where the future of the human race is dependent upon the judgments of a single human pair, the flourishing of creation upon their activity as stewards, and the story of the God of creation upon their limited cultural symbols, finite memories, and selective obedience. It is a story of starts and stops from beginning to end, and yet the character and purposes of God come though clearly as the story unfolds. There is something about particularity and context that reveals the identity and will of God in a way that contextless, universal, generic, and abstract declarations simply cannot. Again, why is that?

From the story we have, it would seem that God could not have done it any other way. God's self-identification and self-giving move from the particular to the universal, from the one to the many—not the other way around. Adam and Eve stand in for the entire human race. Abraham for Israel. The church for the world. Jesus for all creation. The life of the many are constantly implicated in the existence, identity, and actions of the one or the particular. This dynamic runs like a red-thread through the narrative of Scripture, suggesting strongly that God's concern for context is rooted in God's very being and the very nature of the created order. God's concern for context and particularity is personal and material, not simply instrumental.

We might, of course, suggest otherwise, and assert that God's concern with the particular, with context, with culture, is indeed instrumental, and not rooted in any necessity of God's being, or the structure of the created order. That is, we might claim that God comes to the human creature in terms of the particularities of their biology and culture simply because *we* require it, not because it is required of God himself, or that it has any significant role to play in the fulfillment of God's purposes for creation. Thus, we might argue that if God wants to say something to human persons, God has to come to human persons on their own terms, whether he is a particular enthusiast of human culture or not. Culture is simply a socially constructed coping mechanism for finite creatures and is of no abiding interest to God. And since there is no such thing as a generic human speaking a universal language,[13] God accommodates himself to the particularities of our context in order to accomplish an instrumental goal: to communicate with us and to reconcile us to himself in a way that is tangible, powerful, and communicable. Once that instrumental task is accomplished, we might claim, the importance of culture and context is relativized. It enables communication and revelation, but itself is not a by-product of God's work in the world. It is a human necessity, not a divine one. Culture and context enable the mediation of God's work, but are not the end goal of that work. God's work in this case would ultimately transcend context; it does not give rise to it, nor does it ultimately endorse it. This would suggest that true knowledge of God should strive for an objectivity that is ultimately incompatible with particularity; that a "contextual theology" is an oxymoron.

This very approach, however, is itself a deeply contextual understanding of the task of theology, and one rooted specifically in the context of Western modernity. It not only colonizes other cultures who do not share this vision of knowledge, it colonizes God by insisting that God has no ultimate interest in culture or context, and that the further we get from the particularities of culture, the more accurate and devoted our understanding of God.[14]

This seems highly unlikely for a number of reasons, but I will only take the time to concentrate on one theological reason: the God of the Christian confession is triune. Particularity and relationality are essential features of

13. However, the mechanisms of our global economy are busy constructing just such a generic human. It seems that the vision of the generic human that may prevail is one where we are fundamentally consumers whose mother tongue is English.

14. Liberation theologians of all varieties have been chafing against this modernist epistemology for some time. Kevin Vanhoozer, in an excellent essay on theological method in the global church, articulates the dynamics well, in noting that we don't want to decontextualize God or engage in "theological ethnification." In the former, God is universalized, and belongs to no one in particular, while in the latter, God becomes a tribal deity with no universal reference. Both are errors that any theological method needs to be aware of. Vanhoozer, "One Rule to Rule Them All?" 85–126.

PART 1: CONFIGURING CARIBBEAN THEOLOGY

God's very being, not simply instrumental conventions employed when it comes time to deal with human persons. If this is the case that God is tri-une—and the majority of the Christian church has confessed so for centuries—then it would suggest that the only kind of theology that can faithfully bear witness to this God's identity and will is a contextual one. In addition, contextual theologies not only mediate to human persons knowledge of God's identity and will, they themselves are manifestations that the will of God is being fulfilled and advanced, for they provide a kaleidoscopic witness to the identity and creativity of God, the nature of that God's work in the world, and the manifold scope of human stewardship over creation.

Four things, I think, can be said about the importance of the tri-unity of God for our theme: 1) It is the basis for the identity of God; 2) it is the basis for the creativity of God; 3) it is the basis for the identity of creation and the human creature; and 4) it is the basis upon which the Christian community finds the confidence, freedom, and creativity to dingolay new forms of culture that bear witness to God and enable the flourishing of creation. I'll comment on each of these ideas briefly.

That God is triune is the most fundamental, and the most distinctive, claim the Christian community can make about the God to whom it bears witness. The inner-logic of the Christian faith is rooted in this claim, even if the term and the dynamics it describes are absent in explicit form from the biblical witness. The idea of the Trinity itself emerged as a result of some very creative, contextual, theological dingolayin' in the fourth century by those in the church who had to articulate clearly (in the face of confusions both in and outside the church) the nature of their faith in Jesus of Nazareth, and their claim that references in the Bible to a Father, a Son, and a Holy Spirit were references to not only one God, but one God whose very being and identity was grounded in the mutual relationships between three distinct divine persons. The God of the Christian faith did not "play mas"[15] by appropriating differing masks and costumes as the context demanded (one for Father, one for Son, and one for Spirit), but was in fact three distinct persons who, through these three different identities, identifies himself as the one God. In the face of such mysteries it took a great deal of confidence and personal creativity with the conceptual tools offered by the Christian tradition and classical culture, to formulate the distinctive idea of God that the Trinity refers to. It was a concept of God that placed the relational dynamics of particular persons giving and receiving in love at its center, a love

---

15. An expression used in Trinidad to refer to those who participate in the annual Carnival celebrations by assuming the identity of a group, or some other person (a political or cultural figure) or thing (an animal), specifically by putting on costumes of all kinds and "masquerading" along with others in a procession of street dancing.

eternally shared among the Father, the Son, and the Spirit, and generously and personally extended to all creation in a trinitarian chain of embrace and affirmation. That God is triune says important things about the role of contextuality and sociality in the theological witness of the church.

It not only suggests certain truths about the of identity and nature God, but also about the creative activity of God, in that God acts according to God's nature, not according to theoretical possibilities based upon abstract attributes.[16] Divine omnipotence, for instance, just looks different when we consider its meaning from the vantage point of a crucified Jewish male, as opposed to the vantage point of Aristotelian metaphysics. We hinted at this above, in noting that God's concern with context is rooted in personal and material factors, not instrumental ones. Theoretically, according to abstract conceptions of divine power, knowledge, and presence, God could have created a world free of contingency, risk, diversity, and limitation, but simply did not want to. If that were the case, then the shape of the created order would be determined more by our conceptions of libertarian freedom, as applied to God's choosing and willing, than by factors rooted in the very identity and being of God as the triune Creator. The truth is, we know God through the concrete actuality of his particular works, and those works, both general and special, are congruent with a God characterized by relation, particularity, grace, forgiveness, love, freedom, generosity, and abundance. The particular has a unique power to reveal in a way the generic does not, because the triune God is a God of particularity and relation, of story and plot, of harmony and dissonance, and has brought into being a created order characterized by the same.

Theologies that attempt to identify such a God by recourse to abstract generalities bear an ambiguous witness, if not a hegemonic one. The particularity of God's identity as Father, Son, and Spirit, and the particularity of God's engagement with the created order (both of which are grounded in the biblical witness), critique any attempt to define and identify this God in a way that excludes or marginalizes particular persons, events, contexts, and cultures. The theological work of the church should not seek to minimize or obliterate these characteristics, but to incorporate them into her theological reflection and witness. After all, the God we seek to bear witness to was not ashamed of our weak, finite, and culture-bound humanity, so why should we seek to outdo our master by crafting theologies that assume that divinity, rightly described, transcends contextuality?

---

16. Some of these attributes are rooted more in human desires for comfort, control, and cultural validation than God's self-giving and identification in Jesus of Nazareth.

PART 1: CONFIGURING CARIBBEAN THEOLOGY

Perhaps the most profound, and concrete, evidence of God's dynamic nature, and deep connection to creation and context, is that this triune God *became* both Creator and incarnate.[17] No doubt, these possibilities existed before being realized through God's actions, but nevertheless, this is a God who enacts profoundly new things, and does so by involving the created order, and by doing so, redeems it without displacing it. God, in God's very being, does not experience creation and context theoretically, but practically, in becoming Creator and becoming Incarnate. This suggests that there is a qualitative difference between theoretical knowledge of God and knowledge that is based in praxis and experience, and that experience, of creation and context, is a form of praxis-based intimate knowing that cannot be had otherwise. Can the church, again, as student and disciple, be above her master in this regard? This fact would seem to make not only deep exegesis a necessity (as it forces the interpreter of the Bible deep into the linguistic and social particularities of the text), but contextual theology as well.

That God is triune also has important things to say about the nature and identity of the created order God has brought into being, and the human creature entrusted with its care and cultivation. We will develop these two areas of Christian thought below, so it will suffice at this point simply to point out this connection. The tri-unity of God, the contingency of creation, and the creation of the human person in the image of God are all of one fabric, in that the created order and the human creature are what they are by virtue of the fact that they have been brought into being, not by a generic, merely monotheistic God, but by a triune God.[18] True, there is a qualitative difference between Creator and creation, but that ontological distinction, while serving to preserve the freedom of God and the particularity of creation, does not undermine the deep continuities between them. The Scottish Reformed theologian T. F. Torrance gets the balance right when he says that "the reason for the creation is theologically traced back to the free, ungrudging will of God's love to create a reality other than himself which he correlates so closely with himself that it is made to reflect and shadow forth on its contingent level his own inner rationality and order."[19] I will explore more on what these connections mean for understanding the nature and identity of creation and creature below.

Finally, it is the triune God of Jesus Christ who confers upon the Christian community the confidence, freedom, and creativity to dingolay

17. See in particular the discussion by Torrance in *The Trinitarian Faith*, 88.

18. The Catholic theologian Karl Rahner used to bemoan the fact that Christians were "mere monotheists" when they had the richness of a triune God to inform their imaginations and inspire their actions.

19. Torrance, *Divine and Contingent Order*, 35.

new forms of culture that bear witness to God and enable the flourishing of creation. To dingolay requires confidence and creativity, but neither of these qualities are ultimately rooted in the human person. Instead, they are ultimately tethered to the God who gifts to us the security and imagination needed to bear witness to God well.

Without this external tethering of our identity, confidence, and creativity, these gifts usurp their proper boundaries and *telos*, and instead of bearing witness to God (with the flourishing of the human creature as by-product) they assert themselves and by so doing obscure God and subvert the human creature and creation. We base our confidence on ethnocentric arrogance and tether our imaginations and creativity to our own fears and egocentricity, with devastating personal and social consequences. The freedom, faith, trust, risk, and creativity required to dingolay in this fashion arises out of God's embrace of the human creature, an embrace that is not conditioned upon anything other than the love of the Father, the Son, and the Spirit. This unconditioned love liberates the human creature to be what it is (a finite, fragile, and physical image-bearer of the triune God), and to become what it is not yet (faithful, joyful, just, kind, etc.). The triune action of God confers upon the human creature the psychological conditions necessary to dingolay in such a way that the divine freedom and love are embodied in the created order through the agency of the human creature embraced by God and empowered by the Spirit.

A contextual theology can start from any number of points to be *contextual*, but it is not a *theology* unless it is bound and tethered to the triune God of Jesus Christ.

With my most important and defining point made, I will treat the other two notes in a much briefer fashion, and with an eye towards further development at a later time.

NOTE #2: THE CONTINGENCY OF THE CREATED ORDER

A contextual theology is a theological necessity because the created order brought into being by the triune Creator is "contingent," in that it has been created "out of nothing" and as such is a reality that has an integrity of its own, is responsive to the agency of God and humanity, and is meant to reflect, through that agency, the divine design through human designs.

A former teacher at the University of London, the late Colin Gunton, was often fond of referring to the creative activity of the Father as being carried out through his "two hands," namely, the Son and the Spirit. He is, of course, indebted to the second century theologian Irenaeus for this metaphor, which reinforces the early importance of the doctrine of the Trinity for understanding God's creative activity, as well as the nature of the created order that was its consequence. However, the Son and the Spirit are not simply laborers at the behest of the Father, for the Father, the Son, and the Spirit constitute "a fellowship in creative activity" among themselves,[20] a loving communion that is in fact the ultimate basis for the origin of the world, its contingent nature, and its ultimate *telos*. The particularity of each divine Person qualifies the character of God's creative activity, as well as the character of created order that is the result of that activity.

Nevertheless, that qualification in place, and staying with Irenaeus' metaphor, God has created something with his "hands" that we in turn are to manipulate with our own. This is deeply connected to the idea that human persons are created in the divine image, a matter we will address shortly. The reality that God has brought into being has determinate boundaries that suggest design, orientation, and purpose. To ignore, abuse, and violate those boundaries, and to impose a design of our own upon it, is to create structures, social and physical, that subvert the integrity of the created order and undermine the flourishing of creation. To dingolay is not to engage in pure randomness, nor to impose order indiscriminately and insensitively; it is to coax and nurture out of creation an abundance and design that has been placed there by God, and by so doing to find our reason for being, and with that, satisfaction, contentment, and joy. In fact, the freedom found in dingolayin' is not a freedom of unrestrained movement, but purposeful action, where action in accordance with the divine purpose confers a freedom unattainable through sheer randomness and chaos.

Theologizing in context is part of this coaxing and nurture, in that theologizing of this nature seeks to provide persons with the conceptual tools necessary to rightly understand and orient our relations to God, others, and creation, and out of that right orientation, to engage in right action that produces and sustains justice, wholeness, abundance, and beauty.

What conceptual tools can we use to understand the uniqueness of creation as the context for dingolayin' a contextual theology? With regard to God, the conceptual tool I have found most effective in theologically validating contextual theological projects is that God is "triune." With regard to creation, "contingency" is perhaps the broadest descriptor for the unique order God has brought into being as the canvas upon which, and the context within which, our relations to God, neighbor, and creation are constructed and carried out.

20. Torrance, *Theology in Reconstruction*, 220.

T. F. Torrance (a contextual theologian in his own right) understands contingency as an idea that flows out of the theological assertion that the created order was brought into being out of nothing, through the sheer freedom, goodness, and grace of God. The created order as we know it need not exist all, and it need not exist in the form that it does. The reality of the created order, and its particular form, are determined by something outside of itself, and that something is the triune God of Jesus Christ.

Because of this contingent relation, Torrance claims that the Creator confers upon the created order a distinctive intelligibility, freedom, and order,[21] which can be ultimately traced back to the one who has brought it into being.[22] The created order is contingent, because all these qualities derive from, and are sustained by, the good and gracious will of the triune Creator. But, beyond that, it is *intelligible* because the created order can be known by human persons as a reality external to themselves, and with an integrity of its own. Furthermore, it is *free*, because the created order is not a deterministic system that is ultimately governed by immutable laws inherent within its structure, nor wholly determined by a reality other than itself. And, finally, it is *orderly*, in that the structure of the created order suggests an overarching design and *telos* that is reflective of the divine will.

These ideas are rich and suggestive, and deserve further treatment. However, it will suffice, for the scope of this essay, to state that contingency so defined implies two fundamental truths. First, the created order is *reflexive or reciprocal in nature*. That creation is reflexive or mutually reciprocal suggests that it is a relational, flexible, plastic, and multivariable reality that, by divine design, is open and responsive to divine and human agency.

Secondly, the created order is *reflective in purpose*. That creation reflects an overarching divine purpose suggests that it is an eschatological reality, bounded and determined by structures that orient it toward a specific design, *telos*, or goal that ultimately lies beyond its inherent structures to approximate.

Contingency, so defined, has important implications for the development of any Christian theology, but in particular theologies that seek greater theological "space" for the conscious inclusion of contextual elements in

---

21. These three areas of Torrance's thought are developed more fully in his books *The Trinitarian Faith*, *Divine and Contingent Order*, and *The Ground and Grammar of Theology*, as well as chapter 2 of my book *Persons, Powers, and Pluralities*, where the ideas are placed in a broad context for use in a theology of culture.

22. This perhaps sounds simpler than it is, and certainly simpler than Torrance himself develops in his work. One cannot trace the identity of God off the surface of creation. For Torrance, fundamental clues rooted in the revelatory work of God are essential in "tracing back" any connection between the form of creation and its Creator. Nevertheless, a correspondence of some kind can be affirmed.

theological reflection and theologically informed action. The created order as contingent suggests that the created order has been brought into being so that it can be sculpted, coaxed, and stretched toward a determinate end, and that much of this manipulation has to do with divine and human agency, and specifically with the human person whose fundamental task in the created order is to serve as a steward through the creation of cultural forms that approximate, in ever greater ways, the project of creation initiated by God with the creation of the world.

That the created order is "contingent" means that God introduced an interplay between plasticity, multivariablility, and determinancy into the very structure of the created order as its inner logic, and this is a key clue as to the fundamental *telos* of the created order and the vocation of the human creature. These qualities are not incidental to the fundamental purpose of the created order, but in fact constitute the inner logic of that *telos*, in that contingent things are meant to be sculpted and shaped in such a way that they realize a potential they are not able to actualize without "outside" assistance, and that they reflect that potential in such a way that brings glory to Creator and creation alike. Creation as contingent is meant to be coaxed towards its goal and *telos* by a triune God who lovingly interacts with it and sustains it, and by its human inhabitants who are meant to bring its multi-variable structure to cultural form through their interactions with it. The inner logic of contingency suggests that the created order is a responsive reality so that it can be a reflective reality, reflective of the creative purposes of its Creator, and reflective of the creativity of the creatures created in God's image.

This also means that the created order will surrender to a number of different designs, sculptings, and interpretations. Some of those will be theological and all of them will be contextual. This is a by-product of contingency, and of the central vocation of the human person as a culture-maker created in the image of a triune God. This brings us to the third theological note we can use to sound an authentic Caribbean contextual theology.

NOTE #3: THE IDENTITY AND CALLING OF THE PRIEST OF CREATION

A contextual theology is a theological necessity because the human creature, brought into being by a triune Creator and entrusted with a contingent creation, has been created "in the image of God" and assigned a cultural task that necessitates contextual theological reflection and embodiment.

The delicate harmony between plasticity and determinacy required of contingency must also be extended to the human creature, for the human creature is also part of the created order. It is not so plastic that it can be manipulated into whatever form human society sees fit, nor is it so determinate that there are not a multitude of ways to manipulate its physical and social life, and by so doing reflect the divine *telos* for flourishing and shalom. As with the created order in general, contingency is an essential component in the constitution and calling of the human creature, and the inner logic of its life. Contingency makes it possible for the human creature to exist, and to exist as the kind of creature it was meant to be.

Just as the classical theological category of creation *ex nihilo* gave rise to the idea of contingent intelligibility, freedom, and order, so the idea of the human creature as created in the image of God becomes the central conceptual tool for understanding the implications of contingency as applied specifically to the human creature. The human creature is reflexive in nature and reflective in purpose just as the created order, but in a unique way in terms of its constitution and calling. The phrase "created in the image of God" seeks to identify the uniqueness of *human* contingency.

The reflexivity of the human creature is tied up in the fact that the human creature, as contingent, is deeply dependent upon its relations to God, others, and creation for its physical and social existence. This dependency seems evident from the biblical witness, and in particular the creation and fall narratives in Genesis 1–3, where the shalom that characterizes Eden is rooted in an ecology of relations such that the violation of one of these relations has ramifications for all others, just as the health of one of these relations has similar ramifications.

There are continuities and discontinuities aplenty between the created order and the human person, and those cannot be explored within the focus of this essay.[23] Suffice it to say that the *reflexiveness* of the human creature as a relational and social being is essential to its ability to *reflect* and image its Creator, not only as a unique species, but through its work as a species uniquely dependent upon God and the symbolic worlds it both creates and sustains. The human person in the image of God is fundamentally a religious, social, cultural, and doxological creature, setting it apart in identity, nature, and calling from the rest of the created order. This too seems clear from the biblical witness, and in particular the fact that, of all the creatures God had made only one was given a task to complete, a task contingent upon its unique identity as image of God. The human person exists as a continent

---

23. Those continuities and discontinuities occur on a number of levels: physical, social, emotional, etc.

creature like all others, but with an identity and calling unlike all others. It has been created in the image of God in order to image God.

That work (imaging God) is fundamentally one of stewardship, mediation, and priesthood—all exercised through the creation and transformation of culture, and very particular and complex forms of culture at that. Let's expand a bit on this claim.[24]

The image of God is closely associated with the vocation of humanity as a priest of creation or mediator of order. This priestly vocation of mediation is fulfilled through cultural activity, understood in its broadest sense as the formation of conceptual and physical tools with which we order and orient our life together, and with which we apprehend and engage reality. As created in the image of God the human being is essentially a social being, and therefore an irreducibly *cultural being*, for human relations to the world, to God, and to other persons are made possible and held together within a cultural framework that God has not only provided for, but condescends to work within, binding himself to it in grace and love, all the while remaining transcendent over it as its Savior and Lord.

In the words of theologian Robert Jenson, we are uniquely related to God as "his conversational counterpart,"[25] a conversation initiated by the Father, secured by the Son, and sustained by the Spirit. The whole created order is implicated in this conversation, for it provides not only the environment in which the conversation takes place but also the physical and social tools that make its dialogical and embodied character possible. The response that Christ secures and the Spirit enables is fundamentally a cultural response since it incorporates the entirety of our being, as embodied souls and ensouled bodies. Our cultural life is made possible through the agency of the triune God and is intended to reflect that God, and by so doing to sustain the creatures crafted after his image, and the created order in which they are placed (and of which they are a constituent part). These presuppositions necessitate the presence of contextual factors in all theological thinking, whether theoretical, practical, or pastoral. Thought about God is inherently contextual, and contextual according to divine design (not by accident or human necessity), since it is the triune God who has created

---

24. Much could be said at this point to substantiate that the human person is an irreducibly social and relational creature, whose constitution in the image of a social and relational God is directly tied to its fundamental calling as a culture-maker. It will suffice to simply cite the work by one of the editors of this volume as a gateway to the biblical, theological, sociological, and archaeological material on this topic. See Middleton, *The Liberating Image*. For a theologically focused treatment, with specific reference to the Trinitarian theology of Thomas F. Torrance, one could refer to Flett, *Persons, Powers, and Pluralities*.

25. Jenson, *Systematic Theology*, 95.

a creature of this kind, so that it cannot but think contextually about God, neighbor, self, creation, etc.

Thus, there is something unique about the constitution of the human creature that necessitates a cultural environment for its survival, and that generates a cultural environment as an essential aspect of the *telos* of its being. The cluster of relations and capacities this requires, and how they are oriented and put to use, can be understood as "the image of God," and are directly related to the trinitarian understanding of the God developed above. Some of these same anthropological assumptions, although differently described, are central to the work of sociologist Peter Berger.[26]

Berger's theory of culture is deeply rooted in fundamental worldview assumptions about the nature of the human organism, assumptions that are, at significant points, compatible with the theological anthropology developed here. Although Berger would not use the language of "image of God" to describe the anthropological models that inform his cultural theory (let alone explicate what the "image" means by recourse to a trinitarian God), the dynamics of the human organism described in his sociological work are recognizable in the theological work of a number of trinitarian theologians. Of particular interest is Berger's description of the human organism as "incomplete," "open to the world" and "plastic," which I take to be a sociological and naturalistic way of referring to what theologians have described as the fundamental sociality of the human creature as a contingent being and its desire to find meaning beyond itself in its Creator. A brief explanation of Berger's anthropological assumptions, and the cultural theory built upon them, is in order.

According to Berger, the plasticity of the human organism is rooted in the fact that the human species is not born into a species-specific environment but must create one for itself. In addition, the human creature does not have a highly developed instinctual apparatus that will enable it to survive apart from the care and sustenance of others, or apart from a socially constructed environment. These two factors differentiate the human species from other species.

What biology does not provide (a well developed instinctual apparatus, or a species-specific environment) must be compensated for through non-biological means. It is this fundamental necessity that drives the human creature to create a socio-cultural world. This world in turn provides the human creature with a sense of significance and security in the light of its fundamental fragility and meaninglessness. It does this by giving the

---

26. See in particular Berger and Luckmann, *The Social Construction of Reality*, and Berger, *The Sacred Canopy*.

human creature signs, symbols, and institutions as tools with which the human creature builds a stable social world and finds a meaningful role within it. These are relatively uncontroversial and widely accepted assumptions among anthropologists and sociologists.

The clarity and simplicity of Berger's description of this process is what makes his contribution so significant. According to Berger, the constitution of this cultural world comes about through a three step dialectical process, one that he articulates in many of his works, but is succinctly described in his book with Thomas Luckmann entitled *The Social Construction of Reality*.[27]

Berger identifies three distinguishable steps or "moments" in the dialectical process that serves as the basis for his theory of culture; they are externalization, objectivation, and internalization. The specific content of each of these movements is not important. What is important is that they are necessary movements rooted in the plasticity and biological incompleteness of the human creature that give rise to culture, and serve to create a socio-cultural environment that functions as the human creature's primary tool of adaptation and survival.

While Berger and other anthropologists and sociologists ground this three-fold dialectic in human biological incompleteness, I would locate it in the creation of the human person in the image of the triune God and the vocation of the human person as a priest of creation. For Berger, the fundamental plasticity of the human organism leads to a diversity of social constructions, and the necessity of being formed by what the human organism creates.[28] For myself, however, the plasticity of the contingent order as a whole, and the sociality of the human person in particular, becomes the basis for the expression of the image of God and the fulfillment of human stewardship.

Plasticity and sociality make it possible for the human person to take on a concrete cultural identity, and to be part of a concrete cultural collectivity through the socialization process. This gifts the human creature with the capacities necessary to shape the social world in such a way that it will reflect the divine purpose for the creation and the creature. By this process, the human creature is offered a security and significance that is ultimately grounded outside the ever changing boundaries of the socially constructed

---

27. A more condensed version of the process described in *The Social Construction of Reality* may be found in Berger, *Sacred Canopy*, 1–28; with a more condensed version still in Wuthnow, et al., *Cultural Analysis*, 34.

28. Torrance also recognizes the "plasticity" of the human person and understands this plasticity as a quality of personhood: "As person . . . man is the being who is open to others as well as to the world." Torrance, *Reality and Scientific Theology*, 193.

world. This entire process would be impossible apart from the contingency of the human creature as the image of God, and apart from the explicit inclusion of contextual factors in the human persons reflection about God.

Just as plasticity and sociality are essential features of the human creature created according to God's design, they can also be just as much a *threat* to the human person. This is because the very openness of the human person to the world that this requires also opens the human person to being determined by that world. This is why any articulation of a contextual theology must not make context alone the sole focus of its endeavors—if the ultimate purpose of such a contextual theology is to reflect the God of Jesus Christ, enable the flourishing of the human creature, and push the created order toward shalom. Context is important, but it is not enough.

Berger does not seem to be able to account for the threat of cultural determinism, or if he does, it certainly is not solved by recourse to a transcendent reference point. This however, is exactly the move made by Torrance to keep in check the blessings and curses of those who wish to think theologically and contextually. A dialectic of externalization, objectivation, and internalization that is *incongruent* with the divine *telos* for the created world and the human creature would subvert the personal structure of humanity and the vocation of that humanity as priest of creation.

In order to set the human person free to be *determinate* (to have a concrete identity and to fulfill a concrete calling), without being *determined*, a transcendent reference point is required, one that is dynamic and active and that has an objective existence of its own.[29] For Torrance, this reference point is the triune God. It is this reference point that safeguards the personal structure of being human even while safeguarding the *plasticity of the human person* from becoming a vehicle of determinism; instead, this plasticity is the means by which the unique human *telos* is fulfilled. This is summed up by Torrance in the following way: "I submit that it is only through a divine Trinity who admits us to communion with himself in his own transcendence that we can be consistently and persistently personal,

---

29. Perhaps a reminder is in order here. Torrance fully affirms the goodness of being created a determinate being. This is not a negative quality of being human that must be transcended. The determinate nature of human life is rooted, not in the fall or human sin, but in the declaration of the created order as 'good' by its Creator and the assumption, resurrection, and redemption of the created order through the incarnate Christ. For Torrance being *determinate* is good, for it means the realization of God's good purposes for the creature. However, being *determined* for Torrance takes on a different meaning, where the identity and ultimate purpose of the human creature is defined solely by is relation to the created order and one's social environment and not the Creator who brought it into being. Whether something is determinate or determined can only be discerned through an understanding of that object's *telos*.

with the kind of freedom, openness, and transcendent reference which we need both to develop our own personal and social culture and our scientific exploration of the universe."[30]

What Torrance introduces here is the idea that socio-cultural systems, like the human organisms that generate them, are incomplete in themselves. They too are the contingent byproducts of contingent persons shaping a contingent world through cultural activity, and thus are realities that require completion beyond themselves in order to fulfill their reason for being. Berger recognizes this with regard to the human creature, simply through his assertion that the human creature is incomplete, seeking security and significance. But one wonders whether this incompleteness would also extend to the socio-cultural world, and whether Berger can really answer the ultimate question of meaning within the limits of his discipline, for whatever meaning or completion the human creature seeks for itself is ultimately (for Berger) generated by the self. But this hardly seems an adequate place to go for transcendence, and perhaps is a further clue that the created order and the social world are contingent.[31] Though the human creature may need a transcendent reference point as a locus of security and significance (as both Torrance and Berger would agree), for Berger that reference point would never really transcend the dialectical cycle of externalization, objectivation, and internalization. Consequently, it is difficult to see how a determinism of a hard or soft variety can be avoided.[32]

For Torrance, as with Berger, the purpose of the cultural world is to mediate meaning, primarily by placing human persons in contact with an external world and giving the social world stable boundaries. However, the external world they are placed in contact with is as fragile and contingent as the human organism placed in it, and as such cannot bear

---

30. Torrance, *Reality and Scientific Theology*, 196.

31. Notre Dame sociologist Christian Smith notes in his book *What Is A Person?* that even the idea of "social structure," as pervasive and fundamental an idea as it is for many of the social sciences, is little understood in terms of their origins and purpose: "Theorists in recent years have made helpful strides in conceptualizing what social structures are. We have been less successful, however, I think, in explaining the sources and origins of social structures in the first place. What actually gives rise to the social structuring of human life?" See C. Smith, *What Is A Person?* 5.

32. Much more could be said here with regard to the role of the social world in theological reflection and theologically informed action. We have not spoken about the effects of sin on the socially constructed world of the human person, and the problems that presents for the inclusion of contextual elements in theological reflection. This would only further highlight the need for a 'transcendent reference point' in our theological thinking that is dynamic and active, transcending the social contexts in which our theological reflection takes place, but critically validating and endorsing that work where it reflects and overlaps with God's own work.

the meaning-making demands placed upon it by the human creature. A transcendent reference point, it seems to me, is necessary, one that is mediated by a socio-cultural world, but is not ultimately a product of it. The theological anthropology developed in this essay is open to just such an understanding of the social world, while Berger's anthropology seems, in the end, closed to such a possibility. Whether that is simply a limitation of Berger's personal beliefs, I do not know. From his academic work however, it seems to be a limitation of the methodologies he has employed to define his discipline.

What Torrance brings to his work, and to the work of any contextual theologian, is an understanding of the human person as a social and relational being whose cultural activity is not simply a means to provide for itself a stable, meaning-effused social environment. Instead, Torrance helps us see that human cultural activity, in a greater or lesser degree, reflects the character and will of its Creator. Because of this the meaning of socio-cultural activity is lodged in a transcendent ground that liberates the creature for true security and significance, and subsequently results in imaginative cultural exploration and expression that is motivated by love and characterized by freedom, as opposed to socio-cultural worlds motivated by fear and characterized by insecurity, violence, and determinism.

CONCLUSION

I close with the following quote from an essay entitled "The Goodness and Dignity of Man in the Christian Tradition" that Torrance delivered in 1986 at the Lam Chi Fung Memorial Symposium on Christianity and Chinese Culture:

> It is now the role of man in union with Christ to serve the purpose of God's love in the ongoing actualization of that redemption, sanctification and renewal within the universe.... Thus man has been called to be a kind of midwife to creation, in assisting nature out of its divinely given abundance constantly to give birth to new forms of life and richer patterns of order. Indeed, as the covenant-partner of Jesus Christ man may be regarded as the priest of creation, through whose service... the marvelous rationality, symmetry, harmony and beauty of God's creation are being brought to light and given expression in such a way that the whole universe is found to be a glorious hymn to the Creator.[33]

33. Torrance, "The Goodness and Dignity of Man in the Christian Tradition," 387.

PART 1: CONFIGURING CARIBBEAN THEOLOGY

It would seem reasonable to suggest that if we are to engage in the task of developing a contextual theology for the Caribbean, we need to listen to a melody that originates and terminates in the triune God, but not before it has drawn into itself a created order freely brought into being by the will of God and graciously entrusted to a creature crafted after the image of God. It is this creature, peculiarly constituted and uniquely called, that God dingolays and improvises with, in order to draw the created order toward its liberating *telos*. Human dingolaying in the image of God, participating in the divine melody, is a cultural task; it is a task for theologians and laypersons from every cultural context, if it is to be done completely, with integrity, and in a way that reflects the triune God and enables the flourishing of creation.

This dingolaying grounds the development of a Caribbean contextual theology that has theological integrity and local relevance and reference, while fostering social action. Indeed, authentic dingolaying requires all of these three characteristics to be present for any single one to be validated.

Torrance's presentation is critiqued in Yeung, *Being and Knowing*.

PART 2

Interpreting the Bible in the Caribbean

5

Ashley Smith, Carnival, and Hermeneutics
Reflections on Caribbean Biblical Interpretation

ORAL A. W. THOMAS

Ashley Smith is culturally literate. To be culturally literate is to be attuned to the historical and ideological nature of social location, the causes of oppression and exploitation within social location, and the dominating and exploitative influences and agenda at work in social location. In other words, as culturally literate, Ashley Smith is aware that the social circumstances of social location do not come about magically by irruption, but are caused. It is the causal nature of the social circumstances of Caribbean people that has provided a significant "text" not only for Ashley's theological perspectives but also for his struggle for justice where these circumstances become oppressive and dehumanizing.[1]

For instance, Ashley takes the position that contextual realities shape the understanding of who God is. In making the case for a contextual theology, Ashley posits that "assumptions about God and God's relationship with

---

1. "Text" is being used here to name the influences and experiences of one's soico-geographic space or a version of social realities as a source for theological reflection. As such, the "canon" of the socio-historical praxis of the people of God is not confined to the sixty-six books of the Bible. One's culture is also "text" and must be interpreted. Indeed, it is a fundamental resource for theology.

75

and intentions for the world must not only inform but also be informed by the present human conditions and the questions human beings are asking out of the context in which they live their lives."[2]

In what follows, *Carnival* is used as "text" to provide insights into biblical, hermeneutical practices within the Caribbean and a way of knowing and being that foregrounds Ashley's struggles for Caribbean self-determination and self-identification. This approach seeks to advance a hermeneutical principle long practiced by Ashley Smith, that it is out of our social circumstances that who God is takes shape and form and that, further, these circumstances form and inform Caribbean's people's way to view the world of biblical texts.

The French Planter class introduced Carnival in the Caribbean at the end of the eighteenth century.[3] But the manner and content of the masquerade were adopted, and then changed, by blacks during the post-emancipation era, to include African traditions and customs, and Carnival has continued to morph over the years.[4] In its original manifestation, Carnival was a festival in which the French Planters mimicked the *negre jardin*, or field laborer. The French Planters blackened their faces and wore the tattered clothes of enslaved African field workers.[5] But this was no mere mimicry or "play." In reality, it served as another form of dehumanizing the enslaved Africans.

Nonetheless, when the emancipated Africans in their *canboulay* (the old name for Carnival) adopted the festival or midnight procession in which there was singing and dancing, armed with sticks and torches, marching through the streets, this, too, was no mere imitation of the French Planters, but was symbolic and revolutionary in content and intent.[6] Torches symbolized that a new day of freedom had dawned. A transculturation process was taking place as the emancipated Africans turned the *negre jardin*, originally a parody intended to dehumanize them, into a *canboulay*, a mask of a mask, or a liberating practice, a safe way of doing dangerous things.[7] Here, the masquerade's political potential as "rituals of rebellion" was undisguised.[8] Even so, the fact that it also functioned as release from the stress and strain

---

2. A. Smith, *Emerging from Innocence*, 9.
3. Bremer and Fleischmann, *Alternative Cultures in the Caribbean*, 140.
4. Hill, "Traditional Figures in Carnival," 20.
5. See Wüst's thesis, "The Trinidad Carnival from Canboulay to Pretty Mass," for a comprehensive analysis.
6. Wüst, "The Trinidad Carnival from Canboulay to Pretty Mass".
7. Wüst, "The Trinidad Carnival," 152.
8. Capelleveen, "Peripheral Culture in the Metropolis," 140.

of oppressive and exploitative plantation life meant that it did nothing more than affirms the status quo.⁹ In such circumstances, the masquerade was reduced to a state where it is "role serious, not real serious."¹⁰

Such differences in content and intent mean that Carnival, then, as now, was a contested cultural performance.¹¹ On the one hand, there is ritualized role reversal by both oppressor and oppressed, and on the other, "lampooning liberty"¹² by the oppressed. In this regard, the Carnival masquerade seeks to strike a balance between consensus and conflict, control and spontaneity, compliance and subversion.¹³ Where the balance is upset in favor of consensus and control, Carnival is stylized. A stylized masquerade means that power is contested ritually and consequently entrenched. But where it leans towards conflict, spontaneity, and subversion, Carnival is "ritualised resistance"¹⁴—a veritable symbol of freedom as there is a breaking through of the imposed patterns of society, which creates a new understanding of self and society, albeit with gaiety.

It is these two traditions—*negre jardin* and *canboulay*—that are in flux in contemporary Caribbean Carnival culture. While the concept of creating images of images remains—artists and their masqueraders portraying social realities or continuing human experience—the absence of facemasks and the loss of irony have led to a diminution of the critical, political, and revolutionary edge and intent of these traditional elements. Such absence and loss are due in no small measure to middle-class participation, the institutionalizing of Carnival administration, and the branding of Carnival with an emphasis on marketing and profit. Thus, the emphasis has shifted from mimicry and irony to an assertion of selfhood. Gone are the days when mas' was a political action and a revolutionary act. Now, the subverters are subverted.¹⁵ For V. S. Naipaul, "carnival is neither an illusion nor a direct reflection of social reality but a stylized rendering of concerns and values of society."¹⁶ Emphasis is now on color, such that Carnival is a riot of colors, more stylized than political and revolutionary. It is play that has lost its link to subversion and resistance.

---

9. See the analysis in Cohen, "A Polytechnic London Carnival as a Contested Cultural Performance."
10. Barton, *Afro-Creole*, 245.
11. Cohen, "A Polytechnic London Carnival," 37.
12. Turner, "The Sprit of Celebration."
13. Capelleveen, "Peripheral Culture," 140.
14. Ibid., 141.
15. Barton, *Afro-Creole*, 278.
16. Naipaul, *The Middle Passage*, 90.

Accordingly, the Carnival masquerade is reflective of a wider Caribbean struggle or dilemma: economic benefits versus the quest to reflect cultural history and reality.[17] In reality, the Caribbean dilemma is "how to eat and remain human"[18] since the economic seems inimical to the cultural and the cultural to the economic. Such tension between the cultural and economic is a tough struggle, but is nonetheless a version of Caribbean reality. This is our epistemology, our way of knowing and reading into our "text."

What this epistemology means is that "reading" the *biblical* text begins not with the biblical text in isolation, but with the lived realities of the reader and a cultural-literacy consciousness of those realities. The biblical text certainly remains central to the interpretive enterprise. Yet it is not an inert object. The biblical text is already an action, an interpretation of the will and purpose of God. If its readers are to come to grips with the issues involved in that action, then their way of knowing into the biblical text must of necessity influence the process of that understanding. What Ashley Smith understands very well is that readers of biblical texts are not disembodied souls or spirits. No-one comes to the text *tabula rasa*. If biblical hermeneutics within the Caribbean context is not to be limited to the gathering of knowledge for spiritual formation and faith development, which thereby neuters biblical texts, then the whole issue of the cultural meaning of being—the socially and historically conditioned situated reader—must play a critical role in the hermeneutical experience. Interpreting the reader's context is as critical as interpreting the biblical text in its context. The latter without the former leads to escapism, docility, and passivity. It thereby reinforces of the status quo and gives evidence of cultural illiteracy—something that *cannot* be said of Ashley Smith's hermeneutics.

---

17. O'Marde, "Calypso in the 1990s," 40.
18. Lamming, "Opening Address," 6.

6

Islands in the Sun
Overtures to a Caribbean Creation Theology

J. RICHARD MIDDLETON

THE CARIBBEAN IS A region of tremendous natural beauty. It is the sort of beauty that leads Harry Belafonte to poetically address his ideal (though unnamed) homeland ("Oh, island in the sun") and to promise that, "all my days I will sing in praise/ of your forest, waters, your shining sand."[1] Yet for all its undeniable natural beauty, the Caribbean is a region that is increasingly marred by pollution (for example, unsafe levels of toxins in fish in Kingston Harbour) and deforestation (for example, in Haiti, resulting in catastrophic mudslides in Gonaïves during heavy rains). So, the "forest, waters, [and] shining sand" of the pristine Caribbean are becoming more and more compromised by the human footprint. And this does not yet address the impact of natural disasters (over which humans have no control) like Hurricanes Gilbert and Andrew in 1988 and 1992, respectively, or the devastating earthquake in Port-au-Prince in 2010.

The indelible human footprint on the natural beauty of the Caribbean (our impact on the earth), combined with horrendous natural disasters (the

---

1. Although Belafonte popularized "Island in the Sun," the lyrics were written by Irving Burgie (also known as Lord Burgess).

earth's impact on us), gives the lie to any romantic vision of what we moderns have come to know as "nature" (the realm of the non-human); but it also calls into question the sort of popular piety we find in the Caribbean church that imagines a separation between human "salvation" (narrowly conceived) and our earthly environment. Paradoxically, among many Christians, in the Caribbean and elsewhere, we find a decidedly otherworldly, and often individualistic view of "salvation" as the saving of souls from a fiery judgment to spend an eternity with God in an ethereal heaven, combined with a romantic view of nature as a special place to encounter God—witness the photographs on devotional greeting cards and posters, and even the slides projected behind worship lyrics in some of our churches. Yet little if no thought is typically given to the possible connection—or, better, to the disconnect—between an otherworldly salvation and a romanticized nature.

There is no otherworldly salvation in "Islands in the Sun." What we find, rather, is an idyllic picture of nature joined to a naïve, almost primitive view of human society. Thus Belafonte sings, in the first verse, of "my island in the sun/ where my people have toiled since time begun." Apart from the hyperbolic lack of historical precision, since no people (not even the Amerindian Tainos and Caribs) have lived in the Caribbean from the beginning of time, the remainder of the song continues this romantic idealization of toil, whether it is the woman he sees "on bended knee/ cutting cane for her family," or the man he observes "at the water-side/ casting nets at the surging tide," or even the singer himself "lift[ing] my heavy load to the sky."

The juxtaposition of three verses, each mentioning physical toil or labor, with a fourth verse that fondly remembers drumming and Carnival, suggests that the "calypso songs philosophical" the singer mentions might function not to critique the social order, as much calypso has historically done, but as "philosophical" acceptance of the status quo. But perhaps it is not so much philosophical acceptance of the status quo as much as a positive *ignoring* of historical realities, as when the song's chorus states that this island in the sun was "willed to me by my father's hand." What world is or was the singer (or songwriter) living in, where the Caribbean is the natural inheritance of persons of African descent, without the intervention of European colonial powers? One searches this 1957 song in vain for any reference to the historical fact of colonialism or the history of European chattel slavery and later indentured labor, all of which decisively shaped Caribbean societies (these islands in the sun).

And what are we to say of the present economic and social disparities in the Caribbean, fueled by the ideology and institutions of a global culture of consumerism? It is clear that the perspective of the song could not begin to address these contemporary issues.

SUSPICION OF CREATION THEOLOGY

Caribbean theologians are right to express suspicions about any point of view that is blind to the reality of social inequities, especially if this blindness is combined with a romantic view of nature. When theologians and ethicists attempt to address the pressing needs of society, they often (understandably) focus on matters of human justice and injustice, to the exclusion of significant reflection on the natural environment in which people find themselves. There are certainly existential or pragmatic reasons underlying this suspicion of *creation* as a theme for theological reflection. Given the pressing human needs that face Caribbean people every day, it might seem that a theology of creation would take our focus off what is undeniably of prime importance.

But there is also a historical reason for the suspicion of creation as a theological topic. Theology as an academic discipline, both in the Caribbean and throughout the world, has been decisively shaped by a western, Eurocentric habit of mind that distinguishes radically between *history* (people) and *nature* (the non-human). This distinction has it roots in the Renaissance split between freedom and nature, where thinkers like Pico della Mirandola (in his famous *Oration and the Dignity of Man*) began to idealize human beings as transcending the determined and law-bound natural world, and it was fundamental to the rise of modern science in the sixteenth and seventeenth centuries in Europe, epitomized in Francis Bacon's quest for the seduction and conquest of nature by science (which illustrates well Susan Griffin's contention that women and nature have been identified in western thinking).[2]

A theological version of the nature/freedom conceptual framework was given special momentum in the early twentieth century by Karl Barth, who famously distinguished immanent *religion* from transcendent *revelation*. To the former, explained Barth, God has pronounced a decisive *Nein!*[3]

While Barth himself was opposed to the hubris of modern western humanism, the Barthian distinction between religion and revelation nevertheless contributed to a version of the history/nature distinction found in the Biblical Theology Movement, associated with Neo-orthodox theologians like G. Ernest Wright. In the 1960s this movement tried to preserve the

---

2. Pico, *Oration on the Dignity of Man* 7–8; Griffin, *Woman and Nature*.

3. *Nein!* (No!) was the title of Barth's famous response to Emil Brunner's 1934 work entitled *Nature and Grace*, which itself interacted with Barth's earlier work. Brunner had proposed the validity of a creation theology (using the term "natural theology," though without the rationalism assumed by the classical tradition of that name). Both Brunner's proposal and Barth's response are published together in *Natural Theology*.

uniqueness of Old Testament revelation by contrasting debased Canaanite cyclical *nature* religion with the higher monotheistic, linear, *historical* faith of the Bible.[4] A version of this framework surfaces in the early works of Old Testament scholar Gerhard von Rad, specifically in his claim that creation theology was a borrowing from Israel's pagan neighbors, and in his refusal to allow that creation was integrally connected to Israel's salvation history, or *Heilsgeschichte*.[5] The history/nature dichotomy (without the overlaid value distinction) even shows up in Claus Westermann's famous bifurcation between *salvation*, which is a matter of historical deliverance, and *blessing*, which is associated with matters like the birth of children and the fertility of flocks and land[6]—a bifurcation that simply cannot be sustained on exegetical grounds, since salvation in the Bible involves both deliverance from what impedes God's purposes and restoration to flourishing.[7]

One particularly important version of the history/nature dichotomy is found in the prolific writings of Old Testament scholar Walter Brueggemann, who (especially in his early works) programmatically claimed that creation faith served to justify the oppressive status quo both in Israel and its neighbors—the legitimation of order, he called it—while salvation/exodus faith challenged the unjust ordering of the world in the name of a free and transcendent God.[8]

This complex theological inheritance may well constrain theologians either to prioritize a concern for human flourishing over a concern for the earth, or to view creation theology with outright suspicion. But this anthropocentric focus, which separates human well-being from concern about the earth, is an artificial polarization, since people only exist, live, and work *somewhere*; that is, any socio-cultural analysis would show that people both

---

4. Wright, "How Did Early Israel Differ from Her Neighbors?" and *The Old Testament Against Its Environment*. See Middleton, *Liberating Image*, 186–88, for a discussion of the historical grounds why this distinction between Israel and the nations cannot be sustained.

5. See von Rad, "Theological Problem of the Old Testament Doctrine of Creation," 55–61; and idem, *Old Testament Theology*, 1:137–39. Thankfully von Rad later came to an appreciation of the role of creation theology in the Old Testament, evident in his mature work *Wisdom in Israel*.

6. Westerman, *Blessing in the Bible and in the Life of the Church*, 1–14; idem, *What Does the Old Testament Say About God?* 28, 44.

7. See Middleton and Gorman, "Salvation," 45–46.

8. Brueggemann, *Prophetic Imagination*, 39; "Trajectories in Old Testament Literature and the Sociology of Ancient Israel"; "A Shape for Old Testament Theology, I: Structure Legitimation"; and *Israel's Praise*, 101–121. I have challenged Brueggemann's interpretation of creation theology in Middleton, "Is Creation Theology Inherently Conservative?"

impact and are impacted by their environment. It is an artificial polarization from a biblical point of view as well, since humans are consistently understood in the Scriptures as part of the wider cosmos, which is not only created by God, but is the object of God's saving activity.[9]

This is well understood by Caribbean theologian Ashley Smith, whom this collection of essays honors, and his published works often address *creation* as the underlying basis of God's salvation in history. Especially in his seminal 1984 collection of essays, *Real Roots and Potted Plants: Reflections on the Caribbean Church*, we find a pervasive appeal to God as creator of the world and to God's purposes or intentions for creation as an alternative to a sacred/secular dualism and as a prod to appropriate ethical action on the part of Caribbean Christians.[10]

Along these lines, Ashley claims that the church "needs to represent an attitude of affirmation in place of the traditional world-denial. To accomplish this, those who speak for it need to give greater prominence to the doctrine of creation."[11] Or, as he puts it elsewhere, the key question before the Caribbean church is "what kind of ministry it might exercise at this particular time, in the name of him who continually makes all things new, in order that the purposes of his creation might be fulfilled."[12] He clearly states that to deny the goodness of the material world "is contrary to biblical teaching. It contradicts the Christian doctrine of creation and . . . goes against the New Testament understanding of the cosmic implications of the atonement (Rom 8:18–25). . . . The usual division of reality into sacred and secular is anything but Christian."[13]

I believe that Ashley Smith is on the right track in his theological appeal to creation to ground both salvation and ethics. We can no longer afford the luxury of suspicion about creation theology, that is, if we ever could have afforded that luxury. It is not just that we are all, in the Caribbean and elsewhere, faced with the global realities of climate change, toxic waste, over-fishing, air pollution, and so on. Beyond the fact that the stresses humans are placing on the environment impinge on all peoples of the earth, including Caribbean people, it is also clear that our ecological crises are integrally connected to societal injustice. As James Cone, the father of black

---

9. See Middleton and Gorman, "Salvation," 45–54; Fretheim, "Salvation in the Bible vs. Salvation in the Church," 368–69; and Middleton, "A New Heaven and a New Earth," 86–91.

10. A. Smith, *Real Roots and Potted Plants*, 9–10, 15, 33, 34, 38–39, 41, 44, 53, 65–66, 97–98, 100, 101, 104.

11. Ibid., 15.

12. Ibid., 44.

13. Ibid., 97.

liberation theology in the United States puts it: "The logic that led to slavery and segregation in the Americas, colonization and apartheid in Africa, and the rule of white supremacy throughout the world is the same one that leads to the exploitation of animals and the ravaging of nature."[14]

This is a profound observation, which should give us pause. Yet there is something missing from Cone's analysis. I have no intention of denigrating Cone's historical and sociological approach, which is meant to challenge both ecological theologians and theologians who theorize race to take each other's work seriously. Yet one searches Cone's article (of which this is the opening statement) in vain for any substantive theological or biblical analysis following from this important claim.[15]

This is a shame, since the Scriptures consistently interpret the connection between humans and the earth in a manner that positively contributes to a vision of human flourishing—at both individual and societal levels. The Bible is a powerful, and often untapped resource on this topic. This suggests that the time is ripe for a *biblical* Caribbean theology that grounds human liberation in God's intent for creation and envisions a role for the earth within God's purposes.

However, this creation theology would need to move beyond professional theological interest in a public theology that addresses the large societal concerns of our times. Although such theological concerns are laudable and necessary—and many of the essays in this volume address these concerns with great insight—I believe that creation theology should be serviceable, not just for an elite cadre of Caribbean intellectuals, but for ordinary Caribbean Christians, to empower them in the universal priesthood of the believer, that they might live with dignity, compassion, and power in a broken world, as a healing presence and witness to the coming kingdom of God through Jesus Christ.

These points are integrally connected, since the primary mode of access to theology for most Caribbean laypeople is precisely the Bible. We therefore need to develop a robust creation theology through a careful engagement with Scripture that would address the pressing need of ordinary Christians to internalize a vision of being human in God's world. Such a vision would integrally connect people and their societal needs to their bodies and their physical environment—and would connect salvation with God's creational intentions for this world.

14. Cone, "Whose Earth Is It, Anyway?" 23.

15. We find a similar problem in Leonardo Boff's important attempt at a rapprochement between liberation theology and ecology (Boff, *Cry of the Earth, Cry of the Poor*, esp. 104–114); although Boff does engage the question theologically, the Bible plays only a marginal role in the discussion.

In my reflections that follow, I intend to address the otherworldly bent of much popular Caribbean Christianity, by sketching the biblical teaching of the redemption of creation and by grounding this teaching in Scripture's affirmation of the earthly purpose of human life. It is the burden of this essay that a biblical creation theology addressed to Caribbean realities would both affirm the value and dignity of ordinary life and work in the world and would orient life and work toward God's larger redemptive purposes for justice and earthly flourishing.

THE BIBLE'S VISION OF COSMIC REDEMPTION

Central to the way the New Testament conceives the final destiny of the world is Jesus' prediction in Matt 19:28 of a "regeneration" (KJV, NIV) that is coming; Matthew here uses the Greek word *palingenesia*, which both TNIV and NRSV translate as "the renewal of all things," where the addition of the English phrase "all things" correctly gets at the sense of cosmic expectation.[16] Likewise, we have Peter's explicit proclamation of the "restoration [*apokatástasis*] of all things" (in Acts 3:21), which does in fact contain the phrase "all things" (*tà pánta*). When we turn to the epistles, we find God's intent to *reconcile* "all things" to himself through Christ articulated in Col 1:20, while Eph 1:20 speaks of God's desire to *unify* or *bring together* "all things" in Christ. In these two Pauline texts, the phrase "all things" (*tà pánta*) is immediately specified as things *in heaven* and things *on earth*. Since "heaven and earth" is precisely how Gen 1:1 describes the world God created "in the beginning," this New Testament language clearly designates a vision of cosmic salvation, the redemption of the entire created order.

This cosmic vision underlies the phrase "a new heaven and a new earth" found in both Rev 21:1 ("and I saw a new heaven and a new earth") and 2 Pet 3:13 ("we await a new heaven and a new earth in which righteousness dwells"; author's translation). The specific origin of the phrase "a new heaven and a new earth" is the prophetic oracle of Isa 65:17-25, which envisions a healed world with a redeemed community in rebuilt Jerusalem, where life is restored to flourishing and shalom after the devastation of the Babylonian exile (the phrase is found in Isa 65:17 and later in 66:22). The this-worldly prophetic expectation in Isaiah is then universalized to the entire cosmos and human society generally in late Second Temple Judaism and in the New Testament.

---

16. Unless otherwise specified, the biblical quotations that follow will be from the NRSV.

PART 1: CONFIGURING CARIBBEAN THEOLOGY

This holistic vision of God's intent to renew or redeem creation is perhaps the Bible's best-kept secret, typically unknown to most church members and even to many clergy, no matter what their theological stripe.[17] It is therefore particularly helpful to trace the roots of the New Testament vision in the Old Testament, in order to understand the inner logic of the idea.

THE HUMAN CALLING TO IMAGE GOD ON EARTH

We should note that the Old Testament does not place any substantial hope in the afterlife; the dead do not have access to God in the grave or Sheol (Pss 6:5; 30:9; 88:3–5, 10–12; 115:17; Ecc 9:4-6, 10; Isa 38:9–12, 18).[18] Rather, God's purposes for blessing and shalom are expected for the faithful in this life, in the midst of history. This holistic perspective is grounded, theologically, in the biblical teaching about the goodness of creation, including earthly existence. God pronounced all creation including materiality good—and at the end of the creative activity, "very good" (Gen 1:31)—and gave human beings the task to rule and develop this world as stewards made in God's image (Gen 1:26–28; Gen 2:15; Ps 8:5–8).

In Gen 2:15 the original human task is to work and protect the garden (equivalent to agriculture), while in Ps 8:5–8 humans are entrusted with rule over animal life on land, in air and water (the basis for the domestication of animals). And Gen 1:26–28 combines both agriculture and animal husbandry in its vision of humans created in God's image to rule animals and subdue the earth. Theodore Hiebert is correct to note that, "In the pre-industrial age of biblical Israel, it is impossible that the Priestly writer had more in mind in these concepts of dominion and subjection than the human domestication and use of animals and plants and the human struggle to make the soil serve its farmers."[19]

In all these creation texts, the movement is "missional"—from God via humans outward to the earth. The paradox of these texts is that the fundamental human task is both a matter of humble earthly service and yet a task of great dignity, namely, the responsible exercise of power on God's behalf in tending and developing the non-human world.[20]

17. This observation is based on my own experience in many different branches of the Christian tradition, both denominationally and theologically.

18. For analysis of these and other texts, see Wright, *Resurrection of the Son of God*, 87–99.

19. Hiebert, "Re-Imaging Nature," 42.

20. This rule of the earth on God's behalf is precisely what Gen 1:26–28 means by the image and likeness of God (*imago Dei*), as is recognized by most Old Testament scholars. For an account of the history of interpretation of humanity as *imago Dei*, see

It is sometimes shocking for readers of the Bible to realize that the initial purpose and *raison d'être* of humanity is never explicitly portrayed in Scripture as the worship of God or anything that would conform to our notion of the "spiritual," with its dualistic categories. Instead, Scripture portrays the human purpose in rather mundane terms of exercising power over our earthly environment as God's representatives. In the context of the ancient Near East, which is the Bible's original context, rule of the earth refers most basically to the development of agriculture and animal husbandry, which are the basis of human societal organization and ultimately leads to the development of all aspects of culture, technology and civilization.[21] To put it another way, while various Psalms (like 148 and 96) indeed call upon *all* creatures (humans included) to worship or serve God in the cosmic temple of creation (heaven and earth), the distinctive way *humans* worship or render service to the Creator is by the development of culture through interaction with our earthly environment in a manner that glorifies God. That is our fundamental human calling.[22]

By our communal development of culture through interaction with the earth and its creatures, humans function as God's image (*imago Dei*), mediating God's presence from heaven, where the Holy One is enthroned, into the earthly realm—as God's authorized and delegated representatives. By our faithful imaging of God through the ordinary, everyday tasks of human life (work, education, the raising of children, etc.), the human race was intended to bring the earth to its intended destiny as an integral part of God's cosmos-temple, filled with the divine presence and glory.

But in the biblical narrative a complication or impediment prevents completion of the original human purpose. Humans have misused the power God has given them, rebelling against their creator and turning against each other. This misuse of the power of *imago Dei* is manifest most fundamentally

Middleton, *Liberating Image*, chap. 1.

21. For further analysis of the human purpose in Genesis, see Middleton, *Liberating Image*, chaps. 2 and 5; Crouch, *Culture Making*, chap. 6; Cosden, *Heavenly Good of Earthly Work*, chap. 4; Wolters, "Foundational Command," 27–33; and Middleton and Walsh, *Truth Is Stranger Than It Used to Be*, chap. 6.

22. This is not meant to exclude what we call "worship" from the appropriate human response to God. There are two important points to make here. First, the cultural development of the earth, rather than "worship" narrowly conceived, is explicitly stated to be the human purpose in biblical texts recounting the creation of humanity. "Worship" in the narrow sense may be understood as *part of* human cultural activity. Secondly, we should not reduce human worship/service of God to verbal, emotionally charged expressions of praise (which is what we usually mean by the term). Note that Paul in Rom 12:1–2 borrows language of sacrifice and liturgy from Israel's cult in order to describe full-orbed bodily obedience (which, he says, is our true worship). This is the typical emphasis of Scripture.

in disobedience toward the creator (Gen 3), which then blossoms into a pattern of violence and fractured relationships among people (Gen 4–11), which continues to this day. Whereas the early chapters of Genesis do, indeed, record the continuing cultural development of the earth—including the first city (Gen 4:17) and the development of nomadic livestock herding, technology, and music (4:20–22)—we also have the first murder (4:8) and a bigamist (4:19) engaging in revenge killing (4:23–24), until violence fills the earth (Gen 6:11). The biblical tradition understands that human transgression of God's norms leads to death, which is the antithesis of God's purposes for earthly flourishing; our contemporary predicament is that death in its manifold forms has invaded and degraded human life and the entire earthly creation.

SALVATION AS THE RESTORATION OF GOD'S PURPOSES FOR CREATION

The biblical affirmation of earthly life is further articulated in the central and paradigmatic act of God's salvation in the Old Testament, the exodus from Egyptian bondage. Israel's memory of this event testifies to a God who intervenes in the harsh realities of history in response to injustice and suffering. But more than that, the exodus is manifestly a case of *sociopolitical* deliverance from the most intransigent imperial power of the day. And this deliverance is not just *from* bondage, but *to* or *for* shalom, which is attained only when the redeemed are settled in a bountiful land and are restored to wholeness and flourishing as a community of justice living according to God's wise laws.

In line with the creational grounding of salvation, Old Testament legal and wisdom literature reveals an interest in mundane matters such as the fertility of land and crops, the birth of children and stable family life, justice in the city, and peace in international relations. The Old Testament does not spiritualize *salvation* but understands it as God's deliverance of people and land from all that destroys life and the consequent restoration of people and land to flourishing.[23] And while God's salvific purpose narrows for a while to one elect nation in their own land, this "initially exclusive move" is, as Old Testament scholar Terence Fretheim puts it, in the service of "a maximally inclusive end," the redemption of all nations and ultimately, the entire created order.[24]

---

23. Fretheim, "Salvation in the Bible vs. Salvation in the Church," 371–72; Middleton and Gorman, "Salvation," 45, 47, 52–54.

24. Fretheim, *God and World in the Old Testament*, 29.

Although the Old Testament initially did not envision any sort of positive afterlife, things begin to shift in some late texts. Thus in Ezekiel's famous vision of the valley of dry bones (Ezek 37) the restoration of Israel is portrayed using the metaphor of resurrection, after the "death" they suffered in Babylonian exile. But this is arguably still a metaphor, not an expectation of what we would call resurrection. Then, a proto-apocalyptic text like Isa 25:6–8 envisions the literal conquest of death itself at the messianic banquet on Mt. Zion, where God will serve the redeemed the best meat and the most aged wines; this text anticipates the day when YHWH will "swallow up death forever" (cited in 1 Cor 15:26, 54) and "wipe away all tears" (echoed in Rev 21:4). But the most explicit Old Testament text on the topic of resurrection is the apocalyptic vision of Dan 12:2–3, which promises that faithful martyrs will awaken from the dust of the earth (to which we all return at death, according to Gen 3) to attain "eternal life."

It is important to note that this developing vision of the afterlife has nothing to do with "heaven hereafter"; the expectation is manifestly this-worldly, meant to guarantee for the faithful the earthly promises of shalom that death had cut short. The Wisdom of Solomon, chapter 3 is particularly helpful here. This text, which in the Septuagint, though not in the Protestant canon, specifically associates "immortality" with reigning *on earth* (Wis 3:1–9, esp. 7–8); that is, resurrection is a reversal of the earthly situation of oppression (the domination of the righteous martyrs by the wicked, which led to their death) and thus is the fulfillment of the original human dignity and status in Gen 1:26–28 and Ps 8:4–8, where humans are granted rule of the earth.[25]

These ancient Jewish expectations provide a coherent theological background for Jesus' proclamation of the kingdom of God, which he construed as "good news" for the poor and release for captives (Luke 4), and which he embodied in healings, exorcisms, and the forgiveness of sins (all ways in which the distortion of earthly life was being reversed). These expectations also make sense of Jesus' teaching in the Sermon on the Mount that the meek would "inherit the earth" (Matt 5:5) and later in Matthew that "at the renewal of all things" (the cosmic "regeneration") the disciples would reign and judge with him on thrones (Matt 19:27–30). This helps us understand Rev 5:9–10, which envisions a redeemed church from "every tribe and

---

25. Contrary to Leonardo Boff's misreading (*Cry of the Earth, Cry of the Poor*, 79–80), the use of the metaphor of "rule" either in the Bible or in contemporary theology does not automatically legitimate unlimited dominion or exploitation of the earth. Rather, "rule" is an ancient way to speak of the exercise of power, which may be beneficent or destructive. It is used in Second Temple Jewish tradition to dignify human life, often in situations of oppression. Jesus himself suggests (and models) that the normative exercise of rule is humble service of others (Mark 10:42–45).

language and people and nation" constituted as "a kingdom and priests to serve our God, and they will reign on the earth." Also Rev 22:3–5 indicates that when God's throne (which is currently in heaven) is finally established on earth, God's servants will "reign forever." The word "forever" disabuses us of the idea that this might be some sort of temporary millennium, to be followed by an otherworldly eternal state. Rather, what Revelation offers is the eschatological restoration of the original human calling as *imago Dei* to administer and develop this world to God's glory.

The eschatological restoration taught by Jesus and envisaged in Revelation has begun in the church, which is even now being renewed in the image of God (Eph 4:24; Col 3:9–10) to become the "new humanity" (a much better translation than "new self," which we find in most modern translations).[26] This means that day-to-day sanctification is a matter of the restoration of our humanness, with all that entails, as we are called to live up to the stature of Christ, whose perfect imaging becomes the model for the life of the redeemed (Phil 2:5–11; Eph 4:13). The day will come when we are fully conformed to the likeness of Christ (1 John 3:2), which will include the resurrection of the body (1 Cor 15:49).

So when Paul describes Jesus' own resurrection from the dead as the "firstfruits" of those who have fallen asleep (1 Cor 15:20), he claims that the harvest of new creation has already begun, the expected reversal of sin and death is inaugurated. This reversal will be consummated when Christ returns in glory climactically to defeat evil and all that opposes God's intent for life and shalom on earth (1 Cor 15:24–28). Then, in the words of Revelation 11, "the kingdom of this world [will] become the kingdom of our Lord and of his Messiah" (Rev 11:15). At that time, explains Paul, creation itself, which has been groaning in its bondage to decay, will be liberated from this bondage into the same glory God's children will experience (Rom 8:19–22)—that is, the glory of resurrection.

The inner logic of this vision of holistic salvation is that the creator has not given up on creation, but is working to salvage and restore the world (human and non-human) to the fullness of shalom and flourishing intended from the beginning. And redeemed human beings, renewed in God's image, are to work towards and embody this vision in their daily lives.

THE OTHERWORLDLY HYMNODY OF THE CHURCH

The tragedy is that this kind of holistic vision of salvation is found only rarely in popular Christian piety or even in the liturgy of the church. Indeed,

---

26. The KJV has "the new man." This term portrays regeneration as corporate, not just individual.

it is blatantly contradicted by many traditional hymns (and contemporary praise songs) sung in the context of communal worship. This is an important point since it is from what they sing that those in the pew (or auditorium) typically learn their theology, especially their eschatology.

From the classic Charles Wesley hymn, "Love Divine, All Loves Excelling," which anticipates being "changed from glory into glory/ till in heaven we take our place,"[27] to "Away in a Manger," which prays, "And fit us for Heaven, to live with Thee there,"[28] congregations are exposed to—and assimilate—an otherworldly eschatology. Some hymns, like "When the Roll Is Called up Yonder," inconsistently combine the idea of resurrection with the hope of heaven:

> On that bright and cloudless morning when the dead in Christ shall rise,
> And the glory of His resurrection share;
> When His chosen ones shall gather to their home beyond the skies,
> And the roll is called up yonder, I'll be there.[29]

Some hymns even interpret resurrection without reference to the body at all, such as "Must Jesus Bear the Cross Alone?" which in one stanza regards death as liberation ("Till death shall set me free") and in another asserts: "O resurrection day!/ When Christ the Lord from Heav'n comes down/ And bears my soul away."[30]

A hymn like "When We All Get to Heaven" may be too obvious, but notice that "The Old Rugged Cross" ends with the words, "Then He'll call me some day to my home far away/ Where his glory forever I'll share."[31] And "Just a Closer Walk with Thee" climaxes with the lines:

> When my feeble life is o'er,
> Time for me will be no more;
> Guide me gently, safely o'er
> To Thy kingdom shore, to Thy shore.[32]

---

27. Stanza 4 of "Love Divine, All Loves Excelling," written by Charles Wesley in 1747.

28. Stanza 3 from "Away in a Manger," written by John Thomas McFarland sometime between 1904–8 (the author of the hymn's first two stanzas is unknown).

29. Stanza 2 from "When the Roll Is Called up Yonder," written by James M. Black in 1893.

30. Stanzas 2 and 4 from "Must Jesus Bear the Cross Alone?" Stanza 2 was written by Thomas Shepherd (published 1693) and stanza 4 by Henry Ward Beecher (published 1855). Stanza 4 originally read: "Ye angels from the stars come down/ And bear my soul away."

31. Stanza 4 from "The Old Rugged Cross," written by George Bennard in 1913.

32. Stanza 3 from "Just a Closer Walk with Thee," author unknown (this American folk hymn became widely known during the 1930s).

PART 1: CONFIGURING CARIBBEAN THEOLOGY

Likewise, "Come Christians, Join to Sing" affirms that "On heaven's blissful shore,/ His goodness we'll adore,/ Singing forevermore,/ 'Alleluia! Amen!'"[33]

This notion of a perpetual worship service in an otherworldly afterlife is a central motif in many hymns, like "My Jesus I Love Thee," which affirms that "In mansions of glory and endless delight,/ I'll ever adore Thee in heaven so bright."[34] In a similar vein, "As with Gladness Men of Old" asks in one stanza that, "when earthly things are past,/ Bring our ransomed souls at last/ Where they need no star to guide," and in another stanza expresses the desire that "In the heavenly country bright/ . . . There forever may we sing/ Alleluias to our King!"[35]

Thankfully, most hymns no longer have the sixth verse of "Amazing Grace," which predicts:

> The earth shall soon dissolve like snow,
> The sun forbear to shine;
> But God, who called me here below,
> Will be forever mine.[36]

Yet Chris Tomlin's contemporary revision of this classic hymn, known as "Amazing Grace (My Chains Are Gone)," reintroduces this very verse as the song's new climax, ready to shape the otherworldly mindset of a fresh generation of young worshipers unacquainted with hymns.[37]

This overview of hymns just scratches the surface of worship lyrics that portray the final destiny of the righteous as transferal from an earthly, historical existence to a transcendent, immaterial realm. As the popular theologian and preacher A. W. Tozer is reputed to have said: "Christians don't tell lies; they just go to church and sing them."[38] Perhaps that is too harsh; nevertheless, I can testify to the steady diet of such songs that I was exposed to, growing up in the church in Kingston, Jamaica, which certainly reinforced the idea of heaven as otherworldly final destiny.

---

33. Stanza 3 from "Come, Christians, Join to Sing," written by Christian H. Bateman.

34. Stanza 4 from "My Jesus I Love Thee," written by William R. Featherston in 1864.

35. Stanzas 4 and 5 from "As with Gladness Men of Old," written by William C. Dix ca. 1858.

36. Stanza 6 from "Amazing Grace," written by John Newton, published 1779 (originally entitled "Faith's Review and Expectation").

37. This version of the song was released in 2006.

38. This quote is found all over the Internet, without an explicit citation from Tozer's works. Noted Tozer scholar James L. Snyder admits that while it may not be found in a specific published work, the quote accurately echoes what Tozer has said in some of his sermons (available in audio recordings): "it is Tozer and it expresses his feelings on the subject" (personal communication, December 20, 2010).

ECHOES OF CREATION THEOLOGY IN CARIBBEAN MUSIC

I am, however, perpetually grateful that along with such exposure I came to know, through sheer proximity, the this-worldly theology of Rastafarianism, especially as mediated through the music of Bob Marley and the Wailers. While I am a committed Christian and thus cannot affirm everything found in Rasta theology, I nevertheless discern a deeply rooted biblical consciousness in the lyrics of many Wailers' songs.[39] For example, the song "We an' Dem" claims that, "in the beginning Jah created everythin'/ and he gave man dominion over all things," and "Pass It On" asserts that, "In the kingdom of Jah/ man shall reign."[40] These lyrics express (in androcentric language, admittedly) the biblical vision of this-worldly dignity granted humans at creation, a dignity that will be restored in the kingdom of God.

And Peter Tosh's version of "Get Up, Stand Up" (a song he co-wrote with Marley), understands well the implications of a creation-oriented eschatology for ethics, when it contrasts the doctrine of the rapture with a desire for justice on earth:

> You know, most people think,
> A great God will come from the skies,
> And take away every little thing
> And lef' everybody dry.
> But if you know what life is worth,
> You would look for yours
> Right here on earth
> And now we see the light,
> We gonna stand up for our rights.[41]

The song goes on to critique the "preacher man" for taking the focus off earthly life and affirms that the singer is "Sick and tired of this game of theology,/ die and go to heaven in Jesus name." This is the very theology that leads Marley, in the song, "Talkin' Blues," to admit, "I feel like bombing a church,/ now that you know that the preacher is lying." But if Tozer is right, it isn't just

---

39. I have explored the theology of a number of songs by Bob Marley, Peter Tosh, and Bunny Wailer in, "Identity and Subversion in Babylon."

40. *Jah* is the shortened form of the divine name YHWH (Yahweh/Jehovah) found in expressions like "hallelujah!" (which literally means "praise YHWH!"). Rastafarians love to quote Ps 68:4 in the KJV: "Sing unto God,/ sing praises to his name:/ extol him that rideth upon the heavens by his name JAH,/ and rejoice before him."

41. These lyrics are transcribed from Tosh's *Equal Rights* album (1977); the song first appeared on the Wailers' *Burnin'* album (1973) with slightly different lyrics. The lyrics are different again on Tosh's *Captured Live* album (1984) and on Bunny Wailer's *Protest* album (1977).

the preacher who is lying, but also the worshipers who blithely sing hymns of escape to an ethereal heaven—when the Bible teaches no such thing.

PRACTICAL IMPLICATIONS FOR THE CARIBBEAN CHURCH

Yet the preacher without a doubt bears the larger share of guilt. As Jas 3:1 warns: "Not many of you should become teachers, my brothers and sisters, for you know that we who teach will be judged with greater strictness." Here the culpability of Caribbean Christian leadership is evident. For it is the mandated responsibility of church leaders to teach "the whole purpose of God" (Acts 20:27), rather than some truncated version of this purpose. Of course, the otherworldly orientation of popular Caribbean theology could easily (and legitimately) be blamed on our colonial past, since we learned this theology from our European colonizers. But to shift the burden of responsibility to others would be to let ourselves off too lightly. The Caribbean church must engage in serious self-examination and come to terms with the fact that its own leaders have perpetuated an escapist theology that entrenches ordinary Christians still further in despair and paralysis, as they pine for a heavenly home distant from the everyday realities of Caribbean life.

Historically, the otherworldly vision that has been inculcated into the consciousness of the Caribbean church allows for little or no explicitly Christian norms to guide life in contemporary society (with the prominent exception of sexual mores). In particular, an otherworldly focus on heaven hereafter prevents the biblical gospel from addressing the economic and societal realities of our time. Thus when Caribbean preachers begin to speak (as they are now doing) to the genuine need to overcome poverty among their congregations, their preaching often echoes the idolatrous greed and selfishness of Western consumer culture, baptized with a thin veneer of Christian language.

While it is laudable to motivate church members to move beyond acquiescing in poverty, the so-called prosperity gospel that is gaining ground in the Caribbean church is a betrayal of the biblical vision of shalom, which ought to direct the church towards communal care for neighbors and the earth. The point is that simply casting out the old demons of otherworldliness, without an engagement with a truly biblical spirit or ethos, allows the wandering spirits of the age—unclean spirits—to inhabit our very souls. Today the Caribbean church is in danger of buying into the worst elements of consumerist individualism at the heart of Western culture.

We, therefore, need a radical reformation in the Caribbean—in both the teaching and worship of the church. I propose that if the church's teaching and worship were grounded in a biblical creation theology that addresses earthly concerns in a holistic manner, this would have the potential to guide the church's life in the contemporary world in at least three ways.

First of all, a biblical creation theology can provide a foundation and orientation for the value and holiness of daily life as we live out our identity as *imago Dei* in society. This identity, as it is renewed in Christ, obliterates the artificial split between "sacred" and "secular" and gives meaning to the mundane challenges of life, work, family and education, interpreted as the outworking of our sacred calling to be human in God's world. As Ashley Smith so eloquently puts it:

> The enlightened or awakened Christian who is aware of the biblical doctrines of creation and redemption is liberated from the fallacy that there is a part of the world which is outside of the sphere of God's activity and his love, and therefore, inherently, unholy and under condemnation. Being aware of the holiness of all creation and of God's concern in all that happens in the world, the Christian ... participates wholeheartedly, joyfully and responsibly in all the affairs of his community.[42]

Secondly, biblical creation theology can provide an ethical challenge to the present unjust and corrupt status quo. Understanding the biblical vision of God's original intent for life on earth can allow us to discern a world out of whack with how things were meant to be. Creation theology thus provides the church with a critical principle of dissent from the injustice in the world, so that we do not simply baptize the present as God's will.

Finally, a biblical creation theology provides an empowering vision of God's purposes for shalom that can energize church members—both as individuals and in community—to utilize their gifts and opportunities to make a difference in the world by how they live. A church that has its eyes firmly fixed on the coming of God's kingdom from heaven to earth, rather than on leaving earth for heaven, will seize the moment (the *kairos*) and seek to contribute to healing, justice, and earthly flourishing in the whole range of human life and activities. In this way, the church in the Caribbean may grow into a living foretaste of the coming of God's kingdom to this our beautiful—yet broken and needy—earthly home.

---

42. A. Smith, *Real Roots and Potted Plants*, 38–39.

7

Jesus' Healing of the Paralytic
Luke 5:17–26 and the Jamaican Church

DAVID PEARSON

THE GOSPEL OF LUKE is a favorite for liberation-minded interpreters because of the evangelist's focus on the blessings of God for the outcast. A typical statement often highlighted from the Gospel is drawn from Mary's Magnificat (Luke 1:46–56). Two verses of significance to our discussion are recorded below:

> He has brought down rulers from their thrones
> but has lifted up the humble.
> He has filled the hungry with good things
> but has sent the rich away empty. (Luke 1:52–53; NIV)

Along with Mary's statement, we have Jesus' overview of his mission, seen in the context of his preaching in his hometown of Nazareth, towards the very beginning of his public ministry (Luke 4). Having been handed the scroll of Isaiah, he quotes from the prophet, and then indicates the significance and nature of his ministry as possessing a focus on the outcast, which is a fulfillment of God's messianic plan. The passage reads:

> He went to Nazareth, where he had been brought up, and on the Sabbath day he went into the synagogue, as was his custom. And he stood up to read. The scroll of the prophet Isaiah was handed to him. Unrolling it, he found the place where it is written:
>
>> "The Spirit of the Lord is on me,
>>> because he has anointed me
>>> to preach good news to the poor.
>> He has sent me to proclaim freedom for the prisoners
>>> and recovery of sight for the blind,
>>> to release the oppressed,
>> to proclaim the year of the Lord's favor."
>
> Then he rolled up the scroll, gave it back to the attendant and sat down. The eyes of everyone in the synagogue were fastened on him, and he began by saying to them, "Today this scripture is fulfilled in your hearing." (Luke 4:16–21; NIV)

When the rest of Luke's Gospel is read in light of these two passages, we find confirmation of Luke's interest in portraying Jesus as the deliverer of people on the fringes. More than any of the other evangelists, Luke emphasizes Jesus as the deliverer of women, the poor, the indigent, and the foreigner. Luke is fond of showing Jesus' concern for those who would have been considered undeserving of God's love and attention (especially in the context of a culture that viewed health and prosperity as indicators of God's rewards for righteousness).

Luke reveals his concern by juxtaposing those deemed to be righteous with others who are outcasts; there are at least twelve such episodes throughout the book. These comparative sketches often occur in confrontational encounters between Jesus and the supposedly righteous. In every case, those deemed to be more righteous and deserving of God's love are shown to lack the basics for truly receiving blessings from God. The series of confrontations finally ends with the climactic episode of the religious leaders turning Jesus over to the Roman authorities to be crucified on a charge of blasphemy (Luke 22:66–70).[1]

---

1. This statement might be mistakenly understood to suggest that those considered "righteous" in the time of Jesus are always portrayed negatively in Luke. There are three occasions when the religiously righteous come in for praise (implicitly or explicitly) by the evangelist. The book begins with the description of Zacharias as "righteous before God, blameless according to all the commandments and regulations of the Lord" (Luke 1:6; author's translation), though he is chided for not believing the angel of God about the fact that his wife would conceive. At the end of the Gospel (Luke 23:50–51), Joseph of Arimathea, a member of the council, is described as "good and righteous" and did not agree with the "plan and action" of the religious to have Jesus crucified. In between these is Jairus, the ruler of the synagogue, who receives back his daughter from the dead

PART 1: CONFIGURING CARIBBEAN THEOLOGY

It is the purpose of this paper to examine one passage (Luke 5:17–26) where the dramatic "reversal" depicted in Mary's Magnificat and embodied in Jesus' focus on the outcast is clearly demonstrated. I intend to show that in reading the text as traditional Christian scholarship often does, we downplay the importance of Jesus' ministry to the outcast; this is typically done by focusing on matters peripheral to the text's intent. The paper also suggests that the Jamaican church's current lack of relevance to the community is born out of this mistaken way of reading the gospel, where the church stresses a need for right doctrine (orthodoxy) and downplays the importance of right action in society (orthopraxy). I do not intend to pit orthodoxy against orthopraxy, since both are crucial; yet this is exactly what the Jamaican church has in large measure done, thus nullifying or minimizing its potential impact on the well-being of society.

TRANSLATION AND EXPOSITION OF LUKE 5:17–26

> And so it was that on one of the days he was teaching and sitting, there were Pharisees and teachers of the Law, having come from out of all the towns of Galilee and Judea, and Jerusalem. And the power of the Lord was on him for healing. And behold, men, bearing upon a bed a man who was a cripple, were seeking to carry him in and to lay him in front of Jesus. And not finding a way that they might carry him through the crowd, they went upon the roof and let him down with the bed through the tiles into the midst of the crowd and in front of Jesus.
>
> Seeing their faith, Jesus said to him, "Man, your sins have been forgiven."
>
> And the Scribes and the Pharisees began to reason saying, "Who is this that is speaking blasphemies? Who is able to forgive sins except God only?"
>
> But Jesus, having known their reasoning, answered, saying to them. "Why are you reasoning in your hearts? Which is easier to say—'Your sins are forgiven' or to say 'Get up and walk'? But in order that you might know that the son of man has authority on the earth to forgive sins . . ."; he said to the paralytic, "I say to you, get up and take your bed and walk to your house." And instantly, having stood up in front of them and having taken up the bed he was lying upon, he went away to his house glorifying

---

(Luke 8:49–56) because he chose to believe Jesus rather than obey the strictures of the Law of Moses, which forbade anyone being in the presence of the dead until the time of purification.

God. And ecstasy took hold of them all and they glorified God, and they were filled with fear, saying, "We have seen a paradoxical thing today." (author's translation)[2]

The spreading fame of Jesus is the backdrop to our passage, along with a growing measure of opposition. In the previous chapter, he was angrily rejected in the synagogue in his hometown, despite the fact that elsewhere his popularity was growing. But, as his popularity spread, so did the idea that he performed miracles without consideration for the Law of Moses. Luke 4:31–40 shows Jesus involved in a number of healing encounters on the Sabbath, first with a man with an unclean spirit, then with Peter's mother-in-law, and then with many others. Luke 6:6–11 shows the fury of the religious leaders when Jesus healed a man with a withered hand in the synagogue on the Sabbath. Additionally, in 5:12–16 Jesus heals a leper by touching him and, in the process, making himself ceremonially unclean. The leper then fails to fulfill the obligations of Moses in that he does not present his offering to the priest, as prescribed by Leviticus 14.

At this early stage of his ministry, Jesus' reputation as a healer is developing but a healer who has little regard for the Law, and the religious leaders are concerned. This may explain a peculiar phrase in the first verse of our passage. It was just another day of Jesus' ministry, yet coming to hear him were religious leaders "from out of all the towns of Galilee and Judea, and Jerusalem" (Luke 5:17).

The make-up of this group (Pharisees and teachers of the Law) demonstrates that this was not a typical meeting at which Jesus was teaching. David Gooding indicates that the Greek term "teachers of the Law" (*nomodidáskaloi*), a specialist term used only three times in the New Testament, indicates that Luke wants his readers to see that Judaism's top experts in the Torah were present.[3] Additionally, they had come with Pharisees from all over, including as far away as Jerusalem, the religious headquarters of Israel. It seems obvious that they had come to test Jesus, to see how his teaching and actions stood up against the Law of Moses. This apparently was an expedition for a first-hand encounter with Jesus, rooted in a growing concern for guarding the truth (as they saw it). That they were *sitting* while Jesus taught has been variously understood; they may have taken the appropriate posture of those being taught at the feet of a Rabbi or they may have been

---

2. From this point on, unless otherwise stated, all translations of the New Testament are the author's.

3. Gooding, *According to Luke*, 107.

sitting in judgment, listening to test the authenticity of what was being said.[4] The rest of the account suggests the latter view.

As Jesus was teaching, a peculiar incident happened. Some men brought a paralytic friend on a small bed to place him before Jesus to be healed. But they could not get him through because of the crowd. Of interest is the identification of the crowd that blocked the way for the men to get to Jesus. A few indications in the passage highlight the crowd's composition precisely as the religious leaders identified at the beginning of the passage. Note that the plural article *hoì* in verse 17 (*the ones* having come from . . .) shows that it was the religious leaders and not the sick who had come from the entire countryside of Galilee, Judea, and Jerusalem. Bruce Metzger indicates that this difficult but correct reading has led copyists to alter the text to make it more acceptable. According to Metzger: "The difficulty of the reading supported by the overwhelming mass of witnesses (according to which the enemies of Jesus had come from every village of Galilee, Judea, and Jerusalem) prompted some copyists to omit *hoì* altogether (ℵ* 33) and others to replace it with *dé* (D it[d. e] syr[s]), so that it is the sick who have come from all parts to be healed."[5]

But it was the religious leaders who crowded inside the building, and verse 19 states that they blocked the men with their paralyzed friend from getting in. This was the same crowd in whose midst the man was lowered in front of Jesus. That the crowd was on the inside (or perhaps more so on the inside than the outside) is also seen from the man's friends being able to reach the outside of the building to get to the roof. Thus, the religious leaders in the story sitting around Jesus are blocking the path of the true seekers.

The passage indicates that when Jesus saw the faith of the men who took extreme measures to get their friend to him, he pronounced the man's sins forgiven. This created grave concerns among the religious leaders; they grumbled in their thoughts about Jesus' claim of authority to forgive sins, which to them was a clear sign of *Jesus*' sin: "Who is this that is speaking blasphemies? Who is able to forgive sins except God only?" (verse 21) But Jesus sends them into a tailspin by identifying their thoughts, and demonstrating his authority to forgive sins by healing the man.

This healing apparently led to praise and glorification of God's name among the religious leaders—at least that is how Luke 5:26 has traditionally been understood. Precisely at this point scholars often locate the emphasis of the passage on the divine identity of Jesus, demonstrated in the healing and forgiving of sins, recognized by the religious leaders. Donald Miller

4. Green, *The Gospel of Luke*, 240.
5. Metzger, *A Textual Commentary on the Greek New Testament*, 114.

devotes much space of his brief discussion of this passage to explaining the significance of Jesus' act to his divine self-identification,[6] a stance supported by David Gooding, Joel Green, and Leon Morris,[7] although Morris also emphasizes the faith of the paralytic's friends (as the text itself does). Earl Ellis has an emphasis similar to Morris, though he devotes significant space to the discussion on Jesus' self-identification as "the son of man" (verse 24).[8]

The above scholars are not incorrect in their interpretations, as much as they are incomplete in understanding the intent of the passage. They are right that the account would have shown to Jesus' audience the divine credentials of his ministry and the importance of faith. But in light of Luke's emphasis on the outsider, the text also suggests the danger of defending orthodoxy while neglecting orthopraxy. Luke's original readers would have seen that religiosity can be an enemy to what God wants to do with people, especially those on the outside (like the paralytic and his friends).

It is precisely by comparing the religious leaders with the friends of the paralytic that Luke makes his point concerning the inadequacy of religiosity. Indeed, there are two significant points of comparison in the passage. First, the need for healing of the religious leaders is contrasted with the actual healing of the paralytic (through the faith of his friends); second, the response of the religious leaders is contrasted with the response of the paralytic to the healing.

Near the beginning of the narrative, while Jesus was teaching—*before* the paralytic is in view—we are told that "the power of the Lord was on him [Jesus] to heal" (verse 17).[9] This follows the best Greek texts, which contain the word *auton* ("him"), here understood as the subject of the verb for healing.

The Textus Receptus, however, has the variant reading *autous* ("them"), which changes the reading slightly to say that "the power of the Lord was present for healing *them*" (here *them* is taken as the object of the verb for healing). The Textus Receptus has the effect of making the healing of the paralytic man full of irony, since the Lord really wanted to heal the sick among the religious leaders, but they would not receive from him, and so an outsider comes and benefits from the power of God.

---

6. Miller, *The Gospel According to Luke*, 71.

7. Gooding, *According to Luke*, 108–109; Green, *The Gospel of Luke*, 239–43; Morris, *The Gospel According to St. Luke*, 116–17.

8. Ellis, *The Gospel of Luke*, 104–6.

9. It is very interesting that Luke describes the power as being the power of *God* and not of Jesus. The healing power is presented as the divine prerogative of the Father, and Jesus apparently uses it only at God's prescribed times.

As tempting as it is to accept this reading, it is to be rejected on the weight of the textual evidence for *auton* ("him"),[10] making the earlier identified translation more correct. But the desired sentiment of the variant reading is not lost on the correct translation, though now the implication is more distant. The fact is that the passage clearly shows that Jesus' desire to heal was present *before* the paralytic showed up, and that the paralytic's benefit from this power to heal indicated that *faith* was necessary to activate this power (faith that the religious leaders did not have). Thus, in contrasting the religious leaders and the paralytic's friends, Luke is showing that to receive healing from Jesus requires a commitment of faith.

It is interesting to note that without this commitment on the part of the religious leaders, two negative indicators follow—they not only miss out on benefiting from Jesus' presence but the motivation of their presence (to test Jesus) makes them so oblivious to human need that they block the path of those who came to receive from Jesus.

The second point of comparison, namely, between the religious leaders and the paralytic himself, appears at the very end of the passage (in verses 25-26). "And instantly, having stood up in front of them and having taken up the bed he was lying upon, he went away to his house glorifying God. And ecstasy took hold of them all and they glorified God, and they were filled with fear saying, 'We have seen a paradoxical thing today.'"

The NIV translates verse 26 as follows: "Everyone was amazed and gave praise to God. They were filled with awe and said, 'We have seen remarkable things today.'" This seems a rather odd way of representing the conclusion to the passage, since it makes positive what is not so in the original. The miraculous healing of the man stunned the religious leaders to the point of spontaneous praise: "And ecstasy laid hold of them all." They were not in control of their emotions when they saw the miracle unfold literally in front of them; they burst out in praise. But the last two clauses of verse 26 show that this praise was of a different sort than that of the paralytic. Whereas he had responded to Jesus' commanded instantly and left glorifying God (verse 25), their response is characterized by "fear" (*phóbou*), not the more positive "amazement" of the NIV.[11] This is because they had seen "paradoxical things" (*parádoxa*), not the "remarkable" things as suggested by the NIV.[12]

---

10. Metzger, *A Textual Commentary on the Greek New Testament*, 145.

11. Bauer, et al., *A Greek English Lexicon of the New Testament*, 863. It is interesting to note that though the semantic range of this word does include the idea of "reverence" or "respect" as seen in Philippians 2:12, BAG identifies the meaning in the Luke passage as more akin to "alarm, fright." This no doubt comes from the context of the passage as Luke describes it.

12. Ibid., 615. A similar point has to be made with the semantic range of *parádoxa*,

The NIV gives the impression that it is the miracle itself that is uppermost in the mind of the religious guardians. The passage however makes it clear that it is the miracle's *impact on a hallowed belief* that has left them perplexed. The fact is that Jesus has just defied one of the central tenets of their belief system, namely that only God can forgive, so anyone (other than God) who claims to forgive must be blaspheming. But Jesus had just publicly forgiven and healed the paralyzed man, right in their midst. Did this mean that Jesus had come with divine authority? If indeed this were so, then just maybe their opposition to him was also an opposition to God.

But to admit such would be an admission that their religious heritage, and what they were thinking about Jesus, was (at least, in part) incorrect. Since keeping the Law was paramount for the religious leaders who witnessed the healing of the paralytic, William Barclay is undoubtedly right when he explains their dilemma:

> First, for the scribes and Pharisees these rules were a matter of life and death; to break one of them was deadly sin. Second, only people desperately in earnest would ever have tried to keep them, for they must have made life supremely uncomfortable. It was only the best people who would even make the attempt.
>
> Jesus had no use for rules and regulations like this. For him, the cry of human need superseded all such things. But to the scribes and Pharisees he was a law breaker, a bad man who broke the law and taught others to do the same.[13]

The rest of the book of Luke reveals several instances where the religious authorities clash with Jesus over his teachings.[14] The fact that according to Luke 5 there were so many religious leaders present—from such a widespread region—at this early stage of Jesus' ministry, and that Luke shows their ongoing confrontations with Jesus throughout the gospel, indicates that in this first incident the religious leaders neither responded to Jesus in faith nor to his healing of the paralytic with true praise. Luke uses

---

which includes the diverse understandings of "contrary to opinion or expectation, strange, wonderful and remarkable." This time, however, we have to disagree with BAG that the meaning in our passage is "wonderful things," given the behavior of the religious leaders throughout the rest of the book. That they were thrown into confusion over their cherished understanding being overturned suggests that they would view the incident as "contrary to opinion or expectation" or indeed "strange." And again, the rest of the gospel seems to bear this out.

13. Barclay, *The Gospel of Luke*, 60–61.

14. Miller, *The Gospel According to Luke*, 72, is one interpreter who understands the perplexing nature of the miracle on the religious leaders. He too asserts that their spontaneous praise should not be misunderstood, but should be read with their later attitude of rejecting Jesus message and ministry.

PART 1: CONFIGURING CARIBBEAN THEOLOGY

the crippled man and his friends for two points of comparison with the religious leaders, and in both the latter are found wanting. This is not strange for Luke, since he has deliberately set out to show Jesus' preferential option, so to speak, for the outcast.[15]

LUKE 5 AND THE JAMAICAN CHURCH

There are various indications that if the Jamaican church has read this passage in Luke 5, it has not grasped Jesus' challenge to the church's own religiosity. If we were to take even a cursory glance at the ideas that dominate many of our churches, we would see some attitudes and teachings consistent with that of the religious leaders in Luke 5:17–26. In the discussion that follows, I will examine three trends found in a vast number of Jamaican churches—all of which are problematic from the point of view of our text.

The Message of Prosperity

Though there are voices of local Christian thinkers warning against the dangers of flirting with prosperity theology, the phenomenon remains in many of our churches, especially the Charismatic and Pentecostal, but also with a growing number of evangelical churches. Rev. Roderick Hewitt has scolded many pastors and churches for their continued insistence in preaching this "false gospel."[16] His position is that the obedience the biblical gospel requires is costly, demanding, and involves submissive living—often in the midst of severe economic hardships. There is no promise from the gospel that faithful adherents will suddenly find their financial realities much improved, merely because of their faith in Christ. But where has this message come from to dominate masses of Jamaican churches?

Canon Ernle Gordon has shown that much of the message of the Jamaican church is an imposed and unbiblical spirituality.[17] He argues that it is a form of cultural imperialism by the United States to quell the rise of the

---

15. Such a preferential option is for Luke a function of real human need in the presence of God and not some romantic notion of the godliness or virtue of being poor and outcast. Luke 18:1–29 makes it clear that it is the dangers that come with being rich and respected, in terms of how this makes one think too highly of oneself, that is the real enemy of dependence on God. Apparently, the poor and outcast have little to fall back on and so find faith easier.

16. Hewitt, in a 2010 sermon commemorating the fiftieth anniversary of Hope United Church, Kingston, Jamaica; reported in Walker, "False Gospel."

17. Gordon, "The Church and Religious Imperialism."

liberation movements within the Caribbean and Central America, since the early 1970s. Through satellite broadcasts, a kind of "feel good" Christianity is propounded that dulls people's concern with present realities as they imbibe a puerile individualistic faith. Gordon shows that the number of U.S. brand fundamentalist churches have actually increased in Jamaica since the 1980s; the same cannot be said of the mainline, traditional denominations, which, Gordon suggests, preach a more biblical message at this point.

One cannot deny that fundamentalist churches have grown in Jamaica during the period highlighted by Gordon. The access to cable television has also increased over this time, with many of the gospel channels beaming preachers committed to the message of prosperity. The main tenet of this message is that Christians ought to inherit the blessings of Abraham, both spiritual and material, because of their status as sons of Abraham.[18] This status by itself, however, is viewed as a necessary but not sufficient condition for prosperity, since the believer needs to activate this prosperity in his life by the "positive confession of faith" and by "giving to the Lord." The former is thought to "permit" God to work in the life of the believer, since God had translated authority to the believer himself and will not overstep the authority he has conferred.[19] It is when we "give to the Lord" that he activates the "multiplication" or "reciprocity" principle, where he gives from ten to a hundred times what the believer gave to him in the first place.[20]

The emphasis of this message is what we could get from God if we only had faith. Ill health and poor finances are sure signs of the enemy's attack, and demons are often on the prowl to possess and block the blessings of God in our lives. This has often led to a great emphasis on fasting and prayer, and the manifestation of spiritual gifts to show who is truly spiritual (in effect, a new class of super-Christians). Powerful preachers are rewarded with large churches as a sign of their having arrived, and there is the growing practice of credentialing these faithful men with honorary doctorates and exalted titles—Bishop (instead of Pastor), Prophet, Apostle, and Superapostle. These men (they are usually, but not exclusively, men) are waited

---

18. Jones, "The Bankruptcy of Prosperity Theology." In the footnotes of this online article, Jones comments on the use of the Abrahamic covenant by prosperity theologians: "This important covenant is mentioned numerous times in the writings of the prosperity teachers, i.e., Gloria Copeland, *God's Wills Prosperity* (Fort Worth, TX: Kenneth Copeland Publications, 1973), 4–6; Kenneth Copeland, *The Laws of Prosperity* (Fort Worth, TX: Kenneth Copeland Publications, 1974), 51; idem, *Our Covenant with God* (Fort Worth, TX: Kenneth Copeland Publications, 1987), 10; Edward Pousson, *Spreading the Flame* (Grand Rapids, MI: Zondervan, 1992), 158; and Kenneth Copeland, *The Troublemaker* (Fort Worth, TX: Kenneth Copeland Publications, n.d.), 6."

19. "Positive Confession."

20. Robertson, "The Secret of Financial Prosperity."

upon by "Armor Bearers," a growing second but elite class of believers who are next in line for the blessings.

It is interesting to note that the prosperity message suggests there are two tiers of Christian believers. The prosperous believer is a more faithful believer since he has both believed and activated his faith through positive confessions and obedient giving. Indeed, such a Christian is among the elite, as evinced by God's reputed abundance in his life.

Yet with all of this, the church's ministry to those on the outside is still lacking. Luke 5:17–26 is *apropos* of our situation. Like the religious leaders of Jesus' day, we have embraced the idea of an elite who experience God's blessing. Inevitably then, our emphasis is on matters of our own holiness and rightness (as defined by a flawed gospel), instead of that which is truly important to our Lord—the well-being of the outcast. The message of prosperity blinds the church today (just as it did to the religious leaders of Jesus' day) to what God is doing with outsiders.

By outsiders here I mean anyone who does not share a commitment to the prosperity ideal, whether they are Christian or otherwise. Since faithfulness is often also viewed through church attendance, the bulk of outsiders will be truly those who do not attend the church in question or those not affiliated with it. As the faithful congregate around the proliferation of this flawed message, they breed a spiritual elite among themselves, who, like the Pharisees, expect greater blessings from God. And the reverse of this elevation of an elite is a perverse denigration of the outsiders. Based on this theology, the vast majority of our people are seen as spiritual dwarfs at best, and even deserving of their poverty or failures because of their supposed lack of faith.

Emphasis on Praise and Worship

Also relevant to the Jamaican church is the spontaneous praise offered by the religious leaders in light of Jesus revelation of his authority, a praise that was not followed by true faith. As the "feel good" message of our churches increases, so has the greater emphasis on what has come to be called "praise and worship." Although popular chorus singing has always been a part of the Jamaican church experience, the traditional "Chorus Leader" has given way to the "Praise Team." The former was responsible for "warming up" believers at the start of meetings, or for filling the time until enough of the faithful came to worship. After the choruses, the moderator was often heard to say "Let us begin our service with the singing of Hymn # . . ." The point is that the chorus leader was but an appendage (at the beginning) for the more meaty part of the meeting, where more theologically sound hymns were sung in preparation for the delivery of the message. The Praise Team, however, has a different function. It leads the faithful in an uplifting, emotional experience of worship as an integral part of the church's ministry offering. And whereas the chorus time might have taken ten minutes, praise and worship in some churches can last up to an hour. For many believers it has become the most important part of the church's ministry. Many pastors and church boards also believe in its greater importance, seen in their commitment to spend more on instruments for worship than on ministry to the physical needs of people. The reality of this in many of our churches has led Gordon to propound that: "The music ministry has replaced the mission of Jesus."[21]

This music ministry itself is proof that the Jamaican church has imbibed a false and foreign spirituality; this flawed form of worship often insists that praising God requires the words and music of the more spiritually elite foreigners. The average Jamaican evangelical church today trumpets its praise through the strains and strings of North America. That which is local is often ridiculed as being at least inferior and at best demonic. Local believers are then expected to conform to the idea that they only truly worship when this "correct" form of praise is the medium.

But doesn't this mentality lead to us both to blocking out who we really are and to blocking out people who do not find this foreign form of worship appropriate? Like the paralytic, those who are struck with the "malady" that makes them insist on their own culture as appropriate for praise are blocked by the religious guardians of worship from gaining entry. And we thereby miss out on so many possibilities for influencing our people to true praise. We would do well to heed the advice of Ashley Smith that we must "devise ways of capturing the mood of people as it is expressed in their poetry, dance, music and drama."[22]

But let us take heed less we miss perhaps the most important point about praise in our Luke 5 passage. Spontaneous praise means very little to the Lord if it is not followed by a commitment to the demands of the gospel, especially as it reaches out to those in need. The paralytic's praise is followed by immediate and heartfelt obedience, while that of the religious leaders, though spontaneous, does *not* lead to obedience. And it is not enough for our church leaders to leave such involvement up to the goodwill of the people. Our leaders must demonstrate throughout their ministry that authentic

---

21. Gordon, "The Church and Religious Imperialism."
22. A. Smith, *Real Roots and Potted Plants*, 47.

PART 1: CONFIGURING CARIBBEAN THEOLOGY

praise for the things that God is doing must be celebrated and replicated in the church's ministry, especially to those on the outside.

And therein lays the third concern from our passage, one that has repeatedly shown itself throughout our discussion: the church's lack of concern for the people on the outside.

Lack of Concern for Outsiders

The very practical import of the Luke 5 passage suggests that rightness with God is seen precisely in how we treat those on the outside. But this very often goes unmentioned in our churches. Perhaps you will forgive a personal reflection here. In 2006, twelve students from a class entitled "Teaching in the Church" that I taught at the Jamaica Theological Seminary carried out a twelve-week survey in their churches (no two students were from the same local church and there were about eight denominations represented in the class). The point of the survey was to assess the teaching emphases in the "Divine Service" or "Family Bible Hour" of their respective churches. The assumption was that in these services preachers would emphasize what is most important to their church's understanding of their ministry responsibility. Of the one hundred surveys returned, only two made any mention of the church's responsibility to outsiders, other than to share the gospel message with them. Instead the emphases were on such things as "faith," "tithing," "overcoming the enemy," "the importance of praise," and so on. The typical sermon did not even link these themes with caring for others.

Other indications show that the Jamaican church betrays a lack of fidelity to the teaching of Luke 5. For example, while a clear importance is placed on church planting, seen in the sheer number of churches existing in our island nation (Devon Dick has listed 2,674 registered churches in 2004[23]), our common experience is that with the exception of evangelistic crusades and occasional pulpit swaps, our churches have very little in the way of a unified ministry, whether to other believers or to the outsiders of our communities. Most of these churches refuse the call to ecumenism, insisting instead on their particular understanding of the details of the gospel as making them in some way better representatives of the truth than others (in some cases the *only* representatives of truth). It is not uncommon to hear

---

23. Dick, *Rebellion to Riot*, 137–99. Common experience also suggests that our unregistered churches are of a greater number. If we conservatively assume that there are 5000 churches in Jamaica there would be an average of 357 per parish, often two or three existing on the same street. Yet there is little felt impact of the ministry of these churches on our communities.

of pastors who "guard their pulpits" to ensure that whatever is preached there is in line with their church's official positions. How churches existing in this reality could read Luke 5:17–26 without seeing the danger to their insistence on orthodoxy at the expense of orthopraxy defies understanding!

Of course, our churches might respond to the above criticism by showing their record of commitment to social ministry, especially the growth in such ministry over the last twenty years. Church-based clinics, basic schools, skills training centers, and homework centers have basically continued and expanded the trend that shows that no other institution has done more for the social well-being of our people. Thus, it is the common response by church officials and thinkers that the continued attack on the church for its irrelevance to society is unfounded. How then do we explain why so many people who benefit from our churches' social ministries (outlined above) stay away from church and choose lifestyle options detrimental to themselves and the community? Is it sufficient to merely explain this by people's selfishness? Or is there another possible explanation for the churches' lack of impact?

The Jamaican church has unfortunately had a history that demonstrates its support more for middle-class issues and values than for the poor of our community. Lewin Williams shows that from the very beginning of the church in Caribbean freed society the missionary was thought by many to be of a superior social class.[24] Dick suggests that the church never focused on benefiting the poorest among us.[25] Even the Moravian Church distanced itself from the rebellious behavior of Christians like Sam Sharpe and Paul Bogle (who resisted an unjust social order in the name of Christ). And our churches' insistence on preaching to "win souls" while ignoring the deplorable conditions in which these souls live, is an indicator that their social well-being is not a genuine priority. More important for many of our churches is that people dress and behave conservatively—an attitude that still dominates much of our thinking. Formal wear is still expected in many churches and the music of Caribbean culture is often excluded. In short, our churches communicate to average citizens that they are not "good enough" to be a part of us.

Errol Miller calls into question the added value claim of the Jamaican church's contribution to secondary education between 1912 and 1943. He states:

> The structure of the educational provision which offered elementary education to the blacks and Indians and secondary

---

24. Williams, *Caribbean Theology*, 5–6.
25. Dick, *Rebellion to Riot*, 92.

PART 1: CONFIGURING CARIBBEAN THEOLOGY

> education to the other ethnic groups was consistent with the power structure of the Crown Colony. The fact that during this period government subsidized the public education system and that the church schools were included to expand the system made no difference to the structure of the educational provision and its relationship to social stratification in the society.[26]

The point about public secondary education is well-taken; but the issue is even clearer if we address the churches' contribution to primary education, since very few of the people from our communities can afford the fees for their children to access private church preparatory schools and so are excluded access from the primary education deemed by many to be the most crucial plank on the rise up the educational ladder. At the tertiary level, outside of Teachers' Colleges and Theological Schools, our churches have not made a contribution, and even in these institutions we offer very little in the way of scholarships or other financial backing for the average student. Of course, we offer invaluable ministry opportunities in clinics, and skills-training centers, etc., but more often than not these promote the well-being of people only up to a certain point. Our lack of significant funding is often a big hurdle here, but it is not the main one. We still pour millions of dollars in building megachurch structures that often have very little practical use for community development. Additionally, they are more often than not built in a manner that promotes the congregation's responsibility to listen to the truths the pastor has to offer, and where no differences, discussion, or feedback is expected or welcomed. And as an indication of our uncanny resemblance to the religious leaders of Luke 5: 17–26, we make no way for the disabled to enter our sanctuaries and we have no place catering to their unique needs. We very infrequently have facilities for the deaf or ramps for the crippled. We make no provision for the blind, as was demonstrated in one church that was very happy about its newly installed multi-media projection system that beamed all the announcements on the screen, but without any sound. The blind and the illiterate are left on the outside. Of course we are "involved," but often in a way that suggests to outsiders that they are of less value to us. Those outside are left to their own devices to seek benefit from the ministry of the church, instead of the church (like Christ) reaching out to them.

Yet in a culture not dissimilar to ours, people flocked to Jesus. The paralytic's friends went through great pains to get him to Jesus. The rest of the Gospel of Luke shows all sorts of people of less than upright character flocking to him. But they are not flocking to the Jamaican church. Is Jesus

---

26. Miller, "Contemporary Issues in Jamaican Education," 109.

and/or his message absent from our gathering? Or are we doing a better job than the religious leaders of Jesus' day in keeping them out? Perhaps it is a little bit of both.

CONCLUSION

As we read the Gospel of Luke we must recapture the essence of Jesus' message that a demonstration of godly ministry must involve a focus on the well-being of others—especially the outcast—rather than on our own sense of privilege and importance. Like the religious leaders of Luke's day, the church reads and theologizes in such a manner that protects its own self-interest, thus blocking access to God's ministry, especially for those who most need it. Our involvement in things religious is often a sign of our misreading of Scripture more than it reflects our purity of doctrine. In fact, the doctrine we often defend demonstrates a misunderstanding of the very heart of God for those whom we inevitably exclude from the ministry of the church. Perhaps it is little wonder, then, why few outsiders flock to our churches as they did to Jesus. Our reading of the gospel seems to have locked Jesus on the outside of our churches, along with those he has the greatest desire for.

8

Kairos and Kingdom

STEPHEN M. CLARK

WITH UNCOMPROMISING CERTAINTY, AND for some time now, a wide variety of New Testament scholars have insisted that the centrality of Jesus' teaching on the kingdom of God lies at the very heart of his message.[1] Herman Ridderbos explains:

> The central theme of Jesus' message, as it has come down to us in the synoptic gospels, is the coming of the kingdom of God, ... It may rightly be said that the whole of the preaching of Jesus Christ and his apostles is concerned with the kingdom of God, and that in Jesus Christ's proclamation of the kingdom we are face to face with the specific form of expression of the whole of his revelation of God.... for insight into the meaning and the character of the New Testament revelation of God, it is hardly possible to mention any other theme equal in importance to that of the kingdom of heaven.[2]

According to Gerhardus Vos, Jesus

---

1. The most incisive contemporary commentator on this subject is N. T. Wright; see *The Challenge of Jesus*, 34–53; *Simply Christian*, 91–103; *Jesus and the Victory of God*.
2. Ridderbos, *The Coming of the Kingdom*, xi.

declares that the main purpose of his mission consists in the preaching of the good tidings of the kingdom of God.... Its importance will best be felt by considering that the coming of the kingdom is the great event which Jesus connects with his appearance and activity, and that consequently in his teaching which was so closely dependent on his working this event must also have a corresponding prominence ... the kingdom of God forms the supreme object of pursuit, and therefore of necessity the theme about which before all things the disciples need careful instruction.[3]

Indeed, it can hardly be missed. The ministry of Jesus is introduced to us in the Gospel of Mark with these dramatic words: "The time [*kairos*] has come, ... The kingdom of God is at hand" (Mark 1:15).[4] Equally dramatic is Luke's account of Jesus' early sermon in the synagogue at Nazareth. Jesus reads from the scroll of Isaiah (61:1–2) about good news to the poor, liberation of captives, and sight for the blind, all of which amounts to "the year of the Lord's favor" (Luke 4:19). "Then he rolled up the scroll, gave it back to the attendant and sat down. The eyes of everyone in the synagogue were fastened on him, and he began by saying to them, 'Today this scripture is fulfilled in your hearing.'" (Luke 4:20–21)

The centrality of the kingdom of God in the ministry of Jesus is measured not least of all by the number of times it is mentioned in the Synoptic Gospels. It appears thirty-seven times in Matthew, fourteen in Mark, and thirty-two times in Luke.[5]

On the one hand, the kingdom is yet to come: "For I tell you I will not drink again of the fruit of the vine until the kingdom of God comes" (Luke 22:18). On the other, Jesus insists that it *has* come: "But if I drive out demons by the finger of God, then the kingdom of God has come to you" (Luke 11:20). By the 1970s it was already possible for prominent evangelical scholar G. E. Ladd to declare: "The Kingdom of God has received such intensive study during the last few decades that a recent survey of New Testament research can speak of 'the discovery of the true meaning of the Kingdom of God.' There is a growing consensus in New Testament scholarship that the Kingdom of God is in some sense both present and future."[6]

It is the contention of this paper that the evangelical heritage of the Caribbean church has so emphasized the *future* coming of the kingdom that

3. Vos, *The Kingdom of God and the Church*, 9.
4. Unless otherwise indicated, all biblical quotations in this chapter are from the NIV.
5. Hultgren, *The Parables of Jesus*, 384.
6. Ladd, *The Presence of the Future*, 3.

PART 2: INTERPRETING THE BIBLE IN THE CARIBBEAN

we have lost the dramatic implications of its *presence*—both in its initiation of a new time (*kairos*) in the ministry of Jesus and its relevance for our own place and moment in time. To understand that evangelical heritage, and why it has taken such deep root in Caribbean culture, as well as to recover the significance of Jesus' proclamation, we must begin by setting his proclamation in its own cultural context.

JESUS' CULTURAL MILIEU

Galilee was a hotbed of radical political and religious activity. We know this not simply from historians, but from the evidence of the Gospels themselves. One of the twelve disciples was Simon the Zealot (Luke 6:15), a member of a radical party founded by Judas the Galilean who led a revolt against the Romans in AD 6. Jesus lovingly teases two others, James the son of Zebedee and his brother John, whom he calls the "Sons of Thunder" (Mark 3:17). And Jesus repeatedly finds himself in a position where he must steadfastly resist efforts to forcibly draft him to be a king (John 6:15). He weeps over Jerusalem, realizing that the city will not heed his warnings (Matt 23:37–38); and despite the temple's dramatic impression of permanence, he indicates that it will also be destroyed (Matt 24:1–2), as would indeed happen in AD 70.

"APOCALYPTICISM"[7]

Of particular significance is the rise of an apocalyptic culture that was well developed by the time of Jesus.[8] Apocalyptic expectations are generally associated with times of persecution, crisis, alienation, and suffering. The temple had been ravaged by Antiochus Epiphanes in 168 BC and the Jews had been subjugated first by the Greeks and then by the Romans. To make matters worse, Greek language and culture had overcome the proud Jewish culture. In response, bands of the faithful had formed communities out in the wilderness, waiting—as in the case of the Qumran Community that

---

7. We use the term "Apocalypticism" to describe a negative view of the world in which the present is without hope and the future age must be brought in by means of cataclysmic intervention. This understanding of history has had many religious expressions, but can also be found in secular movements such as Marxism.

8. Apocalyptic is particularly associated with Jewish literature dating from approximately 200 BC. In the case of Daniel in the Old Testament, and Revelation in the New Testament, it is a particular expression of prophecy and eschatology that is a revelation of Jesus Christ. As such, it is understood to be a part of the authoritative norm of Scripture that celebrates the presence of God and the victory of Christ in the midst of history.

gave us the Dead Sea Scrolls—for a Teacher of Righteousness, and for "The End." They waited for the kingdom to come.

What we have termed "Apocalypticism" tends to be highly dualistic. It is predisposed to despair of the present and look for redemption in a future as yet unrealized. Selective characteristics[9] include the following:

- Present age is evil — Future age is utopia
- Present age is ruled by Satan — Future age is the age of the Spirit
- Present age characterized by illness — Future age characterized by health
- Present message is judgment — Future age is one of grace
- *Presently, God is at work in Israel* — Future realization of God's rule in world

JOHN THE BAPTIST

"Apocalypticism" explains in part the excitement that attended the ministry of John the Baptist as he appeared out of the wilderness (Luke 3:15). He came as an embodiment of the law and the prophets, of Moses and Elijah, and speaking the words of the Scriptures; both his presence and his message struck a ready cord. He greeted the crowds with these words of judgment: "You brood of vipers! Who warned you to flee from the coming wrath?" (Luke 3:7); but he also insisted that the future age of the Spirit was at hand, and that the one who was coming would "baptize you with the Holy Spirit and with fire." John's message of the coming judgment was unmistakable: "His winnowing fork is in his hand to clear his threshing floor and to gather the wheat into his barn, but he will burn up the chaff with unquenchable fire" (Luke 3:17–18).

It is hard for us to understand where the "good news" is to be found in this message, until we realize that the word "gospel" was already a part of pagan and Jewish culture. "Among the Romans it meant 'joyful tidings' and was associated with the cult of the emperor, whose birth-day, attainment to majority, and accession to power were celebrated as festival occasions for the whole world." It was understood to be "*an historical event which introduces a new situation for the world.*"[10] In other words, John was declaring that the future kingdom was at hand and everything was about to change

---

9. See, for example, Ladd, *Presence of the Kingdom*, 87–93; Jeremias, *New Testament Theology*, 85, 100; Ridderbos, *Coming of the Kingdom*, 8–13.

10. Lane, *The Gospel of Mark*, 42, 43; italics in original.

because the *kairos*, God's great moment of opportunity, was about to break into the world.

THE AGE OF THE SPIRIT

The Gospels leave us with no doubt that the breaking in of God's kingdom comes with the power and presence of the Holy Spirit. In the first three and a half chapters of Luke there are some thirteen references to the Holy Spirit, a dramatic increase compared to the Old Testament. Jesus' baptism is accompanied by the Holy Spirit descending on him in bodily form like a dove (Luke 3:22). Full of the Holy Spirit, Jesus is led out into the wilderness to be tempted of the devil. Recapitulating the history of Israel in the wilderness, the Son will be victorious where Israel was faithless and disobedient. The deliverer had come.

Unmistakably, the future longed-for age of the Spirit (Joel 2:28) had arrived with the coming of Christ and his kingdom. According to Joachim Jeremias, "The presence of the spirit is a sign of the dawn of the time of salvation. . . . The dawn of the consummation of the world is manifested in it. God is speaking his final word."[11]

That same Spirit would also be given to the church as the body of Christ (Acts 2:14-21; 8:12-16). According to the Apostles, it is the presence of the Spirit that will be the defining characteristic of the "last days" (Acts 2:17), understood (as it is in The New Testament) as the period of time from Christ's resurrection to his return. As at the time of John the Baptist, a whole new community would be called into being. Like John the Baptist, Christ is calling out a whole new community, a people among whom the kingdom is to be seen. This new "Israel of God" (Gal 6:16) would be characterized by their life in the Spirit, and by their understanding that this same Spirit witnesses to their being the "sons of God" (Gal 5:16; 4:4-7), heirs of the kingdom (Rom 8:17).

This community is the proof of the coming of the kingdom. Indeed, anyone can claim that their religion, whatever it is, has provided personal peace, but the kingdom has come only if a community can be seen that is radically reconciled both to God and to one another in the power of the Spirit (Eph 2:14-22). A *people* characterized by the presence of the Spirit and by life in the Spirit is definitive are proof that the future age has come.

---

11. Jeremias, *New Testament Theology*, 85.

SATAN

With equal drama Jesus casts out demons. He binds the strongman and sets the demon-possessed free (Mark 3:27; 5:1–20). When the disciples first return from preaching the Good News, Jesus declares, "I saw Satan fall like lightening from heaven" (Luke 10:18).

The exorcisms are to be understood as battles designed to undo the evil one. Joachim Jeremias explains: "They are not isolated invasions of Satan's realm. They are more. They are manifestations of the dawn of the time of salvation."[12] As such, they are foretastes of the *eschaton*, the end. The demons writhe in agony as they acknowledge who Jesus is, because their end has come upon them. Satan is being destroyed, paradise is being opened up. The kingdom of God is breaking in to the present moment (*kairos*).

Jesus' unequivocal assertion is that "if I cast drive out demons by the Spirit of God, then the kingdom of God has come upon you" (Luke 11:20). The apostolic witness is that the mission of Jesus consists in nothing less than setting the captives free from the power of Satan by triumphing over the evil one on the cross (Col 2:15) or destroying the devil and his work (1 John 3:8). Jesus will free the captives (Heb 2:14–15), lead them out as a part of his triumphal victory procession (2 Cor 2:14), and make them citizens of an entirely new kingdom, where he dwells in the power of his Spirit (Eph 2:18–19).

THE MIRACLES

Jesus' miracles were also manifestations that God's kingdom was breaking in as a part of what had been promised by the prophets, and as part of what he was about to do. It is tempting, of course, to think that if we too have enough faith we can walk on water, or that he will calm whatever storm it is we find ourselves in as we go about building our personal lives. Indeed, the miracles repeatedly show Christ's compassion (Mark 1:41; 5:19; 6:34; 8:2), and his interest in our lives should not be minimized. But having said that, the fundamental purpose of the miracles is to assert who Jesus is, and to represent and bring to pass what it is that he has come to do. They prompt the question, "Who is this man?" (Mark 4:34–51); they indicate that he is the Lord over nature, and that his kingdom is about to make all things new.

John calls them "signs." He is generally reticent to designate them as miracles in case they be mistaken for the sort of things associated with

---

12. Ibid., 94.

itinerant miracle workers as they make their rounds.[13] Instead, the miracles are to be understood as nothing less than a resumption of the mighty acts of God on the scale of the parting of the Red Sea. They exhibit God's power over the natural order. The dead are given new life, sins are forgiven, and the captives are set free. They embody the breaking in of the kingdom of God and show beyond a shadow of a doubt that it is God's intention not simply to save the individual soul, but one day to make all things new (Rev 21:5). They are signs of the first blossoming of a new creation that will burst forth on Easter morning. As the Apostle Paul would conclude, "Therefore, if anyone is in Christ, he is a new creation; the old has gone, the new has come!" (2 Cor 5:17).

THE PARABLES

Like the miracles, the parables point to the dramatic entrance of the kingdom of God. They are consistently introduced with the phrase, "The kingdom of God is like . . ." (Mark 4:26, 30; Luke 8:1).[14] For this reason we must avoid the temptation to understand the parables of Jesus as great stories given for the purpose of moral instruction or spiritual implication. Again, that interpretation is not without some truth, but it ultimately misunderstands the purpose of the parables. They address the presence and ultimate victory of God's kingdom.

In the Parable of the Sower, the real point is that despite all obstacles, the seed is so intrinsically powerful that it takes root in the toughest of conditions, and in good soil bears a harvest beyond all normal expectations (Matt 13:3–23; Mark 4:2–20; Luke 8:4–15). In the Parable of the Weeds, the seed is able to hold its own against all competition and be ready for the final harvest (Matt 13:24–30, 36–43). In the Parable of the Seed Growing Secretly, although the plant does not appear to be prospering, the farmer wakes up one morning to discover that it has had remarkable growth (Mark 4:26–29). Similarly, in the Parable of the Yeast, as it works its way through the dough, we discover that nothing can stop the inevitable progress of the kingdom of God (Matt 13:33; Luke 13:20–21). In the Parable of the Mustard Seed (Matt 13:31–32), it will cover the face of the earth. The future age has broken in, and the kingdom of God is like a treasure that, when found, must be procured at any cost (Matt 13:31–32; Mark 4:30–34; Luke 13:18–19).

Jesus strikes the final blow against superficial "apocalypticism" when he asserts that it is not "wars and rumors of war" that represent the coming

---

13. Richardson, *The Gospel According to St. John*, 62.
14. See Hultgren, *The Parables of Jesus*, 383.

of the end of time. These, he indicates, characterize *both* the present and the future. The end will come only when the gospel has been preached to the ends of the earth. Then, and only then, will he come (Matt 24:6, 14). The extension of the gospel over the face of the earth is *the* sign of his coming, and the presence of the kingdom of God among us fills us with motivation, excitement, and anticipation. The *kairos* in which we find ourselves is therefore always a great moment of opportunity, characterized by the coming of the Spirit, the discovery of grace, and the conversion of the nations (Acts 2:14–21).

THE GOSPEL

The preaching of the gospel, with its emphasis on the centrality of the forgiveness of sins (Mark 2:9–12; Matt 18:23–35), is no less a proof than the miracles or the parables that the kingdom of heaven has come.[15] Just as the Word was spoken in the beginning (Genesis 1), Jesus' words bring into being a new creation. The kingdom is spoken into being by the Word.[16]

John the Baptist had a difficult time with this aspect of the good news. When he was in prison and about to be executed, he in effect sent his disciples to ask Jesus, Where is the judgment? I want the kingdom to come in power and our enemies to be destroyed! Jesus replied, "Go back and tell John what you hear and see: the blind receive sight, the lame walk, those who have leprosy are cured, the deaf hear, the dead are raised, the good news is preached to the poor" (Matt 11:25). The age of grace the apocalypticists longed for has broken in!

REVERSAL OF CONDITIONS

The coming of the kingdom brings about a fundamental reversal of conditions. In the kingdom of God the poor are becoming rich and the rich go away empty. As the young peasant girl Mary, the mother of Jesus, declares: The proud are brought down and the humble lifted up (Luke 1:46–55). Possessions become irrelevant, except as they are a hindrance (Luke 12:22–31; Matt 13:22; 19:23). Women are included (John 4:27–30), legalism is rejected, and temptation is resisted from within (Mark 7:18–23). Children are held up as a representative example (Matt 18:1–4), and the greatest in the kingdom are the servants of all (Mark 9:33–35). The sword is repudiated

---

15. Ridderbos, *Coming of the Kingdom*, 71.
16. Ibid., 73.

(Matt 26:52), and prostitutes are pressing into the kingdom ahead of the righteous (Matt 21:31). The poor are especially mentioned, because of God's care for them, but also because the essence of the kingdom is to make the poor to be rich and the weak to be strong. It is, after all, the kingdom *of God*. Everything is being turned upside down.

THE ETHICS OF GRACE

It is important to realize that living in the kingdom is not about a whole new list of commandments to be layered on top of those already given to Moses. Instead, The Sermon on the Mount is a set of examples designed to show us how life is to be lived once we have received the blessing of the kingdom.[17] The Beatitudes begin, "Blessed are the poor in spirit, for theirs is the kingdom of heaven," and it ends with, "Blessed are those who are persecuted because of righteousness, for theirs is the kingdom of heaven" (Matt 5:3, 10).

Discipleship discovers a new motivation. It is a response to grace, a life lived in the freedom, forgiveness, and healing, which the kingdom has brought to us as the most unlikely of all people (Luke 15:11–31; 7:42). In turn, it produces a whole new outlook based on love of God and love of neighbor.

The followers of Jesus discover a fresh way of looking at things because a new order has dawned, there has been a reversal of conditions, and the kingdom is existing already in the midst of the world. The real ethical question becomes, *How do those who belong to the kingdom live in a world which has not yet acknowledged the reign and rule of God?* What immediately becomes clear is that such a people can, for example, afford to "turn the other cheek," and value the poor and dispossessed, instead of the rich and powerful.

Prayer takes on both a new dimension and direction. Indeed, it is utterly transformed. Instead of being the anxious preoccupation of neurotic disciples who are propping up their own kingdoms, it becomes the joyful celebration of the Father, followed by the immediate request: "May your kingdom come, and your will be done on earth as in heaven" (Matt 6:10; author's translation). The real question becomes, *If the Father answers my request, how will that cause his kingdom to come among us?* We begin to live our lives caught up in the purposes of God, and in so doing we find ourselves set free, beginning precisely with our times of prayer.

---

17. France, *The Gospel According to Matthew*, 106–7.

THE KINGDOM OF GOD—A SUMMARY

The question that divided Israel was not whether God ruled, but when and how his rule would be realized upon the earth. In regard to the chronology of the kingdom, or, when it would come, Jesus proclaimed that it is "at hand" (Mark 1:14; ESV), indeed, it is "upon you" (Matt 12:28). It has already come, and its healing is breaking out all around us. That truth becomes our fundamental conviction as we live our lives in a broken and fallen world.

We no longer live under the shadow of "apocalypticism," thinking that this world is beyond hope, but that one day the kingdom of God will come and we will be set free. Instead, we understand that the new creation has begun and that we are a part of what God is already doing in the world. We live as those upon whom "the fulfillment of the ages has come" (1 Cor 10:11). Instead of longing for escape from this world, the final coming of the kingdom fills us with motivation and excitement because we cannot wait to see the King complete what he has already begun, and is already doing in our lives, our communities, and our world.

We understand that the wedding banquet of which the prophets spoke (Isa 25:6) is already taking place (John 2:1–11; Luke 14:15–24). The light shines (Mark 4:21; Matt 5:14), the harvest time has come (Matt 9:38), the fig tree shoots, spring is here (Mark 13:28–30), and the new wine is about the burst the old wineskins (Mark 2:22). The bread of life, understood as a gift of paradise, is being given even to the children of the Gentiles (Mark 7:24–30).[18]

This radical proclamation of the kingdom of God in the Synoptic Gospels is not a new teaching about God but a new activity of God in the person of Jesus Christ.[19] It is not merely the resumption of God's mighty acts in history; it is their coming to their intended fulfillment. It is the beginning of the purposed end.

As such, we understand that Jesus does not envisage the kingdom in limited spatial or geo-political terms (Luke 17:21). It is about reign and rule over all the world, not over some specific realm or nation.[20] The kingdom of God is not so much a particular place in which we live but an activity in which we have been caught up in, which is applicable to every place. The kingdom is to be understood not so much as a noun, but as a verb—or if it is a noun, it designates a reality as comprehensive as creation itself.

---

18. Jeremias, *New Testament Theology*, 106–7.
19. Ladd, *Presence of the Kingdom*, 125.
20. Ibid., 46–47, 130.

It is the kingdom *of God*. As William Lane puts it, "the accent falls upon God's initiative and action"; the kingdom "belongs to the God who comes and invades history in order to secure man's salvation."[21] We do not bring the kingdom to pass; it comes upon us. Technically, we cannot build the kingdom of God, but we can and must participate in it.

Indeed, now we must speak about the church as an eschatological community. That is, a people upon whom "what will be" is already coming to pass. "The Gospels represent him [Jesus] not merely as proclaiming the reign of God but as actually setting up the community of the reign of God, the fellowship of the Messianic rule."[22] This community is a people who already bear the fruits of the Spirit (Gal 5:22–23, Rev 22:1–2), a nation upon whom the kingdom has already come, and upon whom the future is already breaking in. It is a community that not only remembers the victory of Christ, but already participates in the celebration as it sits down at the messianic table (John 6:53–57; Rev 19:7–9), and tastes of the heavenly reality (John 6:48–51), doing so until he comes (I Cor 11:26). We are those who understand "our daily bread" to be our Father giving us tomorrow's bread today.[23] As such, the church understood as the new Israel (Gal 6:16) becomes the people who model life in the kingdom before a watching world. There are no poor among us (Deut 15:4; Acts 4:34) because the grace of the kingdom has turned everything upside down. Rather than being those who can't wait to be "delivered," or who have tied their hopes to some political movement or the other, the challenge before the Caribbean church is to represent an entirely different way of thinking and acting. The church becomes a people-movement that represents the victory of Christ rather than the triumph of materialistic aspirations, and the renewing presence of the Spirit instead of the ongoing decay of culture.

OUR MOMENT IN TIME

As we look at the theme of "*Kairos* and Kingdom," two things come immediately to mind. The first is by way of a warning, the second by way of encouragement.

First, we are always in danger of trying to domesticate both Jesus and his kingdom. It was Albert Schweitzer (1875–1965), the renowned organist, theologian, seminary president, and later missionary doctor, who most

---

21. Lane, *The Gospel of Mark*, 64.
22. Richardson, *An Introduction to the Theology of the New Testament*, 86.
23. See, for example, Ellis, *The Gospel of Luke*, 165; Wright, *The Lord and His Prayer*, 40–41.

dramatically helped us to understand this.[24] As he looked at the Jesus of classical European liberal Christianity he realized that its representation bore little resemblance to Jesus of Galilee. Schweitzer's realization is encapsulated in the famous quote of George Tyrell, commenting on the then reigning German historian, Adolph von Harnack "The Christ that Harnack sees, looking back through nineteen centuries of Catholic darkness, is only the reflection of a Liberal Protestant face, seen at the bottom of a deep well."[25]

In contrast to liberal Christianity, Schweitzer believed that Jesus singlehandedly threw himself upon the wheel of history, and when it turned, it crushed him. Schweitzer's representation at least had the virtue of understanding the central place of the coming of the kingdom in Jesus' ministry, even if it was misunderstood as a tragic moment in the history of "apocalypticism."[26]

The lessons that the church learned from the first so-called "Quest for the historical Jesus" have been all but lost.[27] A cartoonist would have a field day with its present reincarnation in the form of the "Jesus Seminar." In such a caricature, scholars would be seen sitting around a table issuing their latest pontifical decrees on what Jesus really said and did. At the end of it all they would rush outside to meet the hungry media waiting to meet the "real" Jesus, but who are greeted instead by the most recent representation of Western intellectual postmodernism in its most arrogant form.[28]

We are in no less danger. The temptation to remake Jesus into the person who best fits our moment in history, is always there. This is true both our individualistic Western middle-class aspirations and of our more radical Third World interpretations. Jesus' question to his disciples, "Who do people say that I am?" and "Who do you say that I am?" (Mark 8:27–29) are as relevant as ever. Every effort to remake Jesus in our own image always ends up being dashed upon the Rock, and broken. It is never our kingdom. It is always the kingdom *of God*.

---

24. Schweitzer, *The Quest of the Historical Jesus*.

25. Tyrell, *Christianity at the Crossroads*, 44.

26. See Gathercole, "The Critical and Dogmatic Agenda of Albert Schweitzer's *Quest of the Historical Jesus*," 261–83.

27. For a helpful appraisal of our present situation, see Wright, *Victory of God*, 3–124.

28. Not all forms of postmodernism are arrogant; some are genuine attempts to critique the autonomy of modernism. See the discussion in Middleton and Walsh, *Truth Is Stranger than It Used to Be*. The Jesus Seminar, however, is an extension of late modern autonomous rationality applied to the Gospels. For a sober assessment, see Evans, *Fabricating Jesus*.

PART 2: INTERPRETING THE BIBLE IN THE CARIBBEAN

The second implication is inspirational. While I was the pastor of a once thriving North American church now seeking to be relevant to its new multi-cultural context, we discovered that the first immigrant to walk through the doors of our building was a widow from Pakistan. Forty more Pakistanis and then others, including West Indians, would follow her. On one occasion she told us that she was from a town named after the first missionary family to bring the gospel to her region. Two months later I discovered from an elderly family member that the missionary wife was in fact born in Jamaica. Only in the kingdom of God does that happen! Everything gets turned around.

On one occasion a famous apocalypticist visited our church in Jamaica with talk that "Satan is alive and well" on the "late great planet earth," and that two hundred million Chinese troops would come pouring over their borders to precipitate Armageddon, apparently within the present generation. Having just read a book on early Puritan and Protestant understanding of the spread of the gospel and the extension of the kingdom before Christ's return,[29] I recall subsequently exclaiming from the pulpit that it would be more likely that one day there would be two hundred million Chinese missionaries. It was a rash statement, but the generation of which the preacher spoke has now passed, and what it saw was the unprecedented growth of the church in China, in some estimates to as much as eighty to one hundred million members. Indeed, I recently spoke with a Jamaican in China who indicated that he had just met two Chinese Jamaican Christians in that country. This was something that seemed impossible half a century ago when the Christian population stood at one million, and the first Jamaican missionary to China was forced to leave due to the rise of Communism.

God delights to raise up the poor, humble the mighty, and turn everything upside down. Fifty years later, as the humble beginnings of Jamaica Theology Seminary shows, that truth fills us with hope for our present moment and place in the kingdom. The relevance of the Caribbean church lies not in its power or in its numbers, but in its faithfulness to the "gospel of the kingdom" (Luke 8:1; 9:2). As the spread of the gospel in the Acts of the Apostles indicates,[30] nothing can stop the purposes of God. And what we

---

29. Murray, *The Puritan Hope*.

30. The Acts of the Apostles is characterized by a dynamism of movement. In a number of inspiring summary verses (Acts 6:7; 9:31; 12:24; 16:5; 19:20; 28:31), Luke narrates the spread of the gospel from Jerusalem through Judea, to Samaria, into Asia, and finally to Rome as the center of the ancient world. He envisions the continued expansion of the kingdom through the power of the Word and the presence of the Spirit. It will be unhindered, despite problems in the church (5:1–11; 15:1–35) and persecution in the world.

have discovered is that the King delights to sit down at table with those who number themselves among the poor, the maimed, the lame, and the blind (Luke 14:12–14, 21–24), those upon whom the kingdom of God has come.

This breaks our fascination with the world and it structures of power. We refuse to become tied to the social and political "kingdoms" of the world and instead find ourselves members of a radical new community that exists in the midst of the brokenness of our world. The task at hand for the Caribbean church is to be a people who are intoxicated with the kingdom, in love with the gospel, who live by grace, pursue the good of the church, proclaim the good news, share healing with a broken world, and live our lives to the glory of God, in the power of the Spirit.

We are surprised to discover the joys of being a servant and find ourselves no longer wishing to be the master. We find ourselves strangely able to cope with the frustrations of being a part of a still fallen world because we realize that we are caught up in a movement destined to bless the nations, a kingdom that represents the beginning of an entirely new creation (Rom 8:18–25).

May your kingdom come, and your will be done on earth as it is in heaven!

PART 3

The Church in the Caribbean

9

Can Jamaica Be Restored?[1]

LAS G. NEWMAN

IN 1981, THE JAMAICA Council of Churches and leaders of the church in Jamaica had the courage to respond to a time of national crisis and joined forces with others to stage the first National Prayer Breakfast. It was the church's attempt at fostering a climate of healing, reconciliation, and national unity in a country that was in a state of undeclared civil war. Little could they have imagined that this Prayer Breakfast would have continued, and would continue to be necessary, thirty years later. As brief, limited, and imperfect as this annual event has been, over these years it has helped to create some recognition of the need for leaders across all sectors in the nation to come together at the beginning of a new year to spend time in reflection, prayer, and fellowship. Leaders need to pray and be prayed for as they face the enormous challenge of leadership and bear the burdens of office.

---

1. This is the revised text of an address given to the thirtieth annual National Leadership Prayer Breakfast, held at the Pegasus Hotel, Kingston, Jamaica, on January 21, 2010.

PART 3: THE CHURCH IN THE CARIBBEAN

NATIONAL UNITY—"ONE BLOOD"

What has been the message of the National Leadership Prayer Breakfast over these years? There has only been one message: if we are to survive as a nation, then national unity and the integrity of the nation must take center stage. It must be top priority in policy-making and governance. It must be top priority in our leadership behavior. We must unite as a people or continue to hemorrhage the goodwill that is ours. Amidst all our divisions and our unrelenting tendency towards disunity, the very survival of our collective lives in Jamaica is at stake. For, as one of our more conscious entertainers, Junior Reid, puts it, "the whole a we a one blood." A few excerpts from his song lyrics are worth quoting:

> Yuh coulda come from Rema or yuh come from Jungle
> Coulda come from Fiyah House or yuh come from Tower Hill
> One blood . . .
>
> Yuh coulda come from uptown or you come from out a town,
>
> Coulda come from Hannah Town or you come from Browns Town,
>
> One blood . . .
>
> You coulda be a Bobo Dread or a Iyabinghi, . . .
>
> One blood . . .
>
> The fussing and fighting, tribal war, racial war
> Cause blood[2]

To that, we say, Amen! That's what the church has been saying these past thirty years and more. Our unity is an imperative as much as it is a challenge.

CHALLENGE FOR LEADERS

We meet at a time of extraordinary challenges for leaders. Here in our own country and throughout the world, the demands and complexities of the decisions that leaders are called upon to make are perhaps more overwhelming than ever before. There are no easy choices. No easy answers. These are extraordinary times. And extraordinary times demand extraordinary leadership, the kind of leadership that experts like Peter Drucker define as

---

2. Junior Reid, "One Blood." Reid, a Jamaican international reggae artist, produced this signature song in 1989, out of his deep experience of living in the inner-city community of Waterhouse, and nurtured by the spiritual teachings of the Bobo Shantis within the Rastafarian movement.

"lifting a person's vision to higher sights, the raising of a person's performance to a higher standard, the building of a personality beyond its normal limitations."[3] For some leaders the challenges and outlook for this New Year are daunting. Even those who normally are optimistic by nature and personality are not so buoyant at the prospects for this New Year. Our leaders in the public and private sectors, and in communities across Jamaica, are under enormous pressure. So too are the people who look to leaders for direction. Many are fearful and worried. Some have lost their jobs, their livelihoods, and life savings, even their homes and personal assets. Families are suffering. These are perilous times. So what do we do? How should we respond? How should we prepare ourselves to face whatever further challenges are sure to come our way this year and in the years to come?

WE CAN . . . WITH GOD'S HELP

The theme for this thirtieth Prayer Breakfast is *With God, we will overcome*. This is not a theme of undue optimism. It is not a theme that invites positive thinking regardless of the circumstances and realities that we may face. Instead, it is a theme—based on the Judeo-Christian faith—that calls for sober reflection. It is a theme that expresses confidence in the power of Almighty God. It is a theme that challenges us as leaders to know the basis on which we can expect to rise above and triumph over whatever the tasks and challenges that confront us—for rise we must. Things cannot continue as they are without the most disastrous consequences upon the people of this nation.

With this in mind, I bring you the encouraging words of a Hebrew prophet of the seventh century BC, the prophet Habakkuk. Since his book is catalogued as one of the Minor Prophets, comparatively little attention has been given to Habakkuk's life and message. Habakkuk lived at a time when he and his people were faced with national crisis. His nation was under siege in all directions, politically from the invading forces of the Babylonians, economically and morally from its own internal forces. The presence of evil, injustice, and oppression was overwhelming. Habakkuk agonized over this problem and asked, How long must this continue? He knew the challenges and the difficult prospects facing his people. As a faithful Israelite he even questioned his God, as he took issue with Yahweh. In the first chapter of his prophecy Habakkuk asked:

> How long, O LORD, must I call for help,

---

3. Drucker, *Management*, 288.

PART 3: THE CHURCH IN THE CARIBBEAN

> but you do not listen?
> Or cry out to you, "Violence!"
> but you do not save?
> Why do you make me look at injustice?
> Why do you tolerate wrong?
> Destruction and violence are before me;
> there is strife, and conflict abounds.
> The law is paralyzed,
> and justice never prevails.
> The wicked hem in the righteous,
> so that justice is perverted. (Hab 1:1–4)[4]

And yet, despite these depressing circumstances, Habakkuk ends his prophecy with these amazing words:

> Though the fig tree does not bud
> and there are no grapes on the vines,
> though the olive crop fails
> and the fields produce no food,
> though there are no sheep in the pen
> and no cattle in the stalls,
> yet I will rejoice in the LORD,
> I will be joyful in God my Savior.
> The Sovereign LORD is my strength;
> he makes my feet like the feet of a deer,
> he enables me to go on the heights. (Hab 3:17–19)

This so-called minor prophet was a man who refused to give in to despair. He refused to give up hope. His prophecy ended as a prayer that expressed a strong and deep faith in God. He concluded that confidence, courage, and trust in the Sovereign LORD is the way to face and overcome the crises that life brings upon us. Only in this way would his nation overcome. In his prayer he affirmed that even if the whole economy collapses, even if the agricultural sector on which so much of life depends should fail, he would still stand on his confidence and trust in the power and sovereignty of Almighty God. Habakkuk's prophecy is a testament of faith and hope. It is a challenge to commitment, especially for leaders, and a call to action by all. This is the word I believe we need at this time. *With God's help, we will overcome.*

---

4. All quotations from the Bible in this chapter are from the NIV.

JAMAICA UNDER SIEGE . . . ON THE WRONG ROAD

Like it was in Habakkuk's time, our nation too is under siege. Jamaica is no longer at a crossroad. It is going down the wrong moral and spiritual road. We have taken a turn down the wrong road that leads to the undermining of all efforts at nation-building. And none of us, like Pontius Pilate the Roman Governor, can wash our hands and proclaim our innocence. This is not the time for futile debates about whose fault it is, whether it is the government's fault, or the church's fault, or the private sector's fault, or the trade unions' fault, or the fault of parents and family life. We are all at fault. We have all watched, witnessed or participated in the disintegration and destruction of the moral fabric of the nation. All of us must accept responsibility. Our youth have lost their innocence. What is reported in the media about the behavior of our youth on the public transportation system is nothing short of a national disgrace.[5] The level of violence in schools is a loud and clear message that something has gone wrong in our society.

JAMAICA—TRIBALIZED

But equally, the behavior of those in leadership and positions of trust, both in the state and in civil society, is—sad to say—less than exemplary. Most often, it is not something of which we as a people are proud. Our economy and society are on the edge of a precipice, just a short distance away from major collapse. We have tribalized our politics and witnessed the effects of tribal politics on the people across Jamaica. We have tribalized everything, including our culture and our entertainment. Communities are being torn apart and our people are divided.[6] Even the gospel of Jesus has been

---

5. Esther Tyson, Principal of a leading Secondary School in Jamaica, drew attention to this problem in her newspaper column, "Transportation Centre: Blessing or Curse?" She writes: "In a meeting held at the Transport Centre with the stakeholders involved in the operation of the centre and representatives from various schools, the number of fights and other anti-social behaviours, which take place among the students, was discussed with a view to finding solutions to the problem. . . . We were told that almost every day there was a fight, not only between boys, but also between girls who are fighting over a boy or a man. We were shown pictures of myriads of weapons taken from students by the police who monitor the centre. We understood how serious the situation was when the managers pointed out that during the school holidays, the centre was a peaceful, pleasant place, but when school was in session, the atmosphere became tense and a hub of conflict because of the behaviour of some students." This phenomenon in Jamaica attracted attention in other parts of the Caribbean. For a Trinidadian comment, see, Downer, "Plans in Place to Curb Wanton Behaviour in Jamaican Buses."

6. The recent musical sparring between two of Jamaica's top DJs, Vybes Kartel and Movado, turned into tribal warfare between "Gully " and "Gaza" that split inner city

tribalized. The landscape of our country is littered with record-breaking numbers of churches, as if St Paul was not at pains to point out that there is only "one body and one Spirit—just as you were called to one hope when you were called—one Lord, one faith, one baptism; one God and Father of all, who is over all and through all and in all" (Eph 4:4–6). We have got to get our act together as a people. Thank God for the new signs of unity and working together among our churches and among the leadership of the umbrella groups. This is a good sign. It must be encouraged. The demanding mission of the church at present and in future requires it.

JAMAICA—A ROGUE STATE?

Some are now wondering, is there any hope of recovery, any hope of redemption for Jamaica? Can Jamaica turn itself around? Is it too late for the nation to find its moral purpose and turn itself around towards real hope for a prosperous and sustainable future? Confronted by the Goliath of crime and violence, many leaders and people of influence are asking, Are we on the verge of becoming classified as a rogue state, a state that is lawless, ungovernable, and out of control?[7] Why should a little country like ours of 2.7 million people have some 268 gangs with over three thousand members operating in sixteen of the nineteen police divisions?[8] According to the Ministry of National Security, a Gang Threat Assessment Survey reveals that these gangs operate prominently in the Corporate Area and in the parishes of St. James, Clarendon, and St. Catherine. They have international connections and figure prominently in murder for hire, human trafficking,

---

communities and led to some deaths in the inner city. The Prime Minister of Jamaica intervened and held talks at Jamaica House on December 8, 2009, involving both camps. The talks included four Government Ministers. Following the talks a Press Conference was held at Jamaica House, December 15, 2009. See World Star Hip Hop, http://www.worldstarhiphop.com/videos/video.php?v=wshhy8oUs8sWHWL9xnU3.

7. Such as in the *Gleaner* editorial entitled, "If Mr Golding Is to Be Great," which asserted: "It is important, therefore, that civil society and the private sector leave the prime minister and his government in no doubt, if it is not obvious to them, that after 47 years of Independence, Jamaica is rappelling towards becoming a failed and rogue state. The Government's obviously transfixed fear in dealing with America's extradition request for west Kingston businessman/community leader/don, Christopher 'Dudus' Coke, for alleged drug and gunrunning, is a case in point." See also Buddan, "The Reputation of the Jamaican State."

8. This figure of 268 gangs in Jamaica has been challenged by the Peace Management Initiative (PMI). Spokesman of the PMI, Horace Levy, contends that the Government figure is inflated, based on an inadequate definition of what constitutes a gang. See Spaulding, "Gang Data Off The Mark—PMI."

prostitution, kidnapping, and firearms trafficking, as well as cyber crimes. There are powerful external and internal forces that are besieging Jamaica, trying to capture the Jamaican state and bend it to their own private wills and agendas. Will they succeed? If it is not yet too late, we must act before it is too late. What must we do?

As leaders in the nation in all spheres of life, we need to rise up and face the challenge before us. This challenge is much more than economic. There is a real battle for the hearts and minds of our people. We need some Davids among us to take on the Goliaths in the name of God and in the interest of the welfare and well-being of the people. We need every Jamaican who is proud of his/her citizenship, who is willing to fight for the preservation of the integrity of this piece of God's creation, to join the fight against evil. We will never succeed if we are divided and confused about the moral principles that should govern our public and private conduct, principles of decency, honesty, justice, fairness, and respect in our dealings with one another, love for God and neighbor. We will never succeed if we continue to harbor and nurture feelings of hatred and bitterness towards one another, especially among those in positions of leadership. We will never succeed if we seek to destroy one another, thinking that that would make us get ahead and advance our leadership position. We must unite.

WE CAN'T HAVE IT BOTH WAYS

As leaders of the nation, and as citizens of this country, as parents, teachers, administrators, church members, church leaders, civil servants, members of the private sector, and public sector, vendors on the streets or in the marketplace—I say to you, it is time for change to put Jamaica on the right road to a more peaceful, law-abiding, and caring society. The problem is, we have been trying to play it both ways. As a people we must understand that we can't have life both ways. We can't, on one hand, scream *We want justice* and, on the other hand, seek to pervert the course of justice by our corrupt behavior in seeking to bribe the police, the jury, or any other representatives of the court, or protect and harbor those among us who are determined to live a life of crime. Life does not work that way. We cannot expect government to deal with the corrosive and vexing problem of corruption, while we ourselves encourage corruption in our personal and corporate dealings. We cannot have it both ways. We cannot demand more from our over-stretched law enforcement and security personnel and, at the same time, undermine and decry the work of those men and women in the security forces who take their job "to serve and protect" seriously. They are out there fighting bravely against the evil of crime and violence in our society. We cannot have it both ways. We cannot block roads and "bun tyre" whenever we feel aggrieved over an act of injustice in our community, and at the same time fight against the police and against the forces that seek to bring justice, peace, and security to our communities. We cannot abuse and abandon our children and at the same time expect them to be our future. Life does not work that way.

Unless we unite on the moral principles and the moral foundation that should govern a nation and lead to the well-being of the people—principles of integrity, equitable and distributive justice, concern for the poor, the destitute, and the most vulnerable in our midst—we will never overcome.

LEADERSHIP MATTERS

This is why leadership matters. I think it is now abundantly clear that Jamaica needs fundamental change. Jamaica must change course and turn in a new and more positive direction or we will all perish together as fools in paradise. Jesus said, "unless you repent, you too will all perish" (Luke 13:3). Where is the leadership for change to come from? Should it come from the legislative agenda of government? Should it come from the programs and leadership of the church? Should it come from the dynamic cultural life of the nation or from our institutions of learning? I say it has to come from all of the above. It is time for each of us to step forward and become leaders of change and transformation in our society.

It is also time that we open the space for new and younger leadership to emerge. They can help us find the way forward. And this is why I affirm and congratulate our Governor General, Sir Patrick Allen, for his *I believe in Jamaica* campaign to inspire new hope for this country, particularly among the younger generation. I believe this is one of those programs that can help us turn the page in our history to a new chapter of hope and inspiration. We must listen to our younger leaders. They too have a role to play in shaping the change we need.

But how will this happen? What do we need to do to make that change? Do we have what it takes to truly liberate ourselves from the crises that we are in and put ourselves on the path towards a better future? I think we have what it takes. We are not short of ideas. We have an excellent national vision outlined to take us to the year 2030. We have the Millennium Development Goals (MDGs) to benchmark our annual progress to the year 2015. We have political manifestos, corporate plans, community action plans, and a new fiscal plan to engage our people in all aspects of our life.

CALLING OUT THE ARMY OF REFORMERS

The fact is the vast majority of Jamaicans are decent, law-abiding citizens who deeply desire a better Jamaica. The question facing us as a nation is how are we to achieve this better Jamaica that we desire? This requires a strong commitment from each of us to be part of the change and transformation we long to see. This commitment arises from our confidence, courage, and trust in the Sovereign Lord that the prophet Habakkuk speaks of. We long to see Jamaica become a country where there is respect for one another, where there is more caring for one another, where each looks out for the other—a place of justice, truth, forgiveness, and peace. We long to see Jamaica become a country of real freedom and transformation, human flourishing and productivity, economic development and spiritual vitality.

For this to happen we need an army of people who are prepared to stand up and join the brigade for change, people who are willing to make a difference right where they are. We need citizens who are prepared to sign a pledge to join in the fight against evil, to be a peacemaker in the home, the community, and at the workplace. We need citizens who are prepared to renounce old habits and the old politics of division that destroy instead of build. We need citizens who are prepared to reconcile, forgive, and unite with their neighbor, instead of seeking revenge and retaliation. We need leaders who will help Jamaica turn the page and write a new chapter in our politics and governance, in culture and entertainment, in our treatment of one another, and in the preservation and development of our communities, including our treatment of the environment.

Can your leadership make a difference this year? For that to happen, I urge you not to give in to cynics. I urge you not to give in to despair. You can make a difference if you are prepared to take steps to trust in the Sovereign Lord, to set aside and renounce those old ways, those habits and behaviors that have kept us back and undermined our potential as a people. The old politics and the old habits have been around too long. Today, I challenge you to make that commitment to change.

PRAYER FOR RENEWAL

Habakkuk's prayer included a prayer for the renewal of his nation. With the strong heritage of his people in mind, Habakkuk prayed:

> LORD, I have heard of your fame.
> I stand in awe of your deeds, O LORD.
> Renew them in our day.

PART 3: THE CHURCH IN THE CARIBBEAN

> In our time make them known.
> In wrath remember mercy. (Hab 3:2)

If ever there was a time that Jamaica needs to be renewed that time is now. This is the forty-eight year of our Independence and the one hundred and seventy-second year of our Emancipation. Soon we will be celebrating our fiftieth birthday, our Jubilee, as an independent, sovereign nation. Jamaica's Jubilee will be the same year and at the same time as the London Olympics of 2012. All eyes will be focused on Jamaica. The whole world will be cheering this country. The question for us is, will we be worthy of the respect of the world? Often it seems that we are lacking in self-respect. It is time to grow up. As St. Paul says, "When I was a child, I talked like a child, I thought like a child, I reasoned like a child. When I became a man, I put childish ways behind me." (1 Cor 13:11) As we move closer to age fifty it is time to renew the nation.

If we want every Jamaican citizen to feel that they belong here, that they have a role to play in the restoration and development of the fabric of this nation, if we want to increase the productive capacity of our people and get ourselves out of this economic mess that we are in, we must seize this moment. We have an opportunity right in our hands at this time to turn Jamaica around. We had this opportunity in 1838 with Emancipation and we failed. That failure led to the crisis of the Morant Bay Rebellion in 1865.[9] We had this opportunity in 1962 with Independence and we failed. That failure led to the crisis of the nineteen-seventies.[10] God has given a new opportunity in 2012, our Jubilee year. We must not fail again. We cannot let this opportunity pass.

NEW SPIRIT, NEW DAY

We must begin to look forward to and prepare for that milestone, that time of Jamaica's Jubilee in 2012. And as we do, we must take into account how good the Lord Almighty has been to us. Over these fifty years we have struggled, we have worked hard, and we have achieved much in our journey towards building the nation we desire. Yes, we have failed in many areas. We have missed opportunities for nation building. But we most certainly have

---

9. Heuman, *The Killing Time*.

10. One way to understand the conditions of post-independence Jamaica in the nineteen-seventies is through docu-dramas such as *Better Mus' Come*. The World Premiere of *Better Mus' Come* took place at the 2008 Flashpoint Film Festival, June 7, 2008, Port Royal, Jamaica. See http://www.jamaicans.com/news/events/flashpointpolitic2008.shtml.

reasons to celebrate our achievements in health and education, in science and technology, in politics and industry, in arts and culture, in our athleticism and the glory of sports that have won us the admiration of the world. Who can ever forget the spirit of deep pride and unity that swept through the nation when Usain Bolt, Shelly Ann Fraser, and our wonderful team of athletes brought the world to its knees in sheer admiration of Jamaica's excellence in world athletics in Beijing and Berlin in 2009? This is the time to summon that spirit and call the people to renewal of the nation. This is the time to move aggressively towards the building of the Jamaican spirit through programs for the uplifting of the poor and the marginalized. This is the time to unleash the vast potential that is Jamaica. If not this time, when?

Let us not miss this moment. Let us not lose this opportunity. Renewal must begin right where we are, in our 4-H clubs, our neighborhood watch and citizen associations, our societies and fraternities, our business places, our institutions of learning, our churches, synagogue, mosque, and temple. We must seize this opportunity for renewal of our family life, of ourselves, and our institutions.

As we renew our spirits and ourselves, let us draw upon the inspiration provided by those among us who are making a difference; like Shaggy and Friends who are making a difference to an institution like the Bustamante Children's Hospital that desperately needs all the help it can get; like Vilma Clarke, President of The West Green Citizens' Association in St. James, under whose leadership that organization made such a difference to the lives of the people of the community through strong defense of their community.[11]

I am so proud of those men and women and young people of the church who, for the compelling love of Christ and their desire to see a better Jamaica, volunteer their time and energy to feed the hungry, rehabilitate those from prison, and spread the good news through their evangelistic activity; those who teach in basic school education for little or no remuneration. When I see the courage and perseverance of these young people in organizations like Hear the Children Cry, that is passionate about protecting and rescuing our children who are at risk, and Little Brothers of St Andrew, that is giving hope and meaning to inner city youths, and many other groups and individuals throughout Jamaica engaged in helping the most vulnerable to gain a grasp on life, I believe there is hope for Jamaica. I admire their dedication. It is a sign of hope that we can renew. But we need to do much more. We need more people who are prepared to volunteer their time and energy towards making a difference. Too much is at stake for us

---

11. Cummings, "No Cell Tower 'Roun Here!"

not to make this dedication to each other, our fellow Jamaicans, more commonplace. Is this is it achievable? Yes, it is.

COMPASSION AND SACRIFICE

Just before Christmas we witnessed the most remarkable incident of the year, the crash of American Airlines flight 331 at the Norman Manley International airport and the miraculous survival of all on board. What a miracle that was! The Sovereign Lord had his angel in place. Annette Howard, that brave female JUTC bus driver who, on the night of December 22, witnessed this amazing event while on duty, and felt she had no choice but to respond to the cries for help from those frightened passengers who astonishingly emerged from the crashed airplane.[12] Annette Howard made a difference to what could have been a much more tragic situation. Her response symbolized the true spirit of compassion, self-sacrifice, and service embodied in our people. She has inspired her local community and us by her example. This is the difference of one. Annete Howard is here with this morning a special guest of the National Prayer Breakfast Committee. We want to recognize her and say thank you Annette for your inspired example. Annette Howard made a difference. You too can make a difference.

Can Jamaica be restored? Yes, it can. With God's help it will. Jamaica can be restored, parish by parish, community by community, if we have leaders and people who are prepared to chart a new future, a future of immense possibilities and hope. Jamaica can be restored if we have leaders who are prepared to lead with clean hands and a pure heart, leaders who lead with integrity and compassion, who lead with strong vision and courage, who lead for change and transformation. God is at work trying to form a nation that will honor him, one in which he will be pleased to be their God. He is in the transformation business. For God's sake, and our nation's sake, let us respond to his call. Let us heed the call for change, in our lives, in our leadership, and in our nation. The question is, will we?

---

12. Dunkley, "The Hero of AA Flight 331."

10

Evangelicalism as a Sociological Phenomenon?

A Movement in Search of a Caribbean Identity

DELANO PALMER

OVER THE PAST SEVENTY years the movement widely known as evangelicalism has assumed global significance. But what in the world is evangelicalism? And what is the movement doing in the world—particularly Jamaica? The primary purpose of this paper is to address the second question. However, before doing so, some attention must be given to the first. The paper will also propose a way forward for doing evangelical theology, both in Jamaica and in the rest of the Caribbean.

OVERVIEW OF EVANGELICALISM

Evangelicalism is not a religion or a denomination.[1] It is a movement within the ranks of Christianity, encompassing all the major denominations.

---

1. It is becoming increasingly difficult nowadays to define the term *evangelicalism*. With some confidence Alister McGrath identifies six characterizing features: (1) belief in the supreme authority of Scripture; (2) the deity, humanity, and salvific ministry of

In other words, there are evangelical Christians to be found in both Catholicism and Protestantism (the two major dimensions of the Reformation divide), though the majority stands outside the Catholic enclave and the traditional Protestant denominations.

The roots of evangelicalism may be traced to European soil. The Evangelical Revival that took place in the United Kingdom back in the eighteenth century is thought by some to be the fountainhead of the modern evangelical movement. "What happened then was a rediscovery of the gospel and its power" to address the human condition of alienation. Thus, "it spread across denominations."[2]

However, some, like Byang Kato, would trace the roots of evangelicalism even further back, to the first couple of centuries of the Christian era. Although in modern times missionaries from Europe and North America took the gospel to Africa, they were not the first representatives of Christianity on that continent. As a matter of fact, history shows that Christianity's ties are closer to Africa than with Europe or North America. Kato makes the amazing claim that "we can, therefore, rightly call Christianity an African religion."[3]

At the end of the last decade of the nineteenth century nearly 50 percent of the African population had some affiliation to Christianity.[4] That number has since grown. But while evangelicalism is not entirely responsible for that figure, recent reports have attributed a great deal of it to the movement.[5] So, although Kato's claim may be considered exaggerated, the continent today is experiencing a Christian presence that is unprecedented.

Turning to Latin America, a predominantly Roman Catholic domain, we also see a significant growth of evangelical Christians, particularly among the Pentecostal and Charismatic churches.[6] However, in contrast

---

Jesus Christ; (3) the lordship of the Holy Spirit; (4) the need for personal conversion; (5) the priority of evangelism, individually and corporately; and (6) the importance of the local church for spiritual maturity (McGrath, *Evangelicalism*, 54–87).

2. I. Howard Marshall, "Methodism and the Evangelical Tradition," cited in Allan, *The Evangelicals*, 36.

3. Kato, *Biblical Christianity in Africa*, 32–39, cited in Allan, *The Evangelicals*, 54.

4. Allan, *The Evangelicals*, 54.

5. Of course, Islam is also on the rise in many parts of Africa; for the challenge this poses, see, for example, Glaser, "Authority, Identity, and the Establishment of the Kingdom of God," 77–91. One of the most famous evangelical ministers in America, Rick Warren, prayed at the inauguration of the forty-fourth U.S. president, whose father was Kenyan.

6. For the Pentecostal influence in Jamaica, see Austin-Broos, *Jamaica Genesis*, and Smith, *Pentecostalism in Jamaica*. According to Winston Persaud: "As it looks to the twenty-first century, the church in the Caribbean cannot avoid serious wrestling with

to the strong social concern exhibited in other latitudes, evangelicalism in Latin America "has had the effect of insulating believers from the world, filling up their time with church activities and imposing strict social regulations upon them so that their contribution to society was limited."[7] Interestingly, in the 1980s,

> some South American dictators with an extremely dubious civil rights record were friendly to the growth of Pentecostalism, because it distracted the attention of the masses from the inequality in society. Not all Pentecostalism was like this, however; and other evangelical denominations have also taken seriously the need for agents of peace and justice in a hopelessly unfair society (in Latin America close to 20% of the population receive 66% of the total income).[8]

A relatively recent development in evangelicalism worldwide is the formation of regional bodies to consolidate and promote its concerns. In Asia, the leading evangelical witness is found in South Korea, such as in the famous "Full Gospel Central Church . . . which claims no less than 250,000 members and Presbyterian congregations with over 50, 000 in one city"; these churches are considered sure signs of revival in a country that in a previous century was said to be impervious to Christian influence.[9] One of the positives of South Korean evangelicalism, directed by the Evangelical Fellowship of Asia, is the self-reliant basis on which it was formed. Another positive is the fact that the movement is credited with an overall beneficent influence on the society, with believers strategically placed in parliament and the sports arena. The Korean paradigm appears to be catching on in other Asian countries and has certainly become a model of social engagement for Christians worldwide.[10]

Several factors, such as the need to create an authentic African theology and the desire to pool resources led some African evangelicals to organize

---

the current phenomenal growth of Evangelical and Pentecostal Christianity in Latin America and the Caribbean. It is a phenomenon that especially, though not exclusively, touches the masses of the suffering, poor, powerless, exploited, marginalized, and dislocated. It is a phenomenon of liberation, of new found 'free space,' new found spiritual and socio-psychic healing in the midst of fragmentation and chaos. It is a phenomenon of division, a spiritual and social separation" ("Caribbean Response to Globalization in Theological Education," 49).

7. Allan, *The Evangelicals*, 113.

8. Ibid., 114.

9. Ibid., 94.

10. For more on Asia, particularly South Korea, see Lee, *Holy Spirit Movement in Korea*; and McGrath, *Future of Christianity*, 30–31.

themselves into a unified force. In Kenya and Uganda, the motivation was different. Their unity gave a sense of solidarity and security in the face of grave danger. Yet out of differing motivations came in 1966 the Association of Evangelicals in Africa and Madagascar (AEAM). "Today AEAM is recognized as a major voice speaking for evangelicals throughout Africa."[11]

The kind of evangelicalism that preceded AEAM, though lacking in organizational structure, nevertheless contributed significantly to the demise of the African slave trade as well as giving itself "to a myriad of philanthropies."[12] Organizations similar to AEAM are found in Oceania, North America, Europe, and the Caribbean as well.[13] In Central and South America, we have the *Confraternidad Evangelica Latino America*.[14]

THE JAMAICA NEXUS

Arguably, the religious phenomenon with the greatest impact on the Jamaican society, and to a lesser extent the wider Caribbean, is the Rastafarian movement.[15] Many in recent times have sought to chart the course of this movement.[16] Notwithstanding the Rastafarian influence in the culture, the church continues to make its mark, though it seems to some that it is not keeping pace with other institutions of social change.

Rastafari is not as old as the evangelical movement in Jamaica. If it were, there is little doubt that it would certainly have been in the forefront of the fight for "the African-Jamaican on his remote plantation, [helping to] destroy slavery and the West Indian sugar monopoly in England" along with the evangelicals. What is doubtful, though, is that Rastafarians would be establishing white-black alliances based on religious convictions.[17]

The first avowedly evangelical group to arrive in the Caribbean was the Moravian church in the mid-eighteenth century. Like the Anglicans, Baptists, and Catholics before them, the Moravians sought to preach the gospel to the new "native" population. Although they initially owned slaves in Jamaica, they came to disavow slavery and addressed the stark social

---

11. Allan, *The Evangelicals*, 67–8.
12. Isichei, *A History of Christianity*, 81.
13. Johnstone, *Operation World*, 455–86.
14. Noelliste, "The Church and Human Emancipation."
15. See Chisholm, *Revelations on Ras Tafari*.
16. For example, Chevannes, *Rastafari*; Edmonds, *Rastafari*; Edmonds and Gonzalez, *Caribbean Religious History*, 166–69, 183–201; Murrell et al. (eds.), *Chanting Down Babylon*.
17. Sherlock and Bennett, *The Story of the Jamaican People*, 177.

inequality with which they were confronted, particularly among the black population.[18]

Prior to that there were early evangelical Reformists working out of England for the abolition of slavery, including William Wilberforce and Granville Sharp. It is Sharp himself who was instrumental in getting a positive ruling through the courts in the year 1772. On July 22 the chief Justice of England ruled: "The state of slavery is of such a mixture that it is incapable of being instructed on any reasons, moral or political . . . it is so obvious that nothing can be suffered to support it, but positive law. Whatever inconvenience, therefore, may follow from a decision . . . the black man [specifically, James Somerset, the slave represented by Sharp] must be set free."[19]

The decision had devastating consequences for the English slave trade. "As a result of this ruling all 10,000 of the slaves held in England . . . gained their freedom. Encouraged by this ruling, the abolitionists intensified their efforts," an anti-slavery society was formed by an evangelical group, the Quakers, and Wilberforce, an associate of Sharp, convinced the English parliament to abolish the slave trade. This was "the first time in their history the African-Jamaicans discovered that they had allies and friends in the world of white power."[20]

But it is to two black Baptist preachers that the evangelical movement in Jamaica owes its indigenous character.[21] Today that indigenous character is manifest in most if not all denominations and is now partially institutionalized in the structure known as the Jamaica Association of Evangelicals (JAE). This organization came into being one hundred years after a major turning point in Jamaica's history—the Morant Bay rebellion.[22] Unlike the Morant Bay experience, the founding of the Jamaican Association of Evangelical Churches (as it was then called) was far less auspicious. Framers of the organization trace their roots to the revival of the eighteen-sixties, which, ironically, took Jamaica by storm just around the time when the island was experiencing one of its most testing periods, the one which eventually led to

---

18. Arguments justifying slavery were based on a misinterpretation of the so-called Hamitic curse and the notion that whites belonged to a chosen race. Dick, *The Origin and Development of the Native Baptists in Jamaica*, 260; see also his *The Cross and the Machete*, with its insightful foreword by the late Rex Nettleford. For accounts of how descendants of the enslaved rose above the odds, see Newman, "Mission from the Margin." For race relations in the West Indies, see Roper, "Racism and Christianity in the Caribbean."

19. Sherlock and Bennett, *The Story of the Jamaican People*, 179.

20. Ibid.

21. Ibid., 80–81.

22. Black, *History of Jamaica*, 203.

the aforementioned rebellion. Whereas the political directorate of the time was quite insensitive to the plight of the peasantry,[23] the missionaries, few as they were, "laboured tirelessly for fair wages, land settlement, and the establishment of villages," explains Zenas Gerig; they "were also instrumental in establishing schools for the teaching of the three 'Rs.'"[24] Partly out of this social concern and the great spiritual hunger felt at the time, the Moravians in the extreme West of the island were the first to experience the new wave of the Spirit. The rest of the island was soon to come under the new spiritual awakening.[25]

Very early in its history the JAE expressed a deep burden for the social milieu in which it was nurtured. Cited for special mention at the time were "the loose family patterns, coupled with a high percentage of illegitimacy, the growing situation of West Kingston and the high rate of illiteracy," to mention only a few issues. "These ills," declared Gerig, "require the individual and united strength and efforts of the church," which therefore "should aim toward a programme for the total man."[26] Despite its unabashed interest in the proclamation of the gospel, the JAE is still today interested in these social ideals. This is not to say that the movement (and the constituency that it serves) has been entirely consistent with its own aspirations and goals. Therefore, certain questions raised along these lines by its friends looking on ought to be pondered seriously.[27]

In many respects, the standard of living in Jamaica has risen much higher since the 1960s, the decade of Independence. However, this is by no means the total picture. In other areas, things have markedly deteriorated. For example, in the year prior to Gerig's speech to the evangelical clergy gathered in Mandeville, the nation recorded just over a hundred cases of homicide. Today there is a nine hundred percent increase. "The sad thing is that we have now become so immune to the daily occurrences that shock and disgust are seldom expressed until it either affects one's household or is experienced by someone with whom we are closely associated."[28]

In connection with the high level of crime and violence is the widening gap between the poor and the well-to-do, not to mention the growing number of the unemployed. When seen against the backdrop of global

---

23. Ibid., 187–9.
24. Gerig, "Why the Association of Evangelical Churches?," 2.
25. Ibid., 3.
26. Ibid., 7.
27. See A. Smith, *Real Roots and Potted Plants*; and Williams, *Caribbean Theology*.
28. Edwards, "900% Increase in Murder Rate over 30 years," 6.

economic trends, the immediate future for Jamaica, though not hopeless, appears quite bleak.

All this raises the intriguing question concerning the church's role in culture and society, indeed, in nation building. What exactly is the church doing? Is it really relevant to the culture? Is the church a part of the problem of social decay, or what?

I think that clerics of all denominational stripes will agree that the church can do more. However, the church's failure or success in these matters should not be judged merely by individual expectations. Let us remind ourselves that though the church today still struggles with its own identity and mission, it does in fact have its particular *modus operandi* to which, in varying degrees it is committed, although not all church leaders grasp the Messianic mandate in the same way.

For example, evangelicals in the Caribbean basin understand the church's mandate in basically two ways. One group underscores the need to proclaim the gospel as top priority. For instance, "one of the declared objectives of the JAE is to promote evangelism."[29] Another group of evangelicals, however, believes that the mere *proclamation* of the gospel does not exhaust the responsibility of the people of God. One of the chief spokespersons for this position is British theologian, John Stott.

For Stott, evangelism and social responsibility are both grounded, first of all, in the very character of God, because the God of biblical revelation is concerned with the total well-being of all humanity. The second ground for keeping evangelism and social intervention together is the teaching and ministry of Jesus (see especially Jesus' concern for the social needs in Luke 4:16-21). Jesus' ministry, then, as the Gospels testify, certainly did not preclude social action and community service. A third argument is to be found in the very demands of effective contextualization.[30]

It seems that in its embryonic stage the JAE would not have endorsed Stott's position, which, it appears, has been adopted by the majority of evangelicals worldwide. However, later developments have revealed a shift in JAE policy.[31] For example, when Pastor Henry White became president

29. Hall, "Today is JAE Sunday." Observe the sensitivity of the fledgling JAE in this regard: "It is not the intention [of the JAE] to take over the work of evangelism from the church.... Rather, this organization should assist in the promotion of evangelism in whatever way possible" (Gerig, "Why the Association of Evangelical Churches?," 7).

30. Stott, *The Contemporary Christian*, 334-49.

31. It would seem that earlier JAE members were heavily influenced by the approach of McGavran's *Church Growth in Jamaica*, 111, which states: "The church does not need to trouble itself about agricultural production... and the like.... All [they] need to do is to use the structure... inherited... to multiply Christians." Today the JAE's Mission Statement is:

of the JAE in 1979, he not only affirmed the organization's commitment to evangelism as a matter of primary importance, but also announced the establishment of a Relief and Development Commission "to deal with community aid projects." The announcement was made at the fourteenth annual conference of the Jamaica Association of Evangelicals. One year after this report the Jamaican public was informed that the organization had been effective in its objectives of rendering "special services" by way of help to certain flood victims "and relief aid to earthquake victims in Guatemala, as well as [a] gift of $10,000 to the Ministry of Health to help remove the mentally ill from the streets."[32] Evangelicals, like many other Christians everywhere, tend to be reticent about placarding their community involvement. Many observers have therefore missed what they have accomplished. Already we have pointed out ways in which this kind of involvement has taken shape, so a brief review now is in order.

Whereas not much can be said about the social involvement of Jamaican and American evangelicalism in the nineteenth century, the momentum of community involvement on the part of people like Wilberforce was still strong in the United Kingdom. Not that it was needed most there. Conditions in America, in particular, and, to a lesser extent, in Jamaica definitely warranted the philanthropic efforts of all interests. But such organized effort was lacking at the time. In the UK, though, voices of evangelical persuasion could be heard. With the full realization that "the church . . . assisted the privileged classes to keep labour in chains," explains David Bebbington, these voices aggressively addressed societal ills such as "bad housing, inadequate wages and commercial bargaining as frequently as personal sins." Their talk was ably backed up by the Salvation Army and "the extensive institutional philanthropy of the Church of Scotland . . . organized and staffed largely by evangelicals."[33] Regrettably, due to the advent of the First World War and its aftermath, coupled with the attendant apocalypticism among a number of evangelicals at the time, social concern on the part of those associated with the church waned significantly.

In Jamaica during the 1930s, a severe economic crisis ensued, not unlike the global financial meltdown of the early twenty-first century. There had been rapid decline in exports and a serious rise in the unemployment rate. The resulting conditions by the end of the decade, according to David

---

"To provide leadership for Evangelical Christians in empowering them for evangelism, discipleship and *social responsibility* in the nation" (*Kingston Keswick 50th Anniversary Commemorative Magazine 1960–2010*, 27, my emphasis).

32. *Daily Gleaner* (Jamaica), October 11, 1980, 15.

33. Bebbington, "The Decline and Resurgence of Evangelical Social Concern 1918–1980," 175–6.

Panton, included "wide-spread malnutrition, inadequate housing, few educational opportunities for the average Jamaican, and widespread poverty and unemployment," which led to occasional rioting.[34] There was no organized response from the church to address these conditions.

But amidst the mayhem of the period, there was one evangelical clergyman who was to emerge with flying colors. Father Hugh Sherlock,[35] who eventually penned the words of the Jamaican National Anthem, was that man. While not forty years old, Father Sherlock established one of the most effective inner-city institutions, the now famous Boys' Town. Observing the plight of the under-privileged youths, Father Sherlock requested time from the Methodist church to address their needs. Boys' Town was first located in a churchyard in Jones Town but later removed to Central Road, which was subsequently renamed Collie Smith Drive, in Trench Town. The late Nesta Robert Marley (of international musical acclaim) and Collie Smith (who represented Jamaica and the West Indies at cricket) were undoubtedly the brightest stars to have been associated with the institution. Boys' Town was more than a school. It also became a major sports club participating in various Corporate Area competitions, especially cricket and football. For many years, Father Sherlock himself represented Boys' Town at cricket, and the present national Technical Director of Cayman, Carl Brown, represented Boys' Town at football. Brown, like Collie Smith and a host of others, went on to represent his country in the field of his endeavor. For his contribution to football, Brown, who attends an evangelical church, was honored by his country with the Order of Distinction. Later he became the first recipient of the Father Hugh Sherlock Award for Excellence.

Father Sherlock died in 1998. But before his passing he was able to participate in the fifty-fifth Anniversary Thanksgiving ceremony held at the school on November 19, 1995. In his speech on that occasion Father Sherlock noted with pride that, despite set backs, the institution that was on his mind when he penned the words, "Strengthen us the weak to cherish" (from the Jamaican national anthem), is still continuing "to build the mind, body and spirit [of the] underprivileged to gain an opportunity to become good citizens."[36]

Father Sherlock was not the only cleric who saw the potential of education as a means to address some of the challenges in society. Neither was he the first. Some important forerunners include the Rev. Enos Nuttall,

---

34. Panton, *Jamaica's Michael Manley*, 15.

35. For the story of Father Sherlock, see Sherlock and Coke, *Eternal Father, Bless Our Land*.

36. *Sunday Observer*, December 10, 1995, 3.

PART 3: THE CHURCH IN THE CARIBBEAN

who was "the mentor and spiritual father of Percival William Gibson, the founder of Kingston College in 1925, as well as the man who allowed Black men to be ordained as priests of the Church of England in Jamaica. He introduced young Gibson to the world of books, and awakened his thirst for intellectual pursuits."[37]

When Nuttall arrived in Jamaica in the middle of the nineteenth century, he was a Methodist minister like Father Sherlock.[38] But after three years working with that group, he switched to Anglicanism, from where he was to have his greatest influence. Between 1866 and 1895 the man who was once a main attraction at evangelical meetings in his native England was instrumental in organizing the Mico Training School, "permitting more effective training and opening registration to all denominations" and all races. Nuttall was also responsible for the recruitment of black men to the Anglican Clergy, the merging of "Wolmer's with the Kingston Grammar School, to form Wolmer's Boys' School as a secondary institution for day students, and the co-founding of the first degree granting institution in the West Indies (which only lasted for a year)." He also became the Chairman of the Jamaica Schools Commission, "a forerunner of the Department of Education . . . the principal force in establishing education of all types across the island," and took part in the establishment of the Jamaica Church Theological College, "a divinity school for the training of Anglican Clergy," as well as the Shortwood Teachers College, Kingston Technical, Jamaica College, and Cornwall College in Montego Bay. It was indeed Nuttall's efforts that helped significantly to place Jamaica's educational system on a firm footing for the twentieth-century. Can the church do the same for this millennium?[39]

Apart from being the conscience of the nation, perhaps the single most important contribution of the Jamaican church to society is in the area of education. The number of clergymen following in the noble tradition of bishop Nuttall is great. Many have worked hard in and for the nation's schools, particularly at the secondary level. I think it safe to say that some of the best high schools in the island are connected to churches. Apart from those already mentioned, others that readily come to mind are St. George's College, Mt. Alvernia, Immaculate Conception, Holy Childhood, and Campion (all Roman Catholic), Kingston College and Westwood (Anglican), Meadowbrook (Methodist), Calabar (Baptist), Ardenne (Church of God), and Merle Grove (Associated Gospel Assemblies).

37. Johnston, *A History of Kingston College, 1925–1995*, 1–2.
38. Ibid., 7–9 is the source of the quotations in the rest of this paragraph.
39. Considering especially that we need to "develop positive work and service attitudes with a serious commitment to discipline and excellence for students, teachers, and at the work place" (Sangster, "Education and Training," 114).

Although the latter two schools may be classed as evangelical, secondary education has not been the strongpoint of the movement. Traditionally, this has been the forte of the older and more established churches. Over the last twenty years or so, the evangelicals have concentrated their efforts in the setting up of a plethora of basic and preparatory schools islandwide. Four of these, Portmore Missionary, Vaz, Covenant Christian Community Academy, and Mavisville,[40] have done quite well in recent times.

However, while evangelicals have sought to create a niche for themselves in the area of the nation's educational system, they had for the better part of the last century neglected their own intellectual needs in terms of making serious provision for an educated clergy. In fact, some prided themselves in not having been to "college but to Calvary."

The need to provide leaders who could impart intellectual rigor[41] to the movement did not go unnoticed by all, and so in the forties at least two Bible schools were started: the non-denominational Jamaica Bible College in Mandeville and Bethel Bible College associated with the New Testament Church of God. Both institutions offered certificates and diplomas, but it was not until 1960 that the first degree granting evangelical institution was established, Jamaica Theological Seminary.[42]

While evangelical social engagement may be growing in the broad area of education, its concern for social justice and the poor has not kept pace.[43] This tendency appears to be a blot against the movement in several parts of the globe.[44] In an essay entitled, "The Caribbean's Response to the Great Commission," Las Newman, president of the Caribbean Graduate School of Theology, delineates three models of Christian involvement that are pertinent to our survey. The first one he calls the ethnic model "whereby missionary endeavours were focused upon people groups of particular

---

40. Sponsored by "Missa Wildish Maranatha" (Hyatt, *When I Was a Boy*, 21). Maranatha is the original home of the Christian Ambassadors Footballers United (Diedrick, "Christian Ambassadors," 5; Palmer, "Men Reaching Men"; cf. Vassel, *Understanding and Addressing Male Absence from the Jamaican Church*).

41. Noll, *The Scandal of the Evangelical Mind*, and Wells, *No Place for Truth*, have already canvassed the intellectual deficit of American evangelicalism in particular. In recent times some Caribbean evangelicals have been attempting to create a body of literature to fill the lacuna in the region; see, for example, C. A. Thomas, *A Case for Mixed-Audience*, and Middleton, *The Liberating Image*.

42. See Ringenberg, *History of the Jamaica Theological Seminary 1960–1992*; and Roper, "Moving Forward." A professor and graduate (D. Thomas, *Confronting Suicide*) of this institution have launched Choose Life International, an organization with a fourfold purpose that includes suicide intervention.

43. See Oliver, *Salvation as Justice in Amos 5:18–27*.

44. Isichei, *A History of Christianity*, 312.

ethnicities."[45] Several missionaries from the Caribbean went to sub-Sahara Africa under this model. The second model, which emerged in the post World War II era, concentrated its efforts on the youth of the region as potential church leaders. The Inter-Schools/Inter-Varsity Christian Fellowship, Youth for Christ, and Bible school movements all fall under this umbrella. "A third model of Caribbean mission . . . is the contemporary model . . . to the urban poor. . . . Within the first three decades of post-Independence the Caribbean church, in response to the new social and economic order, has been engaged in developing [a] new . . . ministry to the poor. Despite structural adjustment programmes (or indeed because of them) a new class of the poor has emerged. This class is semi-educated, young and urban."[46]

It is the established churches that have given the most telling response under the third model. Here the Catholics boast the Mustard Seed Community (Father Gregory Rakinson), the St. Patrick's Development Foundation (Monsignor Richard Albert), and the Brothers of the Poor (founded by Jesuit priest Father Richard Holung). Since independence, "the Anglican Parish Church of St. Andrew has been engaged in mission work among some 30,000 residents on the fringes of the urban core of the city"[47] and "The United Church of Jamaica and Grand Cayman have several major social projects within its churches . . . one of the largest [of which] is the Mel Nathan Institute . . . located in Hannah Town, a depressed community of about 20,000 people in the inner city of Western Kingston."[48] One could add to the list the effective ministries of the Jamaica Baptist Union and other groups.[49] While individual evangelicals here and there have participated in these ventures, the newer churches they represent seem conspicuous by their absence.[50] But things are changing. Congregations such as Redemption Chapel

---

45. Newman, "The Caribbean Response to the Great Commission," 19.

46. Ibid., 26.

47. Dick, *Rebellion to Riot*, 40.

48. Ibid., 104.

49. "The Jamaica Baptist Union supports an important project of the Bethel Baptist church in Half Way Tree . . . Established in 1970 as a counseling service of the church, the increased demand for the services offered led to the development of a three-pronged ministry involving Counselling Services and Community Outreach to nearby Ambrook Lane where social and basic health education . . . are conducted. . . . The healing Ministry was developed by Jamaican Psychologist Dr. Anthony Allen, and developed over the years under the pastoral leadership of Rev. Burchell Taylor. Some 5,000 persons a year make use of its services" (Newman, "The Caribbean Response to the Great Commission," 28; see Allen's own essay, "The Healing Christ," 86–101).

50. A notable exception, of course, is the Salvation Army one of whose officers, Major Raphael Mason, is a past president of the JAE.

(St James), Holiness Christian Church[51] (Corporate Area), and Portmore Missionary (St. Catherine) are reaching out to their constituents through the sponsoring of clinics and other community-based projects, because "it is important that the church advocates for the social wellbeing of members within its community and complement the existing social services offered by the state. [Consequently] members of the Portmore Missionary Church . . . have implemented a number of social programmes to help improve the lives of those in the . . . area."[52]

Since the beginning of the last decade, the Jamaican Association of Evangelicals (JAE) itself "has expressed concern at the rapid escalation in the cost of living, resulting in severe hardship to the poor, fixed income groups and pensioners." A decision was taken "to encourage the expansion of social services being offered by member churches and, in particular, those in nutrition, health and education. The association [also] decided to take steps with immediate effect to establish grocery outlets with a view to providing basic food items at more affordable prices."[53] More recently, the JAE, like many NGOs, has been playing its part in responding to the Haitian crisis.[54] Evangelicals are deeply involved in models one and two of missions. More consideration needs to be given to model three.

But what about politics? I think it is safe to say that when it comes to Jamaican politics, the actual engagement on the part of evangelical and non-evangelical clergy is very negligible, though their ideological postures may differ quite sharply.[55] Here we have a sharp contrast to the United States, whose head of state, Barak Obama, can, with Christian conviction, write about the "remarkable . . . ability of evangelical Christianity not only to

---

51. Whose former Pastor, Dr Sam Vassel, was an active member of Citizens Action for Free and Fair Elections (CAFFE).

52. Wislon, "Portmore Missionary Impacts Community with Social Outreach." The article goes on to quote the pastor, Garnett Roper: "We believe that church has to approximate the ideals of Christ. It has to show its faith by what it does. So you pick the people who are being left out and are being left behind and you start with them, whether it be the disabled, or the children who are wards of the state or in foster care, or the people in the inner city who don't get the social services."

53. *Daily Gleaner,* November 20 1991, 17.

54. But see Yorke, "Haiti's Rescue"; for Haiti's major historical contribution to Jamaica, see Gosse, "The Impact of the Haitian Revolution on the Emancipation of Slavery in Jamaica."

55 Plummer, "A Survey of Members of the Jamaican Clergy Concerning the Church and Christian Political Involvement," 28–29; Noëlliste and Chung, "A Theology of Political Engagement"; A. Smith, "The Christian Minister as a Political Activist," 24–35; Perkins, *Justice as Equality*; and Campbell and Murrell, "Should Christians be Involved in Jamaican Politics?"

survive but to thrive in modern, high-tech America."[56] He explains further that "evangelical churches are . . . eliciting levels of commitment and participation from their membership that no other American institution can match. Their fervor has gone mainstream."[57]

Interestingly, since 2002 the political Ombudsman of Jamaica, former chairman of the Peace Management Initiative, has been prominent evangelical pastor Bishop Herro Blair.[58] More than a decade before him, a few evangelicals did form The Christian United Party (CUP) but like most third parties on the Jamaican political landscape it withered and died in the harsh and arid climate. Before its demise, CUP, along with The Republican Party "became increasingly vocal through speaking engagements and newspaper adervtisements."[59] One can only imagine what kind of impact a Christian party would have had on the society, if CUP had fulfilled its potential.[60] Three others have tried since CUP, the latest being the New Nation Coalition (NNC), convened by Betty Ann Blaine of Swallowfield Chapel. Blaine wants "to tap into the pool of uncommitted voters and those calling for a change in government," according to a report in a Jamaican daily newspaper.[61] The report continues:

> "The first order of business is to win hearts and minds and to win the trust of the Jamaican people," said Blaine, a self-confessed former supporter of the People's National Party (PNP). Yesterday's launch of the NNC, at the Wyndham Hotel in New Kingston, signaled another attempt by a third party to break the stranglehold the PNP and Jamaica Labor Party (JLP) have enjoyed in Jamaican politics. . . . Blaine, a historian, was a vice-president and founding member of the Antoinette Haughton-led United People's Party (UPP) which was born in 2001 and died soon after the 2002 general election. Third parties have struggled in Jamaica.

Blaine was not deterred, however.

---

56. Obama, *The Audacity of Hope*, 201. The most honorable Portia Simpson-Miller was the first Jamaican head of state to openly profess Christianity. Her political party also boasts a prominent Roman Catholic deacon who serves as a member of parliament.

57. Ibid., 202.

58. Baker, "Of What Use Advocates and Ombudsmen?"

59. Panton, *Jamaica's Michael Manley*, 147.

60. Pastor Al Miller of Fellowship Tabernacle has been spearheading the National Transformation Programme, called "Fresh Start for Jamaica," and a new Governor General (and former Seventh Day Adventist head) Dr. Patrick Allen has been appointed.

61. Lutton, "Time for a New Nation."

"We don't look at failure. We know that since that time (the start of the UPP), things have got much worse in this country and that people want a change. I think the time is ripe and the time is right for a new message, a new mission and a new engagement, and that is what we are focusing on," Blaine said. The NNC, supported by members of the Diaspora and the Church, says it expects to be a major political force when the next general elections, constitutionally due in 2012, are called.[62]

While evangelicals are still ambivalent about politics, they seem to have changed their attitude towards sports and entertainment. Since the start of the new millennium Jamaica has experienced its first taste of having Christians at the helm of a national sporting endeavor, in the persons of Brazilian Rene Simoes and his former assistant Carl Brown.[63] Another evangelical who has gained prominence is recently retired test cricket umpire and former FIFA referee Steve Bucknor, who hails from Montego Bay. Other evangelical sports luminaries further afield include Kaka (who recently turned down a half million pound a week salary to move from AC Milan to Manchester City), Lucio, Bebeto, Ian Bishop, and Ridley Jacobs. In the entertainment field in Jamaica, we have Judy Mowatt, Carlene Davis, Papa San, Stichie, Chevelle Franklin, Winston Bell, Junior Tucker, and Chrissie D, adding to what Alister McGrath calls "The Evangelical Attraction."[64] But McGrath is well aware of the movement's other side as well, such as its leadership crisis, its failure to instill in its constituents a proper sense of belonging based on the *imago Dei*,[65] and, we might add, corruption of the image, as was recently alleged by the Reverend Dr. Roderick Hewitt at the National Prayer Breakfast in January 2009.

A WAY FORWARD FOR EVANGELICAL CARIBBEAN THEOLOGY

Despite these serious setbacks, there are those who are still optimistic that the evangelical movement can become a spiritual and sociological force to be reckoned with, provided that radical corrective measures are put in place and an openness to change is exhibited. In particular, there should be an openness to embrace a new way of doing theology, one that has a

---

62. Ibid.
63. Earle and Davies, *One Love*, 20, 155.
64. McGrath, *Evangelicalism*, 150.
65. This is central to Linton, *What the Preacher Forgot to Tell Me*. For a thorough study of the biblical *imago Dei*, see Middleton, *The Liberating Image*.

greater promise to remove the deficits of Western (or North-Atlantic or First World) theology with which it appears to be enamored.[66]

It would appear that evangelical leaders in the Anglophone Caribbean are unaware that many postcolonial theologians and churchmen are disenchanted with several aspects of North Atlantic theology, and that strong criticisms have also been voiced, especially from Latin American quarters.[67] Some of the weaknesses discerned in Western theology include the dogmatic nature of its approach and perceived straightjacket methodology. This is deemed too humanistic, in that human ingenuity to formulate and articulate the mind of God tends to come to the fore.

Another major weakness of First World theology often mentioned is the excessive specialization and "ivory tower" reflection that characterize its scholars and students alike. Added to the forgoing misgivings, it has also been pointed out that theology from the North-Atlantic is too particularistic in cultural respects, too abstract, and too otherworldly to be of much practical value to Majority World Christians. What has been proposed, then, is that the Caribbean should be looking at the way theology is done in Central and South America.

But all is not necessarily well with Latin American liberation theology either, for when Jürgen Moltmann can say, "we hear severe criticism of Western theology . . . and then we are told something about Karl Marx and Friedrich Engels, as if they were Latin American discoveries,"[68] one ought to be wary of any undue enthusiasm to fully embrace this not-so-new theological endeavor.

Nevertheless, what liberation theology may lack in methodological precision, it has certainly compensated for in its empathy toward the poor and oppressed. Not all is lost. Indeed, there are some who feel strongly that if the movement's starting point (the Latin American context) is legitimate, then that opens up the possibility of doing theology in the Caribbean using the same valid approach. So, despite the reservations some may have concerning Caribbean theology, Burchell Taylor underscores that "it will be in the process of doing theology in the Caribbean for the Caribbean that theological maturity will be fully achieved."[69] There is, then, a definite need for this enterprise to continue with the construction of a theology that

---

66. This is argued in HoSang and Ringenberg, "Towards Evangelical Caribbean Theology"; see also Garnett Roper's essay in the present volume.

67. For a critique from the Caribbean, see Williams, *Caribbean Theology*.

68. Moltmann, "On Latin American Liberation Theology," 59.

69. Taylor, "Messianic Ideology and Caribbean Theology of Liberation," 16.

will meaningfully address our own unique challenges, while avoiding the pitfalls.

The roots of a Caribbean theology may be traced back to the formulation of theological objections against slavery by enslaved Africans.[70] This represents the first and earliest stage of Caribbean theology. The second stage emerged with people like Sam Sharpe in the early nineteenth century, who saw in the words of Jesus ("No man can serve two masters") a powerful broadside against the colonizers who sought to prolong that which was inevitably doomed to fail.[71] But it was not until the middle of the twentieth century that the third stage began, when "a representational gathering . . . of the churches throughout the region" met in 1971 in Trinidad "to analyze the Caribbean's theological inheritance."[72]

One of the discoveries made at that conference was that there were serious "deficits in terms of relevance"[73] attending the brand of theology that was inherited from the North Atlantic region, especially in light of the fact that "the Christian church came to the Caribbean as the religious tradition of the oppressors," raising serious doubts "as to the legitimacy of its claim to be God's agent of salvation/liberation."[74]

It was therefore decided from that point onwards that any theological enterprise in the region should purposefully engage not only academics and clergy, but the *Am ha arets* (to use a Hebrew expression), or "everyday people" (as Sly Stone put it),[75] those we commonly refer in the Christian tradition as the laity. As Harold Sitahal puts it, only a "theology of, for, by and with the '*people*' is a priority for the Caribbean theologian." Sitahal continues: "Theological reflection then becomes part of Christian responsibility to participate in the transformation of the world order to fulfill the requirements of the Kingdom of God. It will eschew theological reflection on the supernatural for its own sake [and include] reflection on how sacred reality acts upon the world, human affairs and history."[76]

In tandem with Sitahal's vision are the words of another Caribbean luminary, Burchell Taylor, who affirms that: "The question of authenticity, situatedness, meaningfulness and effectiveness of . . . [this] theology becomes the question of relevance. Therefore, a relevant theological project

---

70. Williams, "The Indigenization of Theology in the Caribbean," 1–2.
71. Jennings, "'Ordinary' Reading in 'Extraordinary' Times."
72. Williams, "Editorial," 2.
73. Ibid.
74. Sitahal, "Caribbean Theology," 41–48.
75. West, "Nelson Mandela," 15.
76. Sitahal, "Caribbean Theology," 2.

should bear such characteristics. This is what a Caribbean Theological Project must be."[77] As Taylor sees it, such a project is, in terms of methodology, very much "open to the use of multi-disciplinary tools of analysis along with Caribbean-oriented studies for understanding the Caribbean Reality."[78]

With these tools to hand, the Caribbean theologian must address, among other things, the pressing need for a Caribbean social ethic.[79] This social ethic, I suggest, should be grounded in the discourse of the Messianic "I,"[80] despite the call in both Western and Caribbean contexts to abandon any theistic agenda (see the writings of Richard Dawkins and Mutaburka[81]). In an earlier piece Taylor set himself to lay a foundation for a regional ethical praxis in the Messianic pronouncements found in the Apocalypse, particularly chapters 2 and 3. One of the impressive features of the Apocalypse, noted by Taylor, "is the manner in which contextual relevance and universal significance are held together creatively and effectively . . . in the letters. . . . The message [they] convey is not one that is interested in exploring religious themes and ideas without concrete practical reference."[82]

A Caribbean theology should therefore be not only solidly exegetical, but rigorously *contextual* as well.[83] "Contextualization is the process by which Christian truth is embodied and translated in a concrete historical situation."[84] This means for us an appropriate cultural adaptation after serious reflection on both the situational and scriptural horizons.[85] With these considerations in mind, it may be said that a contextual theology is not only possible but also pressing.

77. Taylor, "Theological Relevance," 24.

78. Ibid., 25. See also O. Thomas, *Biblical Resistance Hermeneutics*.

79. Taylor, "Theological Relevance," 69.

80. Palmer, *Messianic "I" and Rastafari in New Testament Dialogue*. Only this "I" can bestow fully the "freedom to be free" (Mandela, *Long Walk to Freedom* 624; see John 8); this is the same One who "might well have learned to walk and talk in Africa. Further . . . [this 'I'] and his Jewish family, being Afro-Asiatic in color and culture, would have appeared more chocolate-brown than Caucasian in complexion" (Yorke, "Biblical Hermeneutics").

81. Dawkins, *God Delusion*; Mutabaruka, "Rasta from Experience."

82. Taylor, *The Church Taking Sides*, 3, 10.

83. And it should be by no means parochial; it should at least draw upon works done by scholars in the African Diaspora such as the essays in Page et al., *Africana Bible*.

84. Tano, "Toward an Evangelical Asian Theology."

85. The order of the reflection here does not necessarily indicate the starting point of the exercise. Recognizing the authority of Scripture, the Caribbean theologian should then remain sensitive to both. Studies in the social sciences would no doubt enhance such sensitivity.

This may be illustrated by the work of a Diaspora Jamaican. As part of his quest to forge a theology that is both reflective of the black experience in general and his own personal response to the divine revelation in Christ, Delroy Reid-Salmon was privileged to have audience with the venerable James Cone, the father of black theology, who encouraged him to pursue a more rigorous path of achieving his goal. This eventually led to further research at the University of Birmingham, where his thesis was successfully defended and subsequently revised and published with the subtitle *The Caribbean Diasporan Church in the Black Atlantic Tradition*. This subtitle is an accurate description of the book's content.[86]

The book is an exploration of the way in which Caribbean-Americans and other Anglophone West Indians in the North-Atlantic Diaspora articulate their self-understanding as part of the new covenant people of God. The experiences of these people as well as the author's own Christian self-awareness are then employed as a source for critical theological reflection.

Reid-Salmon argues persuasively, in my opinion, that the mainstay of several Caribbean immigrants in the United Kingdom and the United States is the strong religious commitment they took with them from home and nurtured within the new environment. This migrant faith is so powerful that he can speak of the "Caribbeanization of American Christianity."[87] The theological perspective drawn from this growing community, the author's own cultural identity, along with the strong intellectual tradition represented by people like Marcus Garvey and C. L. R. James, provided the necessary catalyst for a rigorous theological pursuit culminating in his book *Home Away from Home*. Thus, the author offers a new approach for critical theologizing that will help West Indian theologians construe the relationship between the checkered history of the Caribbean and the rich diasporic tradition that is now unfolding. His approach provides a creative contribution to the ongoing Caribbean Anglophone theological agenda; it is a critical yet

---

86. The book begins with a useful piece of self-disclosure that delineates the author's journey from Jamaica to the United States and his search for an authentic way of doing theology as a Caribbean Christian in a new environment. During his early years of living in the so-called land of the free and home of the brave, "I recall," he writes, "going into my room regularly and standing at full attention before the mirror, singing the national anthem of Jamaica. I did this to nurture and remind myself of my national identity to keep myself connected to my ... homeland" (Reid-Salmon, *Home Away from Home*, 2).

87. Ibid., 4. On page 60 the author points out that Caribbean Christianity is formed from African and European influences. I would add the adverb *mainly* as a qualifier for the following reason: If Jamaica's motto is out of many one people and since this motto is also reflected in the Diaspora, then the Asian contribution—whether Indian or Chinese—however minimal, is to be acknowledged.

constructive theological investigation of the experience of the Caribbean diasporan church engagement.

The book also carefully examines the foundational principles of this engagement and explores its significance for doing theology in the postcolonial era and as a way of making meaningful contribution to society in tandem with African-Americans. This collaborative approach of doing theology is seen as one of the best ways to tackle endemic racism and other challenges unique to that context. The dialectical tradition resulting from the convergence of these religious streams is one of the many worthwhile observations of the book.

The immediate past president of the Jamaica Baptist Union, Stephen Jennings, recently defended his doctoral thesis on the religious nature of globalization. I am reliably informed that at the thesis defense Jennings' position was strenuously opposed by Barry Chevannes, one of his supervisors. The idea that globalization is playing the role of a twenty-first deity appeared strange to me at first, so I could somewhat understand Chevannes' objection. But after reading Reid-Salmon's book, which contains a similar conclusion, I have begun to think differently. In fact, another study, which I think could have helped to strengthen the case for vigilant and vibrant diasporan theology is Burchell Taylor's penetrating publication entitled, *Saying No to Babylon*. It is about the people of God living in the belly of the empire and how they can employ survival strategies to preserve their self-identity while at the same time seeking to transform segments of that Empire open to change. There is a strong sense in which Taylor's booklet and Reid-Salmon's more academic treatise interface theologically and practically.

In this regard, one very important feature that must be addressed as a matter of priority is that of the liberation or emancipation of Caribbean peoples. But in order to appreciate adequately this issue, one must first identify the forces that enslave humankind as well as determine the scope of such dehumanization.[88] This task was taken up with gusto by Gustavo Gutiérrez in his seminal work. According to Gutierrez, humanity is in need of emancipation primarily because it belongs to a "*harmartiosphere* . . . a kind of parameter or structure which objectively conditions the progress of human history itself."[89] In this *harmartiosphere* two elements or "oppressive structures" can be isolated—the exploitation of humanity by humanity and the domination and slavery of peoples, races, and social classes. All this constitutes an awful condition that is the fundamental hindrance to the

---

88. This cannot be done adequately in the compass of this brief essay; what follows is an all too brief sketch.

89. Gutiérrez, *Theology of Liberation*, 175.

kingdom of God and root of all misery and injustice. In short, human beings are in need of freedom from the shackles that bind them, from the sin that is "the breach of friendship with God and others—a human, social, and historical reality."[90] Speaking from the social and historical context of Latin America from which he writes, Gutiérrez can be commended for providing a penetrating analysis of the plight of humanity.

Another worthwhile contribution to the discussion of liberation within the context of the Caribbean comes from the discourse of Rastafari. From Ennis Edmonds' sociological analysis of the movement we learn of its humble beginning in the nineteen thirties, its consolidation in the following two decades, flowering in the nineteen seventies and eighties, and of its global impact particularly in the final decade of the last century. Edmonds argues that the entrenchment of Rastafari was made possible by "(1) the internal development of the movement, (2) the gradual rapprochement between the movement and the wider society, and (3) the impact of Rastafari on the evolution of Jamaica's indigenous popular culture."[91] One notices that Edmonds carried out his sociological analysis so rigorously that there is little or no evaluation of the theological and historical claims of Rastafari. For example, whereas others have pointed out the lack of documentary evidence for the Garvey prophecy concerning the crowning of Ras Tafari, Edmonds appears prepared to defend the prediction by invoking the reliability of the oral tradition that bears it.[92] Edmonds is also optimistic that the movement has a bright future. If this is true, then evangelic Christianity, reshaped and informed by Caribbean theology, should seek to critically engage Rastafari in order to learn from its liberative discourse.[93]

CONCLUSION

I have endeavored to paint with broad strokes the fortunes of evangelicalism in the Caribbean basin, particularly Jamaica. I have also suggested the direction the movement should take in terms of its embracing of an indigenous form of theologizing in order to maximize its impact and greatly reduce its deficits. I affirm, in conclusion, that God's scheme of liberation provides deliverance from destructive forces, that this deliverance is completely accomplished through the Messiah, and that it is made effective by the power

---

90. Gutiérrez, *Theology of Liberation*, 172.
91. Edmonds, *Rastafari*, 4.
92. Ibid., 147n34.
93. See Palmer, *Messianic "I" and Rastafari in New Testament Dialogue*; and Middleton, "Identity and Subversion in Babylon."

PART 3: THE CHURCH IN THE CARIBBEAN

of the Holy Spirit. In sum, the Messianic liberation takes in the whole person and seeks to transform the very structures of society.

PART 4

Caribbean Theology and the Political Sphere

11

Constructing an Egalitarian Society
Women, Social Ethics, and the Policy Imperatives of Michael Manley's "Justice as Equality"

ANNA KASAFI PERKINS

"I believe in the equality of women.... That is why we intend to begin to abolish the various ways in which the law discriminates against women of Jamaica."

MICHAEL MANLEY[1]

---

1. Manley, "The Politics of Change," Budget Speech, May 2, 1973, in *Michael Manley*, ed. Franklyn, 171.

PART 4: CARIBBEAN THEOLOGY AND THE POLITICAL SPHERE

You saw us as
We never saw ourselves
Women and men
Emerging from centuries
Of oppression and denial
Carrying with us
Ancestral memories
That contradict:
At once epitomising
Endurance, strength, resilience
And simultaneously,
Low self-esteem and a victim mentality.

While never denying the historical legacies
You saw us also as victors
Having the capacity to change
And thereby change our country and our world.

You saw us as women and men;
You saw us in our socially constructed roles
Yet you saw us beginning
To change these roles
Created by others
Over space and time

You always knew we could do it.
In death as in life
You so challenge us:
As women—to take up the mantle of leadership
To utilise our courage, wisdom and strength
Forged in centuries of struggle
With our children and men—

To lift our country up and
Take it forward to a place
Where equity and social justice prevail.

Your body has left us
But your spirit remains
To guide us and inspire us.

In giving thanks for your life,
We recommit ourselves to the vision
You upheld on our behalf;
A world where women and men
Walk hand in hand in mutual respect
In loving and caring relationships that
Lead to a country and a world
where all can enjoy a quality of life
that is sustainable and equitable.

Michael, it was wonderful to know you
And be part of the process.

The word is love.

Beverley Anderson-Manley
International Women's Day, 1997

A profound belief in the intrinsic equality of all human beings was a central tenet in the hierarchy of political values of the late Michael Manley (1924–1997), former leader of the People's National Party (PNP) and Prime Minister of Jamaica. His numerous speeches, writings, and policy initiatives revolved around equality to such an extent that Delano Franklyn and others have referred to his political strategy as a "politics of equality."[2] At the heart of his political values was an affirmation of the fundamental equality of all human beings and a commitment to build social, economic, and political institutions that reflected and ensured that equality.

As I have argued elsewhere, it is possible to surface an underlying theory of justice upon which Manley's political articulations and actions are built: "justice as equality."[3] Manley's "justice as equality" is a deeply relational theory of justice that roots fundamental human equality in the relationship to divine transcendence.

According to Manley,

> If you believe that the fatherhood of God expresses the great moral wonder of the unity of the universe, then you will necessarily believe that the fatherhood of God implies the brotherhood of man. And if God is moral, as we believe God is, indeed as we know through faith that God is moral, then a moral God can only be responsible for equal children. Therefore, when people try to suggest that the PNP is anti-God or non-Christian they in fact are reversing the true order of things.[4]

Justice as equality calls for the dismantling of all relationships of oppression and domination, which result when the fundamental equality of all human beings is disregarded. In so doing, it takes account of the multiple dimensions of the human person (social, spiritual, material) and calls a society *just* when it allows for the flourishing of every member, specifically through full participation in the life of the society. A key group that Manley identified as being enmeshed in such relations of domination and oppression are women: "No discussion of an egalitarian society would be complete without consideration of the special position of women.... in many societies women are not equal. Jamaica is no exception."[5]

This analysis presupposes the point made by Portia Simpson-Miller, Jamaica's first woman prime minister, that Manley "correctly understood the

---

2. Franklyn, "Introduction," in *Michael Manley*. Also Bogues, "Reflections on the Political Thought of Manley."

3. Perkins, *Justice as Equality*.

4. Manley, "The Policy of the People's National Party."

5. Manley, *The Politics of Change*, 159.

link between equity for women and true liberation for all . . . [he] defined the struggle for justice as the 'the process by which half of the population achieves its freedom and exercises it for a new creative and mutually-enriching partnership.'"[6] To this end, it is possible to identify his attempts at instituting more egalitarian social legislation, particularly legislation affecting women and families, as part of his key commitments to building a society based on equality. The Jamaican woman has come far since the nineteen seventies, but it is evident that the demands of Manley's justice as equality are even more imperative in the present post-socialist context. His vision calls for a serious re-examination of equality and its place in contemporary social and political ethics. His efforts lend support to the main contention of this discussion that, properly understood, equality can serve as a lodestar for coherent and effective public policy.

The discussion will, therefore, first, draw out some implications of Manley's understanding of "justice as equality" for contemporary social and political ethics, and, secondly, assess and identify the continued relevance of his ideas—particularly his central concern with ending relationships of domination and oppression—in a post-socialist age. The hope is to highlight several aspects of Manley's thought on equality that have continuing relevance today.

MANLEY'S LEGACY TO THE JAMAICAN PEOPLE

It can be demonstrated that many of Manley's most important legacies to the Jamaican people flow from this belief in the centrality of equality, particularly his emphasis on the democratic participation of all members in the political and economic life of the nation (economic and political democracy) and his often-times unsuccessful attempt to find a strategy that would not further entrench class and gender differences and privilege. Beginning in his first year of office (1972), it seemed that Manley was racing against time to correct the injustices of the past. Almost every month a new program or project was launched. The aims of these programs included: lessening income disparity through the provision of Special Employment for the chronically unemployed (the much maligned "Crash Programme"); adding to Jamaica's reservoir of skills through the National Youth Service; and agricultural productivity and access to land through "Operation Grow" and "Land Lease" (idle lands were made available to landless peasant farmers).

---

6. Portia Simpson-Miller, quoted in Russell, "Manley Lauded at Women's Day Opening Ceremony."

Other new initiatives included "free" secondary and tertiary education;[7] the Jamaica Movement for the Advancement of Literacy (JAMAL), which instructed 200,000 people in the first eight years; community health aides; "Put Work into Labour Day"; a lowering of the voting age to eighteen; the National Housing Trust; and the Family Court—just to name a few.

An important piece of labor legislation promulgated was the Labour Relations and Industrial Disputes Act, which enshrined workers' right to be represented by the union of their choice. Another was the Redundancy and Remuneration Payments Act, a measure that at the time could be found in few countries around the globe. The Redundancy Act required workers to be compensated for their time invested in the company to which they are employed at the time of their severance from their jobs.

LEGISLATION FOR WOMEN

Among the significant pieces of legislation that directly affected the lives of women was the setting up of the Family Court, which empowered unmarried mothers in the struggle to have their children financially supported by biological fathers. The importance of this in a nation where the average child is born to parents who are unmarried, and is therefore primarily under the care of the mother, was significant. The Equal Pay Act removed gender bias and allowed women and men to be paid equally whien performing similar jobs. To this end, Manley committed his government to support for women and to ensure that they were given equal wages on all government projects. Maternity leave with pay protected the jobs of women, especially household helpers who often lost their jobs when they and their newborn were at their most vulnerable. Similarly, the Status of Children's Act removed the legal and social barriers faced by illegitimate children. Under the Manley administration the first woman ambassador and the first female puisine judge of the Supreme Court were appointed. Women were allowed into the Armed Forces and a Bureau for Women's Affairs was established and located under the Office of the Prime Minister.

---

7. Some will argue that although as promised by Manley there would be no tuition and other costs to parents for their children accessing education ("free"), the country paid a high price for this. University students who had their tuition covered by the State were expected to volunteer and to offer back service at the end of their studies. Much of this did not materialize. The intention behind "free" education was to ensure that all Jamaican children had a chance to develop their innate talents without artificial barriers like socio-economic circumstances.

PART 4: CARIBBEAN THEOLOGY AND THE POLITICAL SPHERE

"JUSTICE AS EQUALITY" AND SOCIAL ETHICS

Clearly, in Manley's "politics of equality," equality served as a means of evaluating social practices, institutions, and systems. More importantly, equality was a guide for social policy, and such policy was the means of more fully embodying equality in society. His cry for a politics based on principles, or a moral politics, reiterated that there is a need for a firmer ethical foundation for politics, and this in turn will provide a firmer foundation for ethical reflection. Further, his articulation of "justice as equality" is a summons to restore the connections between foundational principles like equality and the overall structure of the just society, and this has implications for social ethics. Undoubtedly, his ideas continue to have currency in an age of political pragmatism where too often principles and practices appear to bear no direct relation to each other. It is refreshing to find a political leader who affirmed that fundamental principles mattered, in particular that religious convictions had a relevance beyond the private domestic sphere.

Justice is about equality, but care must be taken not to misunderstand equality; it should not be simply dismissed as a spent force or viewed as an ideal whose time has passed. More exactly, equality is a highly complex and fruitful notion that requires re-interpretation and reclamation to truly contribute to the transformation of contemporary society for the benefit and flourishing of all citizens.

Manley's portrayal of "justice as equality" has implications for a renewed social ethic that centers on a deeper understanding of the human person as undeniably valuable and possessing a dignity that transcends human-defined roles, possessions, or status. Christian ethics further clarifies the nature of human value by grounding that dignity in direct relationship with divine transcendence. Human beings are not simply the source of their own intrinsic value, but are valuable by virtue of their relationship with the divine. Refusing to appreciate that value (and its source in divine transcendence) has a direct impact on the kinds of societies that human beings create and inhabit, the kinds of relationships that they engage in, and this was thrown into stark relief by Manley's description of the experiences of a postcolonial society like Jamaica. It can be argued cogently that unjust inequalities and relationships of domination and oppression result when there is a refusal to recognize the intrinsic equal worth of all human beings.

Yet, in today's post-socialist context that is so deeply marked by the failure of the so-called grand schemes of socialism, it would be easy to dismiss Manley's ideas and contribution because of the importance he gave to a democratic socialist strategy. Without the *democratic socialist* label and ideological trimmings acting as distracters, however, Manley's ideas on "justice as equality" continue to be of relevance, especially his concern to end relationships of dominance and oppression that disregard foundational human equality and restrict human flourishing and well-being. Indeed, the concern to remedy relationships of domination and oppression has gained increasing urgency in a globalized world where too many people lack the resources to effectively participate in local and international society.

Contributing Religious and Moral Insights

While not himself a "religious" man, Manley incorporated religious insights about the nature of the person in a foundational way in his "justice as equality": human beings are created equal by a divine creator.[8] Unlike Manley's "justice as equality," many influential contemporary theories of justice and equality neglect religious and theological factors; religiously-informed insights and narratives are systematically excluded as a matter of principle.[9] Others shy away from making statements about ultimate truth and either remain silent about deep theory or only hint at it. Amartya Sen, for example, disavows any ability to speak of a deeper metaphysics grounding his call for equality of basic capability for all human beings.[10] But where theories of justice and equality eschew moral and theological insights they tend to be thin and narrow and may be less able to contribute to a full vision of the just society.[11]

All theories of justice, and the public policy they underwrite, in fact, contain a complex interaction of several components that have moral and metaphysical dimensions, which we ignore at our peril. These components may include: an articulation of a set of social values, a view of human nature, groundings of the view of human nature, and ways of mediating between social values and concrete social phenomenon. So, it is simply not sufficient to stipulate, as William Galston does, that "in spite of profound differences among individuals, the full development of each individual—however great or limited his or her natural capacities—is equal in moral weight to that of every other."[12] That raises the question from Vlastos Martian, "Why are they of equal moral weight?"[13] The equal moral value of all human beings cannot simply be assumed, but must be argued for.

8. Manley, "Policy of the People's National Party."
9. Forrester, *Christian Justice and Public Policy*, 2.
10. Sen, *Development as Freedom*.
11. Pojman. "On Equal Human Worth."
12. Galston, "A Liberal Defense of Equality of Opportunity," 171.
13. The importance of answering this fundamental question is clear in Gregory

PART 4: CARIBBEAN THEOLOGY AND THE POLITICAL SPHERE

Catholic social teaching shows that communities of faith can and do provide distinctive visions of human flourishing that take into account human equality, dignity, social relatedness, and well-being that can make an important contribution to public arguments about justice. The substantive approaches of religious communities contribute in at least three ways to public discourse. First, they provide a moral vision and justification for how (in)equality matters and why a public response is necessary; secondly, they give credence to that moral vision by the moral example of people of faith and communities actively engaged in actions of preferential solidarity; and, thirdly, they provide a moral call to action for others to respond in personal and institutional ways to pressing inequalities.[14] Otherwise, explains Douglas Hicks, "where religion becomes a private preference alone, public life lacks the depth of meaning that can generate loyalty and commitment among citizens."[15]

In affirming that fundamental principles matter and that religious convictions have relevance beyond the private and domestic spheres, Manley's works call for openness to the voice of communities of faith in the human project in which they also have an important stake. At the same time, this attention to the contribution of religious communities highlights the inter-relatedness of the various spheres of human life and rejects any attempt to reduce talk about equality and justice simply to the market or to the spiritual or social realms. Rather, "justice as equality" demands an integration of all aspects of human life, including the religious; human life needs to be viewed as a complex whole.

Vlastos's classic discussion of equality and justice ("Justice and Equality"). Vlastos presents his argument partly as a conversation with a "Martian," a being ignorant of the ways of human beings, specifically how human beings view one another. Vlastos explains to the Martian that there is a value attached to a human person as an integral and unique individual, and that this value is something that does not fall under the category of *merit* nor is reducible to it. This irreducible value belongs to the individual solely by having been born human and remains the possession of the person unalterably for life. The value that persons have simply by virtue of being persons, "the intrinsic value," "sacredness," or "the infinite worth" of the human person, has implications in all types of relationship—familial, personal, and most importantly for this discussion, political. Essentially, all human beings are members of a unique rigid "caste" from which a person cannot lose membership or status through any action on her part. There are no second-class human beings or half-castes.

14. Hicks, *Inequality and Christian Ethics*, 200.
15. Hollenbach, "Faith in Public," 5.

Contributing an Integral Vision of the Human Person

The human person is the focal concern of the Catholic social teaching tradition. All social practices, institutions, and systems are judged in terms of their implications for the full human person and for all human persons. The key question is: How do social practices, institutions, and systems contribute to the flourishing of persons—of all persons? Human flourishing is grounded in relationship to God, but in actual reality this relationship is deeply distorted, as is evident in the relationships of domination and oppression, which Manley opposed.[16] This is a truer and more complex understanding of human beings and the institutions they create, which takes into account both the heights and depths of which human beings are capable, while resolutely affirming that human equality is the only basis for true human fellowship. Human beings have multiple dimensions, all of which are essential and in interaction one with the other.[17] In the first place, persons, in virtue of their (potential) relationship with God, have a transcendent dimension. This transcendent dimension informs and transforms all other dimensions of the person: bodily, rational, social, and cultural.

A clearly theological articulation of human nature and flourishing differs from purely philosophical or social scientific articulations; it involves a proper relationship with God, with material things, and with other human beings—in relationships of constant interaction. However, it recognizes that the fullness of human possibilities will not be experienced in this life, and therefore cannot be identified with any social, economic or political structures. This distinctly Christian perspective challenges articulations of human flourishing in which the individual self is made the center of moral concern to the exclusion of concern for the well-being of others, where the self is conceived as the source of all meaning, and where the self tends to deal with others in the fashion that is appropriate for dealing with material things.[18] Similar tendencies were identified by Manley as being at work in the elitist structuring of postcolonial Jamaican society, where certain individuals and groups made their own flourishing and that of their families the main concern, to the detriment of the majority who were socially disadvantaged. This resulted in relationships of domination and oppression that have no place in human relationships, since these ought to be based on "the brotherhood of man which is implicit in the fatherhood of God."

---

16. Lacey, "Catholic Social Thought and Economic Systems," 139.
17. Ibid.
18. Ibid., 142.

Similarly, where the community is overemphasized at the expense of the individual, the person becomes simply a being at the disposal of the forces and the groups in control of the social structures of society. Such subordination of the individual in the face of a powerful bureaucratic state, for example, was critiqued by Manley as a new form of oppression in which individual workers have become the bonded servants of a powerful master. In such circumstances the individual's freedom and participation is subordinated to larger collective goals. The fulfillment open to human beings is, therefore, vastly diminished without a proper attention to human beings as equally valuable selves-in-community, and becomes important when concrete social systems are examined.

The Central Significance of "Justice as Equality"

The central significance of Manley's "justice as equality" remains practically relevant today since it demands the dismantling and resisting of all relationships of domination and oppression in which the fundamental worth of all members of society is not given due regard. The significance of this can be seen by contrasting Manley's "justice as equality" further with other theoretical considerations of justice and equality. The approaches that will serve as a contrast to Manley's "justice as equality" are those that Elizabeth Anderson identifies as having missed the point of equality because of their focus on mostly distributive ends. Anderson groups these approaches under synonymous terms like "equality of fortune" and "luck egalitarianism."[19] These terms will be employed in a general way in drawing a contrast with Manley's "justice as equality."

"Justice as equality" seeks to abolish and redress socially created oppression, while what Anderson calls "equality of fortune" or "luck egalitarianism" aims to correct what it considers to be injustices generated by brute bad luck within the natural order. Approaches to justice that fall under the latter perspective aim at identifying and compensating for inequalities or undeserved misfortunes over which persons have little or no control, such as poor internal endowments, talents which do not command much market value, involuntarily expensive tastes, and so on. Essentially, they focus on the individual and her defective internal assets, while they "blame" those individuals that are socially disadvantaged for their state of being. Such approaches do not express regard for persons and yet assume that individuals have unlimited power to control the outcomes of their lives outside of and in spite of the social situations in which they find themselves.

19. Anderson, "What Is the Point of Equality?," 313.

At the same time, "equality of fortune"/"luck egalitarianism" is a distributive theory that conceives of equality as a pattern of distribution of goods. As such, it regards two people as equal when they hold equal amounts of some distributable good—income, welfare, opportunities. Social relationships are viewed as largely instrumental for generating such patterns of distribution and are rarely questioned.[20]

By contrast, "justice as equality" regards people as intrinsically equal and truly equal when they engage in relationships of mutuality, which allow full participation by all for the development of their talents and the building up society. Of course, as Sen's description of the freedom to achieve makes evident, certain patterns of distribution of goods are instrumental for securing relationships of mutuality, follow from them, or are even constituted by them.[21] Manley's portrayal of "justice as equality," being a deeply relational theory of justice, views (in)equality as a social relationship. Manley is fundamentally concerned with the relationships within which the goods are distributed, rather than simply the distribution of the goods themselves. Goods must be distributed according to principles and processes that express respect for all people; such principles are embodied in the norms of justice that the Catholic social teaching tradition has espoused in recent years and these norms form a part of the underlying structure of Manley's "justice as equality."[22] The basis for distributing goods is not the inferiority or superiority of people, but their recognized equal worth. As such, human need is the primary norm for distribution of the goods of the earth.

The attention that "justice as equality" pays to relationships calls us to ask, "What kind of person will having certain goods allow us to become?" The possession of the goods is not an end in itself, but rather a means towards becoming a certain kind of person: a full and equal participant in society. The flaws in notions of justice that are focused on divisible resources like wealth and income become accentuated in light of this. When the focus is moved from acquiring certain quantities of material goods and placed on the kinds of relationships that people engage in, it then becomes clearer that those goods become meaningful within the context of relationship.

Similarly, there is often an overwhelming focus in many contemporary theories of justice and equality on what is due to the individual, without attending to how what is due is worked out in the context of human relationships or what obligations the individual has within the wider social context. This is evident where the notion of justice is often limited to its distributive

20. Ibid.
21. Sen, *Development as Freedom*.
22. For further discussion, see Perkins, *Justice as Equality*.

and commutative aspects. The aspect of obligation or contribution is neglected, to the detriment of the full participation of many persons in their society. However, human beings are embedded in relationships and are selves-in-community, rather than simply self-sufficient beings engaging in contractual exchanges. Manley's emphasis on individual responsibility towards the national community moves the discourse forward and somewhat beyond such "self-centred" individual claims on the society. At the same time, he did not neglect to aim for balance through a similar attention to the responsibilities that the society has towards every person born within it.

Manley effectively broadened the agenda of equality and justice beyond the distribution of divisible, privately appropriated goods, such as income and resources, or privately enjoyed goods such as welfare, to include wider, more political, concerns. His concerns cannot be accused of being detached from those of present egalitarian movements. In aiming for the creation of a just community defined by relationships in which citizens stand in relations of equality to each other, "justice as equality" effectively integrates principles of distribution and responsibility with demands for equal respect. The demands that citizens make on each other are justified by virtue of their equal humanity, not out of their inferiority to each other. Therefore, the remedies offered by theories of justice should match the kind of injustice being corrected; and attention to the quantity of goods held does not address the injustice in the relationships between people.

Reclaiming Equality

Equality is not about correcting unfairness and inequality in every aspect of human life, only certain kinds of inequality. In this regard, the kinds of inequalities that matter are those resulting from social relations in which there are significant differences in opportunities and power, which limit the participation of many people in society—the absence of a minimum of justice. "Justice as equality" refuses to abstract from the background constraints and circumstances that make it easier for some people to access a larger share of the resources of society because of the privileges gained from these positions of dominance. The fact that one person's choice is often enabled by another's lack of choice, or that one person's success may be dependent on another's failure, is key. Giving people equality of opportunity therefore involves taking into account their life conditions, which affect their ability to grasp the opportunities presented to them—in essence, what Sen refers to as real freedom to achieve.[23] At the same time, "justice as equality" is

---

23. Sen, *Development as Freedom*; Douglas Hicks, *Inequality and Christian Ethics*,

confident that social disadvantage can be removed through social planning and action. This, of course, needs to happen in tandem with changes to the human person—attitudes, responsibilities, expectations.[24]

Nonetheless, "justice as equality" is cautious about simply increasing the formal opportunity that people have to participate in society without altering institutional arrangements and organizational hierarchy. Developing inclusionary strategies should change elitist social and institutional structures built on accepted notions of superior and inferior human worth. Inclusion does not mean simply adding those who are presently excluded to existing standards, but reformulating standards with the poor and disadvantaged as active participants in the process. Consequently, mere assimilation to prevailing norms is to be rejected as a goal. What is demanded is not that everyone be allowed a place at the table once the meal has started, but rather that they be allowed to participate in setting the table before the meal begins.

SOCIAL POLICY

For Manley a central dimension of egalitarian justice was therefore creating the conditions for forms of economic democracy within the workplace that would accompany and make efficacious political democracy. A noteworthy aspect of Manley's concern for economic democracy is the linkage which he saw between economic and political democracy—one led naturally to the other; neither was fully possible without the other. It was to this end that he experimented with various modalities of workplace democracy, from workers owning the sugar plantations to employee share-owning schemes, as means of shifting the balance of power in the workplace. When greater economic democracy happens, social priorities can be decided by the whole society, not by those who own the productivity of the nation. This requires a new social alliance among the members of society, which would provide ordinary working people with a much greater involvement in national development; greater economic democracy enhances labor productivity and this in turn leads to greater welfare for all. In all of this the state has an important role to play in cooperation with the other sectors of society.

Manley was concerned that a society could not be based on competitive acquisitive individualism of the marketplace or on relationships of superiority and inferiority; indeed such a society would be a contradiction in

---

234, maintains that the language of opportunity and capability capture the same spirit of possibility.

24. Manley, "No Turning Back," 295.

terms. Allowing such individualism free rein would make the marketplace the primary mediating point of social relationships and further break down bonds of trust.[25] Rather, a society based on recognition of the equality of all would promote the well-being or welfare of all its citizens and so put the market in its proper place. This is another point of convergence with Sen's rejection of simply possessing certain goods per se. Rather, goods are important for what they do for people; goods allow people to live and be full members of their society.

Further, Manley's approach to equality forces us to reconsider conceptions of the role of government in policy-making. In a nation like Jamaica, where there are severe and increasing inequalities, the state is called upon to have a role that goes beyond formally removing impediments to opportunities and participation; rather, it involves providing substantial resources to allow a minimum of participation and thus the ability to truly capitalize on opportunities. The path towards social change should therefore be defined by the experiences of those who are excluded, particularly women, women with children, unemployed youth, and low-skilled workers. This emphasis on the needs of the economically and politically oppressed/marginalised as being defining of "justice as equality" challenges further some contemporary arguments for exemplary attention to be given to persons who are lazy, irresponsible, have expensive tastes, or are religious fanatics. Indeed, the welfare of the working class, or those who are called the "working poor" in the North American context, was central to Manley's formulation of "justice as equality."

The continued severity of the plight of the working poor was made clear in the conclusions of a 2001 assessment of the living conditions of low-wage workers in Jamaica. The qualitative data demonstrated the impact of the cycle of poverty. The majority of these minimum wage earners came from very poor economic backgrounds and had not been able to improve their own standard of living to any great extent. Similarly, their children were being nurtured in poverty, with limited opportunity for educational advancement. The cycle of poverty remains unbroken. From this analysis, we can see that these workers are not entirely to blame for their condition. They are working, yet they find it extremely difficult to make ends meet.[26]

---

25. Interestingly, on his return to office in 1989 Manley admitted to mistakes in privileging a State-centred approach. He began to see the changing role of the state in a more market-driven international context.

26. Henry-Lee et al., *An Assessment of the Standard of Living and Coping Strategies of Workers*, 39.

WOMEN AND VULNERABLE GROUPS

Jamaican women in particular, in spite of the strides that have been made over the years, continue to be significantly worse off economically and socially than men. Many low-wage earning women express the view that their very motherhood is under threat, as they fear losing their jobs because of pregnancy.[27] This fear exists despite the fact that there are labor laws relating to maternity leave. Such vulnerable groups had very little access to social welfare programs like food stamps; they make no contribution to the National Housing Trust or the National Insurance Schemes. A further consequence of this lack of participation will be that such low-wage earners will be heavily represented among the elderly poor in the future, and their dependents will not be able to benefit from the opportunities made available through education.

Clearly, the government needs to cultivate "justice as equality" through stressing institutions and procedures that meet common needs, but especially the needs of those who are less able to participate in society. These institutional arrangements need to enable the diversity of talents that people possess, their various aspirations, and roles, in a fashion that benefits everyone and is recognized as mutually beneficial. There is a need to broaden and directly target the coverage of social welfare programs. Attention to comprehensive policy-measures will further address what areas are of concern in order for people to stand as equals within the society. Comprehensive policies are necessary to enable all citizens to participate in the society.

Policy measures need to be directed at multiple spheres of life (not just the money-related sphere of income or wealth) without being intrusive in the lives of citizens. This is justified by understanding the integral nature of the person. Full and equal personhood is achieved not solely in the economic sphere, but also in all other dimensions of life that are integrally and significantly related.

The provision of basic needs is fundamental, however, and the government must look towards providing for the most basic socio-economic needs, like food, shelter, health, and education. Policy should therefore include the continuation and improvement of current nutrition schemes like the Food Stamp Programme, compulsory primary education, increased community health care, day care facilities for the children of minimum wage earners.

The criteria for participation in such welfare programs should not result in participants being stigmatized or pitied. Manley, for example, gives special attention to the needs of all children and students in his arguments

---

27. Ibid.

for equality of opportunity for education in a way that emphasizes the importance of providing them with the resources necessary to fully develop themselves. He recognized that institutional arrangements generate people's opportunities overtime and he made these the prime focus of justice.

The preceding policy recommendations attend to questions of distributional inequality, but that cannot be the entire picture. It is important to emphasize, alongside distribution, the importance of production—and the growth of production—of those goods that contribute to the well-being of society and its citizens.[28] The results of the inability of the Manley experiment in the 1970s to substantially increase the productivity of the nation stand as testimony to this need. Productivity is the means by which citizens contribute to their society, an important means of participation and a means of escaping from oppressive entanglements. The precise balance between productivity and distribution can only be arrived at through careful empirical analysis and public discourse, but both must be attended to. Production and distribution serve the normative ends of society of allowing all its citizens to fully develop their talents while contributing to the well-being of themselves, of their family and of their society.

THE INTERNATIONAL DIMENSION

Finally, there is an international dimension that needs to be considered in working out the balance between productivity and distribution in a bid to improve the participation of all citizens in the society. Jamaica is a part of the global economy and the policies of external funding organizations like the International Monetary Fund and the agreements made in light of membership in the World Trade Organization have a direct impact on national policies. Many of the policies of these organizations have been seen to be incompatible with popular democracy and with attention to the basic needs of all people, especially the poor, and instead bring untold suffering on millions across the world, including Jamaicans, who are not able to participate in their societies. Their policies permit little democratic participation in matters that affect the content and quality of people's lives, such as the production and distribution of goods and services, the goals and processes of the workplace, and the kinds of social arrangements that might exist.[29] A vast number of people continue either to be left out (treated as non-persons) or to become instruments of the economic system, and so have no part in shaping the future for themselves or their offspring.

28. Hicks, *Inequality and Christian Ethics*, 207.
29. Lacey, "Catholic Social Thought and Economic Systems," 159–60.

Given the current social realities, what is in the realm of possibilities open to Caribbean states guided by the foundational principle of equality? Jamaica and her Caribbean neighbors need to revisit Manley's call for solidarity among nations that are in a similarly disadvantaged position in the global market, in order to secure a stronger voice and attention to their dilemma. They need to resist the efforts to limit the scope of the state and reduce all transactions to the market. In so doing, they will take a first step in reclaiming a truly complex and multi-faceted equality for the new millennium.

12

Ideology, Religion, and Public Policy in Jamaica

RONALD G. THWAITES

A STORY ABOUT MICHAEL

I remember visiting Michael Manley at his Guava Ridge retreat after his retirement from politics and when his health was failing. I can't remember how the conversation got around to spiritual matters. Keble Munn had come with me to tell him that I was considering joining the People's National Party. Of course, he knew that I was an ordained cleric in the Roman Catholic Church.

Anyway, I ended up quoting that remarkable passage from Isaiah 58 where the Lord inveighs against the false ritual and formalistic practices of the churchical and state order. Let me remind you of some verses:

> Lo, on your fast day you follow your own pursuits,
>   and drive all your laborers.
> Yes, your fast ends in quarreling and fighting,
>   striking with the wicked claw. . . .

> Is this the kind of fasting I wish, . . .
> That a man bow his head like a reed,
> and lie in sackcloth and ashes?
> This, rather, is the fasting that I wish:
> releasing those bound unjustly,
> untying the thongs of the yoke;
> Setting free the oppressed,
> breaking every yoke;
> Sharing your bread with the hungry,
> sheltering the oppressed and the homeless;
> Clothing the naked when you see them,
> and not turning your back on your own. . . .
> Then your light shall break forth like the dawn, . . .
> Then the LORD will guide you always,
> and give you plenty even on the parched land. (Isa 58:3b–8a, 11a)[1]

Michael had a puzzled look on his face. "Is that in the Bible?" he snapped. "Yes," was my reply. His large figure, already reduced by illness, fell silent, almost inert: "But that was what I was trying to do," he eventually said, as if stumbling upon an unthought-of validation of his life's work.

Yes, Michael. That was what you were trying to do, but it seldom came across that way. And is it surprising in this most "churchified" of nations? There has never been a sufficient understanding and identification of Christian philosophical and theological principles as they might relate to political action in Jamaica's pilgrimage towards redemption.

A THEOCRACY?

In the sweep of our modern history, the dominance and great power of the assumptions of colonialism, classism, sexism, and racism—often themselves clothed in religious vestments—have led to an incomplete and often false set of principles undergirding political action and subsequent public policy affecting the majority of our people.

The definition of righteousness in Isaiah 58 has been suppressed, except in the lives of the early national heroes and their kind. And we know what happened to them.

Please don't caricature my point by supposing that I am hankering for some kind of theocracy or rule by fundamentalists and Christian ayatollahs.

---

1. Unless otherwise indicated, all biblical quotations in this chapter are taken from the NAB.

PART 4: CARIBBEAN THEOLOGY AND THE POLITICAL SPHERE

Rather, the contention being advanced has to do with the basic tenets of Christian belief, including personal dignity and responsibility, the primacy of community, and the organization of state activity for the common good; were such beliefs to have been consciously and radically adopted and effected as guiding principles for the nation, they would have produced an altogether better outcome than we are experiencing at present.

OUR EXPERIENCE

Examine this contention with reference, for example, to the ongoing compression of economic life that consigns the majority of our people to degrading hardships, while there are huge reserves of local capital chasing negative interest rates. Consider also the continuing evasion of the disgusting and unjust conditions that incubate crime, while thoughtlessly relying on repression and cruelty. Even ponder the careless waste of the opportunities of popular culture to inculcate wholesomeness of lifestyle, rather than the current elevation of hedonism. Lastly, should we not do penance for the self-imposed myopia of many of us in the churches who preach unity and goodness beyond materialism and extol the Scriptures (which, remember, includes pieces like Isaiah 58 and the Beatitudes), while we ourselves pander to secular gods and find every pretext to distinguish and preserve our denominational phylacteries?

THE KINGDOM OF GOD

The outcome is that in Jamaica today, despite many worthy struggles and the suffering of many martyrs, the Jamaican political economy is more influenced by rough geo-politics and gangster capitalism than principles of the common good espoused by Pope Benedict in his 2009 encyclical letter *Caritas in Veritate*. These principles would find resonance in the philosophies of our own national heroes Sam Sharp, Paul Bogle, George William Gordon, and Marcus Garvey, whom we lionize but hardly emulate.

In his book *The Heart of Christianity*, Marcus Borg defines "the political meaning of the Kingdom of God" as "what life would be like on earth if God were king and the rulers of this world were not. The Kingdom of God is about God's justice in contrast to the systemic injustice of the kingdoms and dominations systems of this world."[2]

---

2. Borg, *The Heart of Christianity*, 132–33.

Ronald G. Thwaites   *Ideology, Religion, and Public Policy in Jamaica*

MUTING OUR TRADITION

We have allowed market forces to mute the strong religious and humanistic tendencies that are even more integrally part of our tradition. The process has been so subtle, and seemingly so inexorable and universal, that many of us think it is normative; others are in denial, preaching a prosperity gospel, which further embeds a sense of insecurity and low self-esteem in the population.

Also, we often confuse charity and justice. Valuable and ethical though our churches are, their work is often relegated to the margins of society, to worship and social work, diluting the mission of the kingdom of God.

My own experience close to government informs me that priorities of public policy today are not grounded in goals of human development, but rather in the pursuit of individual profit and sectoral advantage.

And it is not just persons of religious faith who are sidelined. Trade unions, service and youth clubs, neighborhood watches, and friendly societies—once the loci for authentic democratic participation—are weaker than before. Look at the legislative agenda if you want proof of this. There is urgency to debate issues to do with gambling, abortion, and flexiwork. But try to get space for a discussion on the role of faith-based organizations in the education system or to treat the root causes of crime.

IS GDP GROWTH ENOUGH?

Jamaica is falling prey to the primacy of economism in public policy. Economic growth is considered our heaven. GDP growth, not the avoidance of social destruction, is our major concern.

But the dominant system of political and social economy cannot deliver the goods. It does not speak to the heart. At best it assumes that social engineering can be successful without personal regeneration. At worst, it is satisfied with the continuing transfer of the wealth of the poor to the already rich and the all too common squandering of this on conspicuous consumption and the mad avarice of the ponzi schemes.

Look what we have come to! We had to beg money to enable us to help our neighbors in Haiti—our equivalent of the wounded man on the way to Jericho. We waste untold billions on avoidable underperformance and remediation in our schools and make them into conveyor belts—a phrase used by our prime minister.

A rising tide does not lift all boats. Only the yachts!

PART 4: CARIBBEAN THEOLOGY AND THE POLITICAL SPHERE

A QUESTION ABOUT JAMAICAN POLITICS

A fundamental question for the Christian believer is whether current political structures and behavior can result in an order that is manifestly caring of the dignity and potential of all God's Jamaican creation.

To pose this question is by no means to undervalue the tremendous advances over time led by the nationalist movement and the activity of generations of religious activists. Rather it is to ask whether these are rendered inadequate by the destructive forces of unregulated capitalism and its twin sister, political corruption. Think why it has been so difficult to get that killer poison, tobacco, banned from public places; why establishing paternity for everyone is such a low priority; or why we would rather spend more than a million dollars a year to keep a convicted citizen locked up rather than a far lesser sum to rehabilitate him.

To quote again from Borg: "So long as the wedding of Christianity and the dominant culture continues, Christians seldom engage in radical criticism of the social order. Instead, personal salvation in the hereafter [becomes] the primary message, . . . [which] mutes the political voices of the Bible, thereby domesticating its political passion."[3]

The happy irony is that "bruk pocket" (financial woes) and external pressure from the International Monetary Fund are leading us some way towards a new economic reality. There are new laws regarding fiscal responsibility, tax reform, and an assault on corruption, as well as a retreat from that great medieval sin of usury in the form of the so-called Jamaica Debt Exchange. But we are still celebrating the acquisition of debt, rather than the elevation of earnings from our own increased work and productivity.

A NEW WAY

So in all of this today, where is the church of the Jubilee? Can people of faith get beyond the politics of complaint? Can we recognize the national budget as a profoundly moral document? Will we be heard on the issue of budget priorities, land reform, work, and broad social justice?

It is time for us to fill the ideological vacuum that exists beneath present trends. There is need, in a humble and unpretentious voice, to craft an intellectual, spiritual, and activist construct of a new Jamaican Jerusalem. It will be much wider and deeper than the useful though limited 2030 Vision document for Jamaica.

3. Ibid., 127.

Its character would be sustainedly inclusive and cross-denominational. It is quite impossible for people of faith to say anything credible about political tribalism, for instance, when we ourselves are often so piratical and divided.

A new order and vision for Jamaica will include espousing a simple lifestyle, one where the evangelically integral principle of the common good would be the litmus test—for housing, recreation, the use of capital, transportation, health promotion, education, and everything else.

Values like gratuitousness, solidarity, reconciliation, and habits like self-sacrifice, self-criticism, a willingness both to seek and relinquish power, would be fostered. The task will require a depth, strength, and sense of community beyond mere humanism and secular ideology. We must espouse a national order based on gospel principles, remembering the social order of the Acts of the Apostles and the early, suffering church.

The task bespeaks a faith beyond religious observance, beyond an attachment to the mundane, the immanent, the terrestrial. With strained voices and feet firmly on the ground, we will cry like Peter: "Lord, to whom shall we go? You have the words of eternal life." (John 6:68; NIV)

This journey is what I believe brother Ashley Smith has essayed in his half century of mission. As we say, I want to "follow back a him"! Also, I hope this direction may be what the Jamaica Theological Seminary is engaged in, under the leadership of Garnett Roper. In that hope, I end with Paul's benediction: "Now to him who is able to accomplish far more than we ask or imagine, by the power at work within us, to him be glory in the church and in Christ Jesus to all generations, forever and ever." (Eph 3:20–21).

PART 5

The Relevance of Caribbean Theology

13

Caribbean Theology
A Failed Project?

DEVON DICK

THIS PAPER ASKS WHETHER Caribbean theology is a failed project. I will be arguing that it is a failed project, in a number of senses. First, it has failed to capture the imagination of the Caribbean peoples. Beyond that, Caribbean theology fails because it locates itself in geography rather than in a theme, quality, or value. Furthermore, the attempts at distinguishing Caribbean theology from other theologies are flawed and need more rigorous analysis. The term *Caribbean theology* is also nebulous; it can mean many things to different persons. In response to these failures, I will offer an alternative name for our theology, one that better reflects our experience and ethos, and that has the potential to create and sustain enthusiasm among oppressed Caribbean peoples.[1]

---

1. My claim that Caribbean theology is a failed project does not fault its theological methodology. I am not here arguing along the lines of Alistair Kee, professor of religious Studies of the University of Edinburgh, who indicted the Theology of Liberation for failing to address Karl Marx's critique of religion; hence he proclaimed this theological project a failure. See Kee, *Marx and the Failure of Liberation Theology*. The argument of this book is addressed by Taylor, "Editorial," 2.

PART 5: THE RELEVANCE OF CARIBBEAN THEOLOGY

PROBLEMS WITH CARIBBEAN THEOLOGY

I am not the first person to raise problems associated with Caribbean theology. In the 1990s United Church scholar and former lecturer of the United Theological College of the West Indies (UTCWI), Michael Miller, noted "great concern at the fact that a theological vision which emerged over 20 years ago with great promise, and which invigorated many spiritually and intellectually, appears to have floundered so badly that it has not contributed to Caribbean life in the ways hoped."[2] Lewin Williams made a similar point around the same time. He wondered that "if the issues raised in Caribbean theology are not the issues that interest the people to whom the discourses speak, what good is the enterprise after all? It may tickle the fancy of a few individuals, but is that enough to warrant its own legitimacy?"[3] What a sad commentary! There is no evidence to contradict the findings of the 1990s.

Whatever the reasons, it is clear that Caribbean theology has not had the impact on Caribbean theologians, Caribbean Christians, or Caribbean peoples that many had hoped for. Caribbean theology—its aims and methodology—do not inform any political manifesto, any denominational constitution, and are not in any mission statement of any theological school. In that sense it is a failed project.

There was a hopeful start when in the early 1970s "Caribbean thinkers . . . met in Trinidad to register the region's need of a contextual theology."[4] Indeed, Caribbean theology has had a "gradual but crucial development . . . within the context of the Caribbean since 1971."[5]

There was no symposium on Caribbean theology in the 1980s and only a couple in the 1990s. I believe the Forum on Caribbean Theology at the Jamaica Theological Seminary (JTS) that generated this volume of essays is the first in the twenty-first century. Many persons have expressed shock that JTS was hosting a symposium on Caribbean theology and wondered why. They thought it was not a natural fit for JTS, which is an historically evangelical institution.

But this presumption should be questioned. The Baptist biblical scholar Stephen Jennings notes that there is a "diversity of theologies present in the Caribbean situation."[6] In other words, there are varieties of theologies in

---

2. Miller, "Impulses in Caribbean Theology."
3. Williams, "What, Why, and Wherefore of Caribbean Theology," 30.
4. Williams, *Caribbean Theology*, dust jacket.
5. Ibid. An explanation for why its development was only gradual is that it was "due to the insidiousness of missionary theology from which Caribbean theology sought disengagement."
6. Jennings, "Caribbean Theology or Theologies of the Caribbean," 1.

the Caribbean corresponding to the diversity of cultures and contexts found there. Jennings seems to be suggesting that we should not expect a single, monolithic Caribbean Theology. Nevertheless, he notes that "since the turn of the twentieth century, two related theologies have emerged as forces to be reckoned with—Evangelicalism and Fundamentalism."[7] In separating evangelical theology from Caribbean theology, Jennings seems not to recognize that there are evangelicals who support a form of contextual Caribbean theology.

A case in point is the analysis of Caribbean history and theology by David Ho Sang and Roger Ringenberg, who are no strangers to JTS.[8] Ho Sang and Ringenberg outline the thinking of ecumenical Caribbean theologians in relation to context and praxis under the categories of the Bible, God, Christ, Man, Sin and Salvation, the Church, and Eschatology. They suggest, in general terms, possible lines of an evangelical alternative; they appeal for a theology that is faithful to Scripture and relevant to the needs of the Caribbean. They want to combine orthopraxis and orthodoxy for their understanding of Caribbean Theology.

Former president of JTS, Diumeme Noëlliste, makes a similar argument.[9] Claiming that the issues to be identified in an analysis of the Caribbean context all relate to the overall viability of the Caribbean, he argues that survival can be enhanced if due consideration is given to certain aspects of the classical Christian understanding of creation, redemption, stewardship, and providence. Perhaps evangelicalism should not be seen as an alternative to Caribbean theology; rather, evangelicals have their own understanding of Caribbean theology.

But leading evangelicals have also misunderstood Caribbean theology, believing that it is not concerned with orthodoxy. The point is that there are questions to be addressed about the meaning of Caribbean theology.

CARIBBEAN THEOLOGY AS LIBERATION THEOLOGY

Could Caribbean theology be thought of as a variety of liberation theology? There are some who would argue against viewing Caribbean theology as liberation theology, which originated in Latin America, because the "Caribbean experience has its own contextual particularities which must be reflected in the Caribbean theological enterprise."[10] However, liberation is

---

7. Ibid.
8. Ho Sang and Ringenberg, "Towards an Evangelical Caribbean Theology."
9. Noëlliste, "Faith Transforming Context."
10. Taylor, "Editorial," 2.

adaptable to various contexts and there is no good reason for the term to be dropped from Caribbean theology.

Even Lewin Williams, who is not averse to the term *liberation*, suggests that Caribbean liberation theology must move not only beyond the "missio-colonial" theology of the past Caribbean church, but also beyond the "socio-economic and political aspects of liberation theology," aiming instead to create "The New Caribbean Person."[11] In this, Williams seems to be attempting to distinguish Caribbean from Latin American liberation theology by implying that the latter is guilty of economic or political reductionism. Yet as far back as Gustavo Gutierrez's early *Theology of Liberation* there was a laudable emphasis on the redemptive transformation of the whole person.[12] It seems to me that some Caribbean theologians have not wanted to embrace liberation theology because of fear of being seen as Marxists.

Emmette Weir has suggested that the term "Caribbean Liberation Theology" is adequate to suggest a theology that identifies with "the struggle of the poor and oppressed," since it understands Caribbean reality and thinking, and engages in a careful analysis of the socio-economic realities and spiritual condition of the Caribbean, while also being involved in the transformation of a society.[13] Weir argues that Bertrand Aristide's commitment to the poor and marginalized—an important feature of the faith-commitment of the theology of liberation—was an integral factor in his election as president of Haiti. Perhaps Aristide was kidnapped by French and American forces because they recognized that Aristide wanted liberation. And perhaps because Caribbean politicians fear a similar treatment by American and European forces, some Caribbean theologians have dropped the word "liberation" from Caribbean theology. Even worse, politicians have dropped the theology of liberation from their consciousness.

Any deletion of liberation from Caribbean theology is regrettable, although understandable, because of the fear of being identified with communism. This is supported by Williams' quotation from a theological student: "If Caribbean Theology is identified as liberation theology, with liberation theology being so closely identified with the Marxist analysis, Caribbean theology will have written the blue print for its own demise"[14]

However, liberation has to be central to Caribbean theology. As Robert Beckford, the British theologian, explains: "Liberation is concerned with representing the interests of oppressed people in theological language and

---

11. Williams, *Caribbean Theology*, 150.
12. Gutiérrez, *Theology of Liberation*.
13. Weir, "Towards a Caribbean Liberation Theology," 42, 45–46.
14. Williams, "What, Why, and Wherefore of Caribbean Theology," 31–32.

action. When applied to theology, it expresses a desire to know what God is doing about oppression, and what is the role of the Christian in God's liberative work in the world. Liberation is both internal, concerned with mental emancipation, as well as external, concerned with social justice."[15] The omission of liberation from Caribbean theology demeans the task and undermines the effort at personal and social transformation.

Liberation theology begins with an analytical, sociological, and structural reading of reality that is as scientific as possible. It is a careful analysis of the contemporary world. It involves critical reflection upon praxis in the light of the Word of God. Its aim is to transform society.

Then there is "Black theology" as a form of liberation theology. The term goes back to James Cone, and functions as a theology of liberation because it makes the oppressed community the center of theological discourse.[16] It is a Black male USA-based theology for a minority group. Similarly the "Black Church" movement in Britain developed with reference to a minority group trying to reflect on their particular cultural experience in Britain. Thus Beckford wants to use black culture as "a tool in theological reflection for the Black church in Britain."[17] Beckford urges that "perceptions of resistance, sexuality, ... art, music and prayer" should be used in reflection on God and "identifies dread culture as a concept with radical implications for the Black Christian's understanding of Christ."[18]

The main problem with utilizing either of these movements for Caribbean theology is that it would involve the USA or Britain claiming monopoly on the struggles of peoples of color. This would not work, since in the Caribbean those of African descent are not a minority group. Further, it would be problematic to import Black theology into the Caribbean because it could raise racial tensions; indeed, oppressed persons in the Caribbean are not confined to one ethnicity.

Beyond those issues, *black* is an inappropriate term, since it has historically had a negative connotation, meaning retarded, backward, evil and stupid. *Black* was synonymous with backwardness. In addition, it represented impurity, evil, and wickedness. And many modern scholars have identified the burdensomeness attached to being *black*. Thus the British scholar Catherine Hall notes that, for the missionaries, *blackness* could mean "Africa,

---

15. Beckford, *Jesus is Dread*, 12.
16. Cone, *A Black Theology of Liberation*.
17. Beckford, *Jesus is Dread*, 16.
18. Ibid., from the dust jacket.

superstition, heathenism," which would be in need of transformation. *Black* can also mean non-white, non-rich, powerless, African, or non-human.[19]

In post-independence Jamaica, *black* and *white* denoted not skin color, objectively speaking, but skin color as a symbol of attitudes and status, with *black* being a negative term.[20] This negative connotation was not confined to Jamaica but, as the renowned sociologist Orlando Patterson demonstrates, there was a pattern in both the Latin and non-Latin West Indies of marrying lighter skin color for upward social mobility.[21] *Black* has carried the baggage of negativity.

Womanist theology is a variety of liberation theology that looks at oppression based on gender and class, as well as race. Feminist theological reflection also promotes the "full humanity of women."[22] But neither feminist nor womanist theology would be adequate for the Caribbean; neither would encompass the full range of the struggle and thinking of Caribbean peoples.

DEFINITIONS: WHAT IS CARIBBEAN THEOLOGY?

What is the Caribbean? It is difficult to define *Caribbean*. There are as many definitions for the Caribbean as there are Caribbean territories. Is the Bahamas and Bermuda part of the Caribbean? Is Puerto Rico part of the Caribbean? Should it be territories touched by the Caribbean Sea? Then there is English, Spanish, Dutch, and French Caribbean. How can we have a Caribbean theology when we cannot even identify the Caribbean?

What is theology? In *Jesus is Dread*, Beckford states: 'Theology is essentially God-Talk—an attempt to express the meaning of God in the world. However, theology is never value-free or neutral: because it is human, our language, motives and ambitions affect its expression . . . . theology reflects human interests. In other words, theology tells us as much about God as it does about human beings who are writing about God."[23]

What then could Caribbean theology be? The Moravian scholar Livingston Thompson notes that "Caribbean theology represents an attempt to formulate a theological discourse that would complement the political imaginations of regional independence. Consequently, there is in *Caribbean theology*, a major emphasis on the idea of the decolonisation of theology."[24]

19. Hall, *White, Male, and Middle Class*, 212.
20. Dick, *The Cross and the Machete*, 10.
21. Ibid.
22. Rigby, "Exploring Our Hesitation," 540.
23. Beckford, *Jesus is Dread*, 14.
24. Thompson, "Dr. Lewin Williams and Caribbean Theology," A11, emphasis

This understanding of Caribbean theology, Thompson explains, derives from the struggle for political independence.[25] "The central thought is that the church must also disassociate itself from colonial theology (European/American) if it is to contribute to the social reconstruction in the region."[26]

Lewin Williams, leading exponent on Caribbean Theology and author on the seminal work, *Caribbean Theology*, mentions two important features of Caribbean theology, namely *contextualization* and *indigenization*. Caribbean theology aims to make a meaningful and concrete contribution to "Caribbean self-authentication, self awareness, self development, self-actualization, and self determination."[27]

So what is distinctive about Caribbean theology? Is it that it is contextual? But how is this different from other liberation theologies? In this it is not even different from so-called European theology or missionary theology. European theology/missionary theology is also contextual, only that it supports the context of the status quo.

Stephen Jennings connects Caribbean theology with the theology of liberation, where "the stance is one of 'orthopraxis' rather than 'orthodoxy' as theology is done and demonstrated in the ream of deeds, not mere words and rhetoric."[28] However, I would argue that Caribbean theology is also concerned with orthodoxy. Orthodoxy and orthopraxis are not mutually exclusive. Even European theology/missionary/colonial Theology is concerned about what they perceive as orthopraxis.

CARIBBEAN THEOLOGY AS EMANCIPATION THEOLOGY

I want to propose the idea of *emancipation theology* for the Caribbean. I am not the first to use *emancipation* in this context. Weir notes that theologian Kortright Davis' major point in his 1988 book *Emancipation Still Comin'* is that emancipation is the key to the development of Caribbean theology.[29] Likewise, Hyacinth Boothe uses the phrase *emancipatory theology* when she

---

original.

25. Thompson also mentions two other influences that gave rise to Caribbean theology, including Latin American liberation theology and the 1960s Black Power movement.
26. Ibid.
27. Williams, *Caribbean Theology*, 5.
28. Jennings, "Caribbean Theology or Theologies of the Caribbean," 5.
29. Weir, "Towards a Caribbean Liberation Theology," 49.

discusses culture, gospel, and their interaction in Jamaica.[30] And Ernle Gordon argues that the search for such a theology within the Caribbean context must recognize the African heritage and the effects of plantation slavery.[31]

Some may criticize the concept of emancipation theology based on the fact that different territories in the Caribbean won their freedom from slavery at different times—Haiti in 1801, the British West Indies in 1838, the Dutch colonies in 1863, the enslaved in USA in 1865, Puerto Rico in 1886, Brazil in 1888. The issue would be *which* emancipation date should be the starting point? Different persons can locate emancipation differently, based on their history.

Furthermore, some may claim that there were different motivations for those who resisted enslavement; so how can we determine if it is a Christian motivation for emancipation? For example, the Haitian revolution (1791–1804) was not the same as the 1831 Baptist War in Jamaica. Bookman in Haiti is said to have made petition to the gods of voodoo, while in Jamaica Sam Sharpe was a Christian. How can we perceive God working in all these various religious beliefs and practices? I believe that God moves in a mysterious way and can certainly work through different religious expressions.

Some may question how we can locate a significant theology in the sayings of an enslaved person such as Sam Sharpe, who did not have a developed hermeneutical approach to Scripture based on the canons of recent biblical scholarship. However, in *The Cross and the Machete* I argue that persons such as Sharpe foreshadowed what is today called a reader-response approach to the Bible.[32]

I, therefore, suggest a theological framework that adopts an emancipation paradigm, since emancipatory praxis is central to Caribbean theological methodology. Emancipation theology would be for those who have experienced enslavement and also neo-enslavement. It is for those whose ancestors experienced enslavement and it is for those who have suffered and are still suffering from the consequences of slavery. It is for those working to develop along equal terms with all other ethnic groups. It is for those who see the right hand of God in political emancipation of 1838 in the British West Indies and at other times in other territories.

Since emancipation is central to Caribbean history, it has the potential to excite Caribbean peoples. Barbados' celebration includes various events held at Emancipation Roundabout in the parish of St. Michael. This parish is the site of a statue honoring Bussa, the leader of the slave revolt at

30. Boothe, "A Theological Journey for an Emancipatory Theology."
31. Ernle, "Emancipatory Theology."
32. Dick, *The Cross and the Machete*.

Bayley's Plantation. Both Guyana and Jamaica observe Emancipation Day. And Trinidad and Tobago was the first country in the world to declare a national holiday to commemorate the abolition of slavery.

Other features of emancipation theology would include a theological discourse that would seek full freedom, equality, and justice; indigenous theological formulations; differentiation from colonial theology; respect and tolerance of cultural expressions. It would evaluate historical legacies of injustice and oppression and seek ways to transform the situations, systems, and principalities and powers; it would seek to name, shame, and confront the powers. It should facilitate a better self-understanding under God. The emancipatory theological discourse would draw on the ideals of Jamaican National Heroes such as Sam Sharpe, Paul Bogle, and George William Gordon. It could consider the works on emancipation done by historians, sociologists, and economists concerning the church in the Caribbean. It would affirm all races as equal; it would respect different hermeneutical approaches. Emancipation theology should help people discern the hand of God in their history of suffering and struggle.

This is a call to shift the focus from the geographical region of the Caribbean to re-capture the liberation motif, but under the name *emancipation*. It is to shift the focus from peoples who happen to live, work, study, worship in the Caribbean (a place), in order to re-capture the emancipation motif as a way to talk about and understand God in our context. It is to make formerly colonized people central to the theological discourse. It is to aim for the liberation of the oppressed and oppressors together.

Emancipation theology could be a unique departure in Caribbean theological reflection. Let us re-package Caribbean theology by placing liberation from enslavement as its central theme; this is best done when it is called *emancipation theology*!

14

The Continuing Relevance of a Caribbean Theology

BURCHELL K. TAYLOR

Is CARIBBEAN THEOLOGY RELEVANT? To understand the import of this question, we need first to clarify what we mean by the Caribbean, which is the context or location for doing theology that bears its name as an identifying mark. Is the Caribbean limited to only those island nations in the Caribbean Sea? Or does it include nations like Belize, Suriname, and Guyana, on the Central and South American mainland? And what about islands in the Atlantic Ocean, such as those that make up the nations of Bahamas, Turks and Caicos, or Bermuda? Are they part of the Caribbean? Since defining *Caribbean* can prove both challenging and debatable, it is sufficient for our purposes to note that we are using the term to refer to the entire region that shares a common experience and reality in colonialism and post-colonialism, such that a discussion of the relevance of doing theology within this context can be undertaken profitably without undue preoccupation with the known diversities that otherwise exist.

QUESTIONS ABOUT THE RELEVANCE OF CARIBBEAN THEOLOGY

Next, we need to clarify what exactly we mean by *relevance*, since this raises two issues that are implicit (and sometimes explicit) when the matter is discussed.

Is Caribbean Theology Legitimate?

First, is there any legitimate place or necessity for such a thing called *Caribbean theology*? Indeed, sometimes a specifically *Caribbean* theology is regarded as a non-entity. There is no such thing, for theology is theology. This means that a qualifier that indicates geographical or contextual specificity would transform theology into something else. Whatever this would be, it would not be discourse about and knowledge of God, which is universally applicable without regard for location or circumstances. This is how theology is traditionally perceived.

Ironically, this position is invariably taken by persons who themselves adhere to theological constructs and positions that do bear qualifiers, which have their own geographical or contextual connectedness and influence (though not always stated). What is stated is a historical or a religious-ideological or a denominational or confessional qualifier, such as: ancient, medieval, modern, postmodern; Roman Catholic, Protestant, Evangelical, Orthodox; fundamentalist, liberal, neo-liberal, conservative, neo-conservative. These are all qualifiers that people work with. Theologians often interface and interact with such qualifiers as legitimate, in agreement or disagreement, in terms of the theology they identify. They do not dismiss them as representing theological expressions that are non-entities. Further, qualifiers such as North American, British, or European theologies are taken for granted. Yet theologies from a non-mainstream context, like *Caribbean* theology, are often summarily dismissed as theological non-entities. They are considered irrelevant, theologically.

This matter goes back undoubtedly to who has the entitlement and right to define and determine what is theology. It is invariably the same ones who have always assumed the right to produce and do theology for the rest of the world. Theology undertaken without *their* endorsement is not theology. It is irrelevant. Therefore, Caribbean theology, which is done from a different base with a different perspective and with a different function, is ruled out as irrelevant. This, then, is often the sentiment of those who claim

PART 5: THE RELEVANCE OF CARIBBEAN THEOLOGY

the right to define theology, with the support of those, who even within the context of the Caribbean, concede such a right to them.

This position has long operated on a false basis, probably unselfconsciously so, but nonetheless still false. It has proceeded on the premise that doing theology can be achieved in a thoroughly disinterested and so-called objective manner. The resulting theology itself will therefore be effectively a de-contextualized entity. Such a theology, being of the neutral vintage of the kind it is assumed to be, will always have the versatility to be applied and used in any context anywhere in the world. The truth, however, is that theology is not done in a cultural and sociopolitical vacuum. Whether its practitioners like it or not, or whether they admit it or not, such theology is done in a specific sociopolitical, as well as religious, context, which influences and contributes to the *process* of doing the theology. It does the same to the *substance* and the *content* of the theology itself. Caribbean and similar theologies operate on the basis of this presupposition, with the designated aim of speaking directly to their own constituencies. Relevance is a key factor in this regard.

Is Caribbean Theology Viable in the Present Context?

There is, however, a second issue concerning relevance, namely that of the viability of Caribbean theology, along with its applicability in a sustained manner. Some would claim that at this particular time a specifically Caribbean theology is not viable and so not applicable. For whatever it might have been worth at some stage, it has lost its usefulness. It is therefore not relevant. Circumstances have overtaken it. Presuppositions with which it operated are no larger viable and perspectives which drove it are no longer applicable. In this regard, the fate of Caribbean theology is linked with that of the wider theological family known as the *theologies of liberation*. The self-conscious emergence of Caribbean theology coincided with the emergence of Latin American liberation theology, and subsequently with similar movements in Africa, Asia, and other groups of oppressed peoples in North America and Europe. The link with Latin American theology of liberation was seen to be pronounced and direct. This theology was thus linked with the ideological position of socialism, which included Marxist sociopolitical analysis as one of its prime tools of the social context.

The global geopolitical situation that saw the virtual demise of socialism and Marxism brought with it the claim of the demise of liberation theology, as far as its detractors are concerned. The same fate is pronounced upon

Burchell K. Taylor *The Continuing Relevance of a Caribbean Theology*

Caribbean theology, which is seen to be genetically connected to theologies of liberation. Here, then, the question of relevance emerged.

With the perceived demise of liberation theology in all finality, the claim is that Caribbean theology has lost its viability. Lying in the background here is the assumption of the lack of any independent insight and distinctive feature of Caribbean theology that is sustainable and of enduring value. As usual, the assumption is that whatever is of value in and to the Caribbean must be sponsored and endorsed from elsewhere. The fate of what is viable and meaningful to the Caribbean is tied to the fate of its sponsors elsewhere. The relevance of Caribbean theology inevitably follows this pattern in the minds of some who question it.

Another factor that has caused some to raise questions about the viability and applicability of Caribbean theology has been what appears to be a lack of effective presence and evidence of Caribbean theological activity after the first rush of action. This has been seen as a possible lack of confidence based on awareness of its waning or passed relevance. There has not been any substantial body of works and serious intellectual output. This is taken as a sign of lack of viability and applicability. Coupled with this is a lack of projects and institutions that are devoted to the promotion and advancement of Caribbean theology.

It is sufficient to say at this point that given the nature of Caribbean theology—its methodology, self-expression, and its roots—it is premature to speak of its non-viability in terms of these things that have been considered to make it so. For example, though it does not have the articulation and coherent expression that would be expected of it in the academy and by experts, this doesn't mean that it is not being done and having its impact in a measure. Caribbean theology, by its very nature, as we shall see, takes place and continues to take place among the people in a way that ought not to be ignored.

Yet another thing that has raised questions about the relevance of Caribbean theology in terms of its viability and applicability has been a new wave of religious influence in the latter part of the twentieth century (and on into the twenty-first) that has captured the imagination of a special section of the religious populace in the Caribbean. The old-time religious expressions served by dogmatic influences that undergirded them is no longer engaging the imagination of Caribbean people. This new theological wave puts emphasis on the procurement of personal individual salvation, congregational growth and development, including planting of new congregations, immediate and direct experiences of blessings, resolution of personal issues, and therapeutic experiences. Worship that focuses on facilitating personal expression of celebration and spiritual enthusiasm also forms part of it.[1]

Much of this is not self-consciously contextual. It is pragmatic and caters for what is perceived to be the wants of the people or in response to their expressed demands. The big thing that is claimed for this is its *relevance*. Though much of this is not homegrown, it is made adaptable to wants and desires. *Relevance* in this regard has to do with pragmatism, adaptation, assimilation, and imitation. As far as responding to the challenges and needs affecting people's welfare, the fundamental theological response here is in the form of charitable exercises and reformism relating to existing structures that have systemically stood against the people's welfare and well-being. It is more conformist than critically constructive and transformative. It is more individualistic and experiential than corporate and contextual in outlook and practice. It is more aspectival than holistic and integral in approach. It needs to be made clear that the Caribbean theology project would see, judge, and act significantly beyond the limited understanding of the *relevance* that is portrayed by this new religious wave.

Whether the relevance of Caribbean theology is questioned in terms of its legitimacy, viability, or applicability, the true picture is that the relevance of Caribbean theology, properly pursued and understood in terms of its essential and practical nature and function, is beyond doubt.

THE HISTORICAL ROOTS OF A RELEVANT CARIBBEAN THEOLOGY

But what are the roots of this relevance? In its most basic and rudimentary form, there is to be found in the submerged history and narrative of the Caribbean people the basis and ground of the relevance of Caribbean theology. Long before it came to any coherent articulation and self-conscious expression, Caribbean theology emerged in an antecedent form. It did so in the manner in which the oppressed, enslaved, and exploited people of the region responded to and reflected on the harsh realities to which they were subjected. They did so on the basis of their faith commitment and in the light of their interpretation, understanding, and appropriation of the message of Scripture. This was done, remarkably, over against teachings they were fed that accounted for their lot as predetermined in the purpose of God. Their own reflection led them to a different understanding of God and of themselves, which in turn led them to reject, in their own way, the false

---

1. See the analysis (and critique) of this religious wave in David Pearson's essay in this volume.

identity thrust upon them in the form of the diminished humanity ascribed to them by the teachings of their oppressors.

They did not accept the misplaced significance they were given in the scheme of things, which regarded them as naturally *less than* those who oppressed them, despite the legitimation of this significance by recourse to supposedly biblical teaching and other traditional religious instruction. As now known, the people operated with their own hidden transcripts, inspired by their own reflection on their experience in the light of their own intuitive—as well as critical—understanding of the Scriptures. This served not only as the basis of their own survival, but as the basis of their engagement in, and appropriation of, what made for liberation. What was actually lacking in relevance were the formal teachings and interpretations of Scripture that legitimated their situation. This kind of teaching and interpretation has continued to be irrelevant wherever it is still in evidence. The effectiveness and enduring relevance of Caribbean theology finds its roots in its early beginnings as a theology of protest and resistance aimed at emancipatory accomplishments. Therein also lies its prophetic orientation, along with its public significance. It is all of this that undergirds its rooted relevance.

THE FUTURE RELEVANCE OF CARIBBEAN THEOLOGY

The enduring relevance of Caribbean theology is based on the dynamic movement and process it represents. This is in contrast to the received traditional theological systems and constructs long represented as normative for Caribbean people. Caribbean theology is done with a sense of historical continuity, critical consciousness of, and responsiveness to, cultural realities, and commitment to practical, alternative, and transformative possibilities.

At the point of the self-conscious emergence of the Caribbean theological project, there is recognizable continuity with the antecedent efforts that were made by the enslaved and oppressed to make sense of their faith in God through reflection on the contextual realities to which they were subjected. It was an effort undertaken largely by their own imaginative and intuitive grasp and interpretation of Scripture. The continuity also exists in terms of the persistent socio-economic realities and psychological factors that have lingered on over time. Some of these factors have assumed new forms and shapes, with intensified adverse effects. In addition, there are new factors resulting from current global realities. These have exacerbated the old conditions of injustice and the suffering of the poor in the Caribbean, as elsewhere.

PART 5: THE RELEVANCE OF CARIBBEAN THEOLOGY

There is certainly no diminishing of the need for the Caribbean theology project. To respond adequately to this need, the project will develop a proper reading of the signs of the times with direct bearing on the Caribbean reality. It will seek to give meaning to what is happening by identifying what God is saying and doing; this will include the call to act in solidarity with the suffering poor. It amounts to taking theological responsibility for discovery of, and coming to terms with, what is happening in the Caribbean context.

The project represents God's people responding to the call to act in obedience, as they work for new life and hope for the people in the region. There will need to be the marks of situatedness, meaningfulness, and practical effectiveness that are associated with the theology. These are essential marks of the relevance of Caribbean theology.

In light of the above, the relevance of Caribbean theology can be linked to its methodology and its function within its given context. The following statement would, therefore, locate the relevance more definitely: *Caribbean theology is an ongoing process of giving account of belief in, and relationship with, God in Christ, in the midst of, and in response to, encountering, confronting, and engaging the experiences of the Caribbean reality.* The Caribbean reality is characteristically one of systemic poverty—marginalization, dispossession, deprivation, humiliation, discrimination, oppression, domination, and religious indoctrination—meted out to the majority. In all of this, economic poverty is the most powerful prototypical expression of the phenomenon. The reality also includes a culture of resistance by the poor, a quest for authentic self-identity and self-understanding, and the dynamic expression of creative potential. The process is undertaken intuitively, imaginatively, and reflectively in the light of the Scriptures, with openness to the guidance and inspiration of the Spirit. Multiple sources and creative components are employed in helping to make sense of the oppressive reality, as well as offering motivation and guidance for engagement in transformative action. Interpretation of the Scriptures however, remains the key source of direction.

CHALLENGES AND IMPLICATIONS OF RELEVANCE

To continue to be relevant, the Caribbean theology project needs to manifest certain key characteristics, which will ensure the situatedness, meaningfulness, and rightful effectiveness of the project. Given the constraints of time and space, I offer here a list of five of the more important characteristics or factors.

Burchell K. Taylor   *The Continuing Relevance of a Caribbean Theology*

1. Self-criticism

Given its very nature, Caribbean theology will subject itself to ongoing self-examination and engage in internal dialogue with different partners within the project who share diverse views, but with a shared purpose and common commitment. It will also be mindful of what outside critics are saying and keep the self-critical process going, conscious of all perspectives involved. Caribbean theology is never a complete and settled system. It is dynamic and responsive, bearing in mind the ongoing reality, as well as new complexities and subtleties, that are always developing in the context and making their impact on the reality that impinges on the people's life and the environment in which they live.

2. Ensuring the tools of critical analysis are appropriate and used effectively

The tools of analysis for Caribbean theology will need to be Caribbean-oriented and thus trusted to deliver credible data. These tools will relate to areas covering the Caribbean reality. The social and human sciences, historical, cultural and global studies, and knowledge of the traditions of the people and their religious practices, will be some of the tools of analysis used for understanding of the Caribbean reality and for action as the theological reflection and practice take place.

It is important that these tools are not used only for analysis of the causes of the oppression and suffering visited upon the poor. They must also be used for guidance in terms of historical projects and institutions that may be undertaken in the emancipatory praxis that is close to the heart of Caribbean theology. We must always reckon with the negative potential for such projects and institutions to assume shapes that become more and more part of the problem than the answer, if there is a lack of properly applied information gained from credible and appropriate analysis.

3. Ongoing broadening of scope and range of awareness of the sources and means of oppression

Selectivity and narrowness of focus that ignore realities responsible for the impoverishment of people's humanity and denial of human dignity will undermine the relevance of Caribbean theology. Whereas the economic poor are a powerful prototypical instance of poverty, and represent a vast number of persons, human suffering and oppression affect and afflict people's life and humanity in others ways and in some instances have further implications for economic poverty itself. A relevant Caribbean theology will respond to and even focus on issues related to matters of justice and discrimination on the basis of race, class, ethnicity, gender, sexuality, physical and emotional disablement, diseases, religious beliefs, and practices, as these emerge as aspects of the Caribbean reality. Issues of eco-justice fall in the same category. All in all, there must be ongoing awareness of the signs of the times, which includes being sensitive to the capacity of the powers of the world to create new structures of oppression and suffering.

This raises the matter of the contextual nature of Caribbean theology and how much it may be a limiting factor in terms of human concern beyond its borders. Surely its contextuality is absolutely essential, but it is not a contextuality that limits its vision and sensibility. It can both learn from and contribute helpfully to other contexts of human suffering and oppression through human solidarity that transcends contextual barriers. It is one of the things that present globalism enables. In spite of its negative implications in some stark ways for the already oppressed peoples, globalism can facilitate the possibility of connectedness and solidarity with and among the poor. Caribbean theology must itself be a liberating eye-opener in this regard.

4. Faithfulness to the people-based nature of the Caribbean theology project

The raw material of Caribbean theology is the lived experience of the suffering poor and oppressed. This is the point of departure for the project. Essential to the project is the people's input in terms of their own reflection on their experience in the light of their hearing and understanding of the Bible and their faith-commitment, under the guidance of the Spirit. Caribbean theology has its roots here. It has continued within this framework and on this basis despite various assaults on it by the formal and adopted theology endorsed by the church for a long time. Caribbean theology is also challenged by, and must respond to, lived features of human life in modernity and postmodernity.

Caribbean theology would lose its relevance if it ceases being a theology of the people. This is not a theology that has its roots in the academy or the seminary. These places are refiners, clarifiers, enrichers, and exponents that sharpen the connectedness between, and give order and expression to, the factors that go into given wholeness of the project. But they are not makers of the theology. Those in the academy or seminary are participants with, and listeners to, the people at ground level. This is what will give authentic relevance to what they do theologically.

Thus much of real Caribbean theology is to be discovered in preaching, testimony, and storytelling, as these connect meaningfully to the people's experience. Caribbean theology is done at levels of solidarity with, and in response to, the faith and praxis questions that emerge from reflection on their own lived experience in engagement with the Caribbean reality. It is how people make sense of life's experiences in the light of their own understanding of God's self-disclosure in the daily realities of life. All of this stands over against any theology that is of an abstract, rationalistic nature, considered universally relevant and applicable. Such theology is built on, and determined by, sets of dogmatic constructs or abstract dogma to which trained experts and specialists are made privy. These constructs/dogma in turn are communicated to the people who are meant to appropriate them, whether such constructs relate to their experience or not. The theology of the Caribbean, as a theology of the people, stands as an alternative to this kind of abstract and specialist theology. This speaks centrally to its relevance.

5. Maintaining hermeneutical creativity and integrity

The interpretive approach and practice of Caribbean theology in relation to the Bible is key to the whole theological project and its relevance. Whereas I noted above that a number of interdisciplinary tools and sources will be drawn upon in aiding understanding of the context and in guiding required action, the Bible is the chief source of inspiration, insight, and ideals necessary for decision-making and specific action in line with faith-commitment. It is well known that the Bible itself has been used over time to legitimate and sanction institutions and patterns of life that bent the Caribbean reality towards the systemic poverty and disadvantage that mark it.

It is, however, the early interpretive process undertaken by the people themselves that countered the oppressive readings of the Scriptures they had to contend with. The liberating discernment and insights served them well. In the same vein, there must be interpretation of the Scriptures that will lead to the vision of God as God of justice and liberation, God of life and hope, who acts on behalf of the poor and oppressed and who calls the people of God to share in the emancipatory purpose of the divine will. The integral nature of the emancipatory thrust and experience of Scripture is a critical factor yielded by readings and interpretation that draw upon the meaning and possibilities of the text. These are meaning possibilities that are invariably richer than assumed by traditional popular approaches that posit a single inherent meaning. The emancipatory power of the text is strengthened by the fact that faithful reading and interpretation of the Scriptures will be participatory. This is so in the sense that it expects and presupposes the influence and experience of the community of believers to be part of the interpretive exercise.

At the same time, safeguards based upon respect for the text itself, coupled with the ethics of reading and the reader, will be practiced against misappropriation of the text. This brings together creativity and integrity in working with the text and it ensures relevance that does not embrace compromise at the expense of liberating prophetic truth. In the process, the reading and interpretation will be open to dialogical encounters, not only with diverse others within the Christian community itself, but with other religious groups that form significant elements of the Caribbean context and experience. This is a necessary part of the transformative praxis, which allows religious divisiveness or parochialism to be addressed (and hopefully transcended), while continuing to honor particularity.

CONCLUSION

The relevance of a Caribbean theology will always be displayed as long as it continues to facilitate meaningful understanding of, and discourse about, God in Christ in the power of the Holy Spirit, and contributes to guiding emancipatory and transformative action in response to the Caribbean reality. The nature of the Caribbean reality poses a challenge for various faith issues, including our perception of God. Indeed, Caribbean theology re-appropriates, refines, clarifies, and extends the vision and root experience of God among poor, suffering Caribbean people, so that God is understood as emancipatory and life-transforming for all of life's dimensions. God is reflected on and proclaimed as the God who makes those regarded as no people, not fully human, into a people aware of their humanity and of their capacity to fulfill their humanity in history. This God's self-disclosure in Jesus Christ and witnessed to by the Holy Spirit, is experienced as especially being concerned for the welfare and well-being of the poor and oppressed, the suffering, and excluded. These are people who are put at risk by the dominant historical, social, political, and religious realities of their immediate context, and also by the wider global context, which has made an impact on the immediate context. In a situation like this, Caribbean theology is ever relevant, as an emancipatory exercise in obedience and faithfulness to God.

Bibliography

Abdullah, Clive. "Any Word from the Lord?" In *Troubling of the Waters*, edited by Idris Hamid, 15–20. San Fernando, Trinidad: Rahaman, 1973.

Allan, J. D. *The Evangelicals: The Story of a Great Christian Movement*. Exeter, UK: Paternoster, 1989.

Allen, E. Anthony. "The Healing Christ: His Liberation Destiny in Uncertainty." In *Ministry Perspectives from the Caribbean: Essays in Honor of Horace O. Russell*, edited by Eron Henry, 86–101. New York: Instant, 2010.

Anderson, Elizabeth. "What is the Point of Equality?" *Ethics* 109 (1999) 287–337.

Archer, Michael S., editor. *Manley Farewell: A Scrapbook*. Kingston, Jamaica: Mowtown, 1997.

Arends, Jacques. "The Socio-Historical Background of Creoles." In *Pidgins and Creoles: An Introduction*, edited by Jacques Arends, Pieter Muysken, and Norval Smith, 15–24. Amsterdam: Benjamins, 1995.

Aristide, Jean-Bertrand. *Jean-Bertrand Aristide: An Autobiography*. Translated by Linda M. Maloney. New York: Orbis, 1992.

Austin-Broos, Diane. *Jamaica Genesis*. Kingston, Jamaica: Ian Randle Publishers, 1997.

Baard, Rachel Sophia. "Responding to the *Kairos* of HIV/AIDS." *Theology Today* 65 (2008) 368–81.

Baker, Peta-Anne. "Of What Use Advocates and Ombudsmen?" *Jamaica Gleaner*, January 31, 2010. Online: http://mobile.jamaicagleaner.com/20100131/cleisure/cleisure4.php.

Barclay, William. *The Gospel of Luke*. Daily Study Bible. Edinburgh: Saint Andrew, 1975.

Barton, Richard D. E. *Afro-Creole: Power, Opposition, and Play in the Caribbean*. Ithaca, NY: Cornell University Press, 1997.

Bauer, Walter, et al. *A Greek-English Lexicon of the New Testament and Other Early Christian Literature*. 2nd ed. Chicago: University of Chicago Press, 1979.

Bebbington, David. "The Decline and Resurgence of Evangelical Social Concern 1918–1980." In *Evangelical Faith and Public Zeal*, edited by John Wolfe, 175–86. London: SPCK, 1995.

Beckford, Robert. *Jesus is Dread: Black Theology and Black Culture in Britain*. London: Blackwell, 1987.

Berger, Peter L. *The Sacred Canopy: Elements of a Sociological Theory of Religion*. New York: Doubleday, 1969.

Bibliography

Berger, Peter L., and Thomas Luckmann. *The Social Construction of Reality: A Treatise in the Sociology of Knowledge*. New York: Doubleday, 1966.

Bernard, April. "Emancipating Spirit: Decolonizing the Caribbean Religious Experience." *Wadabagei* 11/2 (2008) 49–64.

Bevans, Stephen B. *Models of Contextual Theology*. Rev. edition. Maryknoll, NY: Orbis, 2002.

Black, Clinton V. *History of Jamaica*. London: Collins, 1958.

Boff, Leonardo. *Cry of the Earth, Cry of the Poor*. Translated by Phillip Berryman. Ecology and Justice. Maryknoll, NY: Orbis, 1997.

Bogues, Tony. "Reflections on the Political Thought of Manley." In *Manley Farewell: A Scrapbook*, edited by Michael S. Archer, n.p. Kingston, Jamaica: Mowtown, 1997.

Boothe, Hyacinth I. "A Theological Journey for an Emancipatory Theology." *Caribbean Journal of Religious Studies* 17/1 (1996) 15–21.

Borg, Marcus J. *The Heart of Christianity: Rediscovering a Life of Faith*. New York: HarperCollins, 2003.

Bremer, Thomas, and Ulrich Fleischmann, editors. *Alternative Cultures in the Caribbean: First International Conference of the Society of Caribbean Research, Berlin, 1988*. Frankfurt: Vervuert, 1993.

Brueggemann, Walter. *Israel's Praise: Doxology against Idolatry and Ideology*. Philadelphia: Fortress, 1988.

———. *The Prophetic Imagination*. Rev. ed. Philadelphia: Fortress, 2001.

———. "A Shape for Old Testament Theology, I: Structure Legitimation." *Catholic Biblical Quarterly* 47/1 (1985) 28–46.

———. "Trajectories in Old Testament Literature and the Sociology of Ancient Israel." *Journal of Biblical Literature* 98/2 (1979) 161–85.

Brunner, Emil, and Karl Barth. *Natural Theology*. Translated by Peter Fraenkel. London: Bles, 1948.

Bryan, Patrick. *The Jamaican People 1880–1902: Race, Class, and Social Control*. Kingston, Jamaica: University of the West Indies Press, 2000.

Buddan, Robert. "The Reputation of the Jamaican State." *Jamaican Gleaner*, October 4, 2009. Online: http://www.jamaica-gleaner.com/gleaner/20091004/focus/focus5.html.

Campbell, Erica. "Christians and Jamaican Politics." In *Romans in Context*, edited by D. Vincent, 255–272. Eugene, OR: Resource, 2011.

Capelleveen, Remco van. "'Peripheral' Culture in the Metropolis: West Indians in New York City." In *Alternative Cultures in the Caribbean: First International Conference of the Society of Caribbean Research, Berlin, 1988*, edited by Thomas Bremer and Ulrich Fleischmann, 131–147. Frankfurt: Vervuert, 1993.

Chevannes, Barry. *Rastafari: Roots and Ideology*. Mona, Jamaica: University of the West Indies. 1995

Chisholm, Clinton. *Revelations on Ras Tafari*. Orlando: Xlibris, 2008.

Cohen, Abner. "A Polytechnic London Carnival as a Contested Cultural Performance." *Ethnic and Racial Studies* 5/1 (1982) 23–41.

Cole, John "What Can the Euro-Christian Churches in the Caribbean Learn from Indigenous Caribbean Religions?" *Caribbean Journal of Religious Studies* 21/1 (2007) 16–27.

Bibliography

Comblin, José. "La Iglesia Latinoamericana desde Puebla a Santa Domingo." In *Cambio Social y Pensamiento Cristiano en América Latina*, edited by José Comblin, José I. Gonzalez, and Jon Sobrino. Madrid: Editorial Trotta, 1993.

Cone, James H. *A Black Theology of Liberation*. Philadelphia and New York: Lippincott, 1970.

———. "Whose Earth Is It, Anyway?" In *Earth Habitat: Eco-Justice and the Church's Response*, edited by Dieter Hessel and Larry Rasmussen, 23–32. Minneapolis: Fortress, 2001.

Cosden, Darrell. *The Heavenly Good of Earthly Work*. Milton Keynes, UK: Paternoster, 2006.

Craig, Dennis R. *Teaching Language and Literacy: Policies and Procedures for Vernacular Situations*. Georgetown, Guyana: Education and Development Services, 1999.

Crouch, Andy. *Culture Making: Recovering Our Creative Calling*. Downers Grove, IL: IVP Academic, 2008.

Cummings, Mark. "No Cell Tower 'Roun Here!" *Jamaica Observer*, December 24, 2009. Online: http://www.jamaicaobserver.com/westernnews/No-cell-tower-24-12-09.

Davis, Kortright. *Emancipation Still Comin': Explorations in Caribbean Emancipatory Theology*. New York: Orbis, 1990.

Dawkins, Richard. *The God Delusion*. Boston: Houghton Mifflin, 2006.

De Vastey, P.-V. *An Essay on the Causes of the Revolution and Civil Wars of Hayti*. Translated by W. H. M. B. 1828. Reprint, New York: Negro Universities Press, 1969.

Devonish, Hubert. *Language and Liberation: Creole Language Politics in the Caribbean*. London: Karia, 1986.

Devonish, Hubert, and Karen Carpenter. "Towards Full Bilingualism in Education: The Jamaican Bilingual Primary Education Project." *Social and Economic Studies* 56/1–2 (2007) 277–303.

Dick, Devon. *The Cross and the Machete: Native Baptists in Jamaica: Identity, Ministry, and Legacy*. Kingston: Randle, 2010.

———. "The Origin and Development of the Native Baptists in Jamaica and the Influence of their Biblical Hermeneutic on the 1865 Native Baptists War." PhD diss., University of Warwick, 2008.

———. *Rebellion to Riot: The Jamaican Church in Nation Building*. Kingston, Jamaica: Randle, 2002.

Diedrick, Andrew. "Christian Ambassadors." *The Alternative* (1997) 5.

Downer, Andrea. "Plans in Place to Curb Wanton Behaviour in Jamaican Buses." *Trinidad & Tobago Guardian Online*, January 11, 2009. Online: http://www.guardian.co.tt/archives/features/life/2009/01/11/plans-place-curb-wanton-behaviour-jamaican-buses.

Drucker, Peter F., with Joseph A. Maciariello, *Management: Tasks, Responsibilities, Practices*. Rev. ed. New York: HarperCollins, 2008.

Dunkley, Alicia. "The Hero of AA Flight 331." *Jamaica Observer*, December 27, 2009. Online: http://www.jamaicaobserver.com/news/The-hero-of-AA-flight-331.

Dussel, Enrique. *Teologia de la Liberacion: Un Panorama de Su Desarrollo*. Mexico City: Potrerillos Editores, 1995.

Earle, Robbie, with Daniel Davies. *One Love: The Reggae Boyz and the 1998 World Cup*. London: Andre Deustche, 1999.

Bibliography

Edmonds, Ennis. *Rastafari: From Outcasts to Culture Bearers*. Oxford: Oxford University Press, 2003.

Edmonds, Ennis, and Michelle Gonzalez. *Caribbean Religious History*. New York: New York University Press, 2010.

Edwards, Webster. "900% Increase in Murder Rate over 30 Years." *Jamaica Observer*, September 14, 1998.

Ellis, E. Earle. *The Gospel of Luke*. New Century Bible Commentary. 1974. Reprint, Eugene, OR: Wipf & Stock, 2003.

Evans, Craig. *Fabricating Jesus: How Modern Scholars Distort the Gospels*. Downers Grove, IL: InterVarsity, 2006.

Flett, Eric G. *Persons, Powers, and Pluralities: Toward a Trinitarian Theology of Culture*. Eugene, OR: Wipf & Stock, 2011.

Forrester, Duncan B. *Christian Justice and Public Policy*. Cambridge Studies in Ideology and Religion 10. Cambridge: Cambridge University Press, 1997.

France, R. T. *The Gospel according to Matthew*. Grand Rapids: Eerdmans, 1985.

Franklyn, Delano, editor. *Michael Manley: The Politics of Equality*. Kingston, Jamaica: Barnes, 2009.

Fretheim, Terence E. *God and World in the Old Testament: A Relational Theology of Creation*. Nashville: Abingdon, 2005.

———. "Salvation in the Bible vs. Salvation in the Church." *Word & World* 13/4 (1993) 363–372.

Galston, William. "A Liberal of Equality of Opportunity." In *Equality: Selected Readings*, edited by Louis Pojman and Robert Westmoreland. Oxford: Oxford University Press, 1997.

Garvey, Marcus. "Speech of Marcus Garvey." In *The Marcus Garvey and Universal Negro Improvement Association Papers*, edited by Robert A. Hill and Barbara Bair, 7:788–94. Berkley: University of California Press, 1990.

Gathercole, S. J. "The Critical and Dogmatic Agenda of Albert Schweitzer's *Quest of the Historical Jesus*." *Tyndale Bulletin* 51/2 (2000) 261–83.

Geffré, Claude, and Gustavo Gutiérrez, editors. *The Mystical and Political Dimensions of the Christian Faith*. Concilium 96. New York: Herder & Herder, 1974.

Gerig, Zenas. "Why the Association of Evangelical Churches?" Paper Prepared for Discussion at the July 2 meeting of Pastors at the Emmanuel Missionary Church, Mandeville, Jamaica, 1969.

Glaser, Ida. "Authority, Identity, and the Establishment of the People of God: Understanding the Political Challenge of Islam." *Binah* 2 (1997) 77–91. Online: http://www.biblicalstudies.org.uk/pdf/binah/02_077.pdf.

Gooding, David W. *According to Luke: A New Exposition of the Third Gospel*. Grand Rapids: Eerdmans, 1987.

Gordon, Ernle. "The Church and Religious Imperialism." *Jamaica Observer*, January 15, 2003.

———. "Emancipatory Theology (A Theological Journey)." *Caribbean Journal of Religious Studies* 17/1 (1996) 22–37.

Gosse, Dave St. Aubyn. "The Impact of the Haitian Revolution on the Emancipation of Slavery in Jamaica." *Caribbean Journal of Evangelical Theology* 9 (2005) 79–96.

Green, Joel B. *The Gospel of Luke*. New International Commentary on the New Testament. Grand Rapids: Eerdmans, 1997.

Bibliography

Griffin, Susan. *Woman and Nature: The Roaring Inside Her*. New York: Harper & Row, 1978.
Gutiérrez, Gustavo. *The Power of the Poor in History: Selected Writings*. London: SCM, 1983.
———. *A Theology of Liberation*. Maryknoll, NY: Orbis, 1973.
Hadjiantoniou, George. *Learning the Basics of New Testament Greek*. Chattanooga, TN: AMG, 1998.
Hall, Catherine. *White, Male, and Middle Class*. Cambridge: Polity, 1992.
Hall, William. "Today is JAE Sunday." *Jamaica Gleaner*, October 11, 1981.
Henry-Lee, Aldrie, et al. *An Assessment of the Standard of Living and Coping Strategies of Workers in Selected Occupations Who Earn a Minimum Wage*. Kingston, Jamaica: Planning Institute of Jamaica, 2001.
Heuman, Gad. *The Killing Time: The Morant Bay Rebellion in Jamaica*. London and Knoxville, TN: University of Tennessee Press, 1994.
Hicks, Douglas A. *Inequality and Christian Ethics*. Cambridge: Cambridge University Press, 2000.
Hiebert, Theodore. "Re-Imaging Nature: Shifts in Biblical Interpretation." *Interpretation* 50 (1996) 36–46.
Hill, Errol. "Traditional Figures in Carnival: Their Preservation, Development, and Interpretation." *Caribbean Quarterly* 31/2 (1985) 14–34.
Hollenbach, David. "Faith in Public." In *The Global Face of Public Faith: Politics, Human Rights, and Christian Ethics*. Washington DC: Georgetown University Press, 2003.
HoSang, David, and Roger Ringenberg. "Towards Evangelical Caribbean Theology." *Evangelical Review of Theology* 7/1 (1983) 125–47.
Hultgren, Arland. *The Parables of Jesus: A Commentary*. The Bible in Its World. Grand Rapids: Eerdmans, 2000.
Hyatt, Charles. *When I Was a Bway*. Kingston, Jamaica: Institute of Jamaica, 1984.
"If Mr Golding is to Be Great." Editorial. *Jamaica Gleaner*, December 14, 2009. Online: http://www.jamaica-gleaner.com/gleaner/20091214/cleisure/cleisure1.html.
Isichei, Elizabeth. *A History of Christianity in Africa*. London: SPCK. 1995
Jennings, Stephen C. A. "Caribbean Theology or Theologies of the Caribbean." *Caribbean Journal of Religious Studies* 8/2 (1987) 1–9.
———. "'Ordinary' Reading in 'Extraordinary' Times: A Jamaican Love Story." In *Reading Other-Wise: Socially Engaged Biblical Scholars Reading with Their Local Communities*, edited by Gerald O. West. Atlanta: SBL, 2007.
Jenson, Robert W. *Systematic Theology*. Vol. 2, *The Works of God*. Oxford: Oxford University Press, 1999.
Jeremias, Joachim. *New Testament Theology: The Proclamation of Jesus*. New York: Scribner's, 1971.
Johnston, Anthony. *A History of Kingston College, 1925–1995: The Building of Character*. Kingston, Jamaica: Teejay, 1997.
Johnstone, P. J. *Operation World*. 4th ed. Kent: Send the Light Trust, 1986.
Jones, David. "The Bankruptcy of Prosperity Theology." Bible.org. Online: http://bible.org/article/bankruptcy-prosperity-gospel-exercise-biblical-and-theological-ethics.
Kato, Byang H. *Biblical Christianity in Africa*. Lagos, Nigeria: ACP, 1985.
Kee, Alastair. *Marx and the Failure of Liberation Theology*. London: SCM, 1990.

Bibliography

Kingston Keswick 50th Anniversary Commemorative Magazine 1960-2010. Kingston, Jamaica, 2010.

Kraft, Charles H. *Anthropology for Christian Witness*. New York: Orbis, 2001.

Lacey, Hugh. "Catholic Social Thought and Economic Systems: Capitalism and Socialism." In *Rerum Novarum: A Symposium Celebrating 100 years of Catholic Social Thought*, edited by Ronald F. Duska, 135-64. Lewiston, NY: Mellen, 1991.

Ladd, G. E. *The Presence of the Future: The Eschatology of Biblical Realism*. Grand Rapids: Eerdmans, 1974.

Lamming, George. "Opening Address, The Plenaries, Conference on Caribbean Culture in Honour of Rex Nettleford." *Caribbean Quarterly* 43/1-2 (1997) 6.

Lane, William. *The Gospel of Mark*. New International Commentary on the New Testament. Grand Rapids: Eerdmans, 1974.

Lee, Youg-hoon. *The Holy Spirit Movement in Korea: Its Historical and Theological Development*. Eugene, OR: Wipf & Stock, 2009.

Linton, Faith. *What the Preacher Forgot to Tell Me: Identity and Gospel in Jamaica*. Pickering, Ontario: Bay Ridge, 2009.

Lipner, Julius. "Religion and Religious Thinking in the New Millennium." In *Plurality, Power, and Mission: Intercontextual Theological Explorations on the Role of Religion in the New Millennium*, edited by Philip L. Wickeri, Janice K. Wickeri, and Damayanthi M. A. Niles, 83-97. London: Council for World Mission, 2000.

Lutton, Daraine. "Time for a New Nation." *Jamaica Gleaner*, August 5, 2010. Online: http://mobile.jamaica-gleaner.com/gleaner/20100805/lead/lead3.php.

Mandela, Nelson. *Long Walk to Freedom: The Autobiography of Nelson Mandela*. Boston: Back Bay, 1995.

Manley, Michael. "No Turning Back." Budget Speech, May 12, 1976. In *Michael Manley: The Politics of Equality*, edited by Delano Franklyn. Kingston, Jamaica: Barnes, 2009.

———. "The Policy of the People's National Party." Unpublished speech given at Denbigh, Jamaica, 1974.

———. "The Politics of Change." Budget Speech, May 2, 1973. In *Michael Manley: The Politics of Equality*, edited by Delano Franklyn. Kingston, Jamaica: Barnes, 2009.

———. *The Politics of Change: A Jamaican Testament*. Rev. ed. Washington, DC: Howard University Press, 1990.

McGavran, Donald A. *Church Growth in Jamaica*. Upper Punjab, India: Lucknow, 1962.

McGrath, Alister. *Evangelicalism and the Future of Christianity*. Downers Grove, IL: InterVarsity, 1995.

Mendes, John. *Cote Ci Cote La: Trinidad and Tobago*. Rev. ed. Trinidad: New Millenium, 1986.

Metzger, Bruce M. *A Textual Commentary on the Greek New Testament*. 2nd ed.; London: United Bible Societies, 1994.

Middleton, J. Richard. "Identity and Subversion in Babylon: Strategies for 'Resisting against the System' in the Music of Bob Marley and the Wailers." In *Religion, Culture, and Tradition in the Caribbean*, edited by Hemchand Gossai and N. Samuel Murrell, 181-204. New York: St. Martin's, 2000.

———. "Is Creation Theology Inherently Conservative? A Dialogue with Walter Brueggemann." *Harvard Theological Review* 87/3 (1994) 257-77.

———. *The Liberating Image: The Imago Dei in Genesis 1*. Grand Rapids: Brazos, 2005.

———. "A New Heaven and a New Earth: The Case for a Holistic Reading of the Biblical Story of Redemption." *Journal for Christian Theological Research* 11 (2006) 73–97. Online: http://www.luthersem.edu/ctrf/JCTR/Vol11/Middleton_vol11.pdf.
Middleton, J. Richard, and Michael J. Gorman. "Salvation." In *New Interpreter's Dictionary of the Bible*, edited by Katharine Doob Sakenfeld et al., 5:45–61. Nashville: Abingdon, 2009.
Middleton, J. Richard, and Brian J. Walsh. *Truth Is Stranger than It Used to Be: Biblical Faith in a Postmodern Age*. Downers Grove, IL: IVP, 1995.
Miller, Donald G. *The Gospel according to Luke*. The Layman's Bible Commentary 18. Atlanta: Knox, 1959.
Miller, Errol. "Contemporary Issues in Jamaican Education." In *Education in Central America and the Caribbean*, edited by Colin Brock and Donald R. Clarkson. New York: Routledge, 1990.
Miller, Michael. "Impulses in Caribbean Theology." Paper presented at the Meeting of the Network on Theological Inquiry, Hong Kong, China, 1998.
Moltmann, Jürgen. *A Broad Place: An Autobiography*. Translated by Margaret Kohl. Minneapolis: Fortress, 2008.
———. "On Latin American Liberation Theology: An Open Letter to José Miguez Bonino." *Christianity and Crisis* 36 (1976) 57–63.
Morris, Leon. *The Gospel according to St. Luke: An Introduction and Commentary*. Tyndale New Testament Commentaries. Grand Rapids: Eerdmans, 1974.
Müller-Fahrenholz, Geiko. *The Art of Forgiveness: Theological Reflections on Healing and Reconciliation*. Geneva: WCC, 1997.
Mulrain, George, "The Use of Senses in Worship." *Caribbean Journal of Religious Studies* 17/2 (1996) 32–38.
Murray, Iain. *The Puritan Hope*. London, UK: Banner of Truth Trust, 1971.
Murrell, Nathaniel Samuel, William David Spencer, and Adrian Anthony McFarlane, editors. *Chanting Down Babylon: The Rastafari Reader*. Philadelphia: Temple University Press, 1998.
Mutabaruka. "Rasta from Experience." In *Rastafari: A Universal Philosophy in the Third Millennium*, edited by Werner Zips. Kingston, Jamaica: Randle, 2006.
Muysken, Peter, and Norval Smith. "The Study of Pidgin and Creole Languages." In *Pidgins and Creoles: An Introduction*, edited by Jacques Arends, Pieter Muysken, and Norval Smith, 3–14. Amsterdam: Benjamins, 1995.
Naipaul, V. S. *The Middle Passage*. London: Deutsch, 1962.
Nettleford, Rex M. *Mirror, Mirror: Identity, Race, and Protest in Jamaica*. Kingston, Jamaica: Collins & Sangster, 1970.
Newman, Las. "The Caribbean Response to the Great Commission: History and Models." *Caribbean Journal of Evangelical Theology* 1 (1997) 16–32.
———. "Mission from the Margin: A Critical Analysis of the Participation of West Indians as Agents of Christian Mission in the Western Missionary Enterprise in Africa in the Nineteenth Century, with Special Reference to their Conception of Christian Mission." PhD diss., University of Wales, 2007.
Noëlliste, Dieumeme. "The Church and Human Emancipation: A Critical Comparison of Liberation Theology and the Latin American Theological Fraternity." PhD diss., Northwestern University, 1987.
———. "Faith Transforming Context: In Search of a Theology for a Viable Caribbean." *Evangelical Review of Theology* 20/4 (1996) 327–42.

Bibliography

———. "Transcendent but Not Remote: The Caribbean." In *The Global God: Multicultural Evangelical Views of God*, edited by Aida Besancon Spencer and William David Spencer, 104–26. Grand Rapids: Baker, 1998.

Noëlliste, Dieumeme, and Sung Wook Chung. "A Theology of Political Engagement." In *Christianity and Political Engagement*, edited by Dieumeme Noelliste and M. Daniel Carroll R. [Rodas], 33–47. Denver, CO: Vernon Grounds Institute of Public Ethics, 2009.

Noll, Mark. *The Scandal of the Evangelical Mind*. Grand Rapids: Eerdmans, 1995.

Obama, Barack. *The Audacity of Hope*. New York: Vantage, 2006.

Oliver, Anthony. "Salvation as Justice in Amos 5:18–27: Implications for Jamaica." MA thesis, Caribbean Graduate School of Theology, 1991.

O'Marde, Dorbrene E. "Calypso in the 1990s." *Antigua Carnival Souvenir Magazine* (1990).

Page, Hugh R., Jr., et al., editors. *The Africana Bible: Reading Israel's Scriptures from Africa and the African Diaspora*. Minneapolis: Fortress, 2009.

Palmer, Delano Vincent. *Messianic "I" and Rastafari in New Testament Dialogue: BioNarratives, the Apocalypse, and Paul's Letter to the Romans*. Lanham, MD: University Press of America, 2010.

Panton, David. *Jamaica's Michael Manley: The Great Transformation (1972–1992)*. Kingston, Jamaica: Henry, 1993.

Payne, Clifford. "What Will A Caribbean Christ Look Like? A Preface to Caribbean Christology." In *Out of the Depths*, edited by Idris Hamid, 1–8. San Fernando, Trinidad: St. Andrews Theological College, 1977.

Perkins, Anna Kasafi. *Justice as Equality: Michael Manley's Caribbean Vision of Justice*. American University Studies Series VII: Theology and Religion 309. New York: Lang, 2010.

Persaud, Winston. "Caribbean Response to the Globalization of Theological Education." In *Caribbean Theology: Preparing for the Challenges Ahead*, edited by Howard Gregory, 35–50. Kingston, Jamaica: University of the West Indies, 1995.

Petrella, Ivan. *The Future of Liberation Theology: An Argument and Manifesto*. London: SCM, 2006.

Pico della Mirandola, Giovanni. *Oration on the Dignity of Man*. Translated by A. Robert Caponigri. Chicago: Regnery, 1965.

Plummer, Orville. "A Survey of Members of the Jamaican Clergy concerning the Church and Christian Political Involvement." Unpublished paper, Jamaica Theological Seminary, 1996.

Pojman, Louis. "On Equal Human Worth: A Critique of Contemporary Egalitarianism." In *Equality: Selected Readings*, edited by Louis Pojman and Robert Westmoreland, 282–99. Oxford: Oxford University Press, 1997.

"Positive Confession." Watchman Fellowship. Online: http://www.watchman.org/articles/other-religious-topics/positive-confession/.

Rad, Gerhard von. *Old Testament Theology*. Vol. 1, *The Theology of Israel's Historical Traditions*, translated by D. M. Stalker. New York: Harper & Row, 1962.

———. "The Theological Problem of the Old Testament Doctrine of Creation." In *Creation in the Old Testament*, edited by Bernhard W. Anderson, 55–61. Philadelphia: Fortress, 1984.

———. *Wisdom in Israel*. Translated by James D. Martin. Nashville: Abingdon, 1972.

Reid-Salmon, Delroy A. *Home away from Home: The Caribbean Diasporan Church in the Black Atlantic Tradition*. Cross Cultural Theologies. London: Equinox, 2008.
Richardson, Alan. *The Gospel according to St. John*. London: SCM, 1959.
———. *An Introduction to the Theology of the New Testament*. London: SCM, 1966.
Ridderbos, Herman. *The Coming of the Kingdom*. Philadelphia: Presbyterian & Reformed, 1962.
Rigby, Cynthia L. "Exploring Our Hesitation: Feminist Theologies and the Nurture of Children." *Theology Today* 56/4 (2000) 540–54.
Rigenberg, Roger. *History of the Jamaica Theological Seminary 1960–1992*. DMiss diss., Trinity International University, 1993.
Robertson, Pat. "The Secret of Financial Prosperity." CBN.com. Online: http://www.cbn.com/spirituallife/CBNTeachingSheets/Pat_Perspective_financial_prosperity.aspx.
Rodman, Selden. *Haiti: The Black Republic*. 2nd ed. Old Greenwich, CT: Devin-Adair, 1973.
Roper, Garnett. "Moving Forward: Celebrating 50 years." *Jamaica Theological Seminary Anniversary Newsletter*, 2010.
———. "Racism and Christianity in the Caribbean." In *The Cambridge Dictionary of Christianity*, edited by Daniel Patte, 1044–45. Cambridge: Cambridge University Press, 2010.
Russell, Horace O. "The Emergence of the 'Christian Black' Concept: The Making of a Stereotype." *Caribbean Journal of Religious Studies* 2/1 (1979) 1–17.
Russell, Sherina. "Manley Lauded at Women's Day Opening Ceremony." In *Manley Farewell: A Scrapbook*, edited by Michael S. Archer, n.p. Kingston, Jamaica: Mowtown, 1997.
Sangster, Alfred. "Education and Training: Key Elements in the Development Process." In *Jamaica: Preparing for the Twenty-first Century*, edited by Patsy Lewis. Kingston, Jamaica: Randle, 1997.
Schweitzer, Albert. *The Quest of the Historical Jesus*. Edited by John Bowden. Translated by W. Montgomery et al. Minneapolis: Fortress, 2001.
Seaga, Edward. "Popular Religion: Its Dimension and Types." *Caribbean Quarterly* 43/1 (1997) 88.
Sen, Amartya. *Development as Freedom*. New York: Anchor, 1999.
Sherlock, Hugh. *Eternal Father, Bless Our Land: Father Hugh Sherlock*. Kingston, Jamaica: Henry, 2000.
Sherlock, Philip, and Hazel Bennett. *The Story of the Jamaican People*. Kingston, Jamaica: Randle, 1998.
Sitahal, Harold. "Caribbean Theology: Of the People/for the People." *Caribbean Journal of Religious Studies* 20/2 (1999) 3–17.
Smith, Ashley. "The Christian Minister as a Political Activist." *Caribbean Journal of Religious Studies* 19 (1998) 4–13.
———. *Emerging from Innocence: Religion, Theology, and Development*. Mandeville, Jamaica: Eureka, 1991.
———. *Pentecostalism in Jamaica: A Challenge to the Established Churches and Socitey*. Mandeville, Jamaica: Eureka, 1993.
———. *Real Roots and Potted Plants: Reflections on the Caribbean Church*. Mandeville, Jamaica: Eureka, 1984.

Bibliography

Smith, Christian. *What Is A Person? Rethinking Humanity, Social Life, and the Moral Good from the Person up.* Chicago: University of Chicago Press, 2010.

Smith, Donald K. *Creating Understanding: A Handbook for Christian Communication across Cultural Landscapes.* Grand Rapids: Zondervan, 1992.

Spradley, James P. *The Ethnographic Interview.* Belmont, CA: Wadsworth, 1979.

Spaulding, Gary. "Gang Data off the Mark—PMI." *Jamaica Gleaner*, February 22, 2010. Online: http://www.jamaica-gleaner.com/gleaner/20100222/lead/lead6.html.

Stott, John R. W. *The Contemporary Christian.* Leicester, UK: InterVarsity, 1992.

Tano, R. D. "Towards an Evangelical Asian Theology." *Evangelical Review of Theology* 7 (1985) 175–87.

Taylor, Burchell K. "Abolished but Not Destroyed: Remembering the Slave Trade in the 21st Century." Lecture delivered at Runaway Bay, Jamaica, 2007.

———. *The Church Taking Sides: A Contextual Reading of the Letters to the Seven Churches in the Book of Revelation.* Kingston, Jamaica: BBC, 1995.

———. "Editorial." *Caribbean Journal of Religious Studies* 12/1 (1991) 2.

———. "Engendering Theological Relevance." *Caribbean Journal of Religious Studies* 20/2 (1999) 24–30.

———. "Messianic Ideology and Caribbean Theology of Liberation." In *Chanting Down Babylon: The Rastafari Reader*, edited by Nathaniel Samuel Murrell, William David Spencer, and Adrian Anthony McFarlane, 390–414. Philadelphia: Temple University Press, 1998.

———. "Stepping Out of the Shadow of Empire." The Swope Lecture, delivered at the University of Puget Sound, Tacoma, WA, March, 2004.

Thiselton, Anthony C. *The Two Horizons: New Testament Hermeneutics and Philosophical Description.* Grand Rapids: Eerdmans, 1980.

Thomas, C. Adrian. *A Case for Mixed-Audience with Reference to the Warning Passages in the Book of Hebrews.* New York: Lang, 2008.

Thomas, Donovan. *Confronting Suicide.* Kingston, Jamaica: Choose Life, 2010.

Thomas, Oral A. W. *Biblical Resistance Hermeneutics within a Caribbean Context.* London: Equinox, 2010.

Thompson, Livingstone. "Dr. Lewin Williams and Caribbean Theology." Guest column. *Jamaica Gleaner*, October 1, 2006.

Torrance, T. F. *Divine and Contingent Order.* Oxford: Oxford University Press, 1981.

———. "The Goodness and Dignity of Man in the Christian Tradition." In *Christ in Our Place: The Humanity of God in Christ for the Reconciliation of the World. Essays Presented to Professor James B. Torrance*, edited by Trevor A. Hart and Daniel P. Thimell, 369–87. Allison Park, PA: Pickwick, 1989.

———. *Reality and Scientific Theology.* Vol. 1, *Theology and Science at the Frontiers of Knowledge.* Edinburgh: Scottish Academic, 1985.

———. *Theology in Reconstruction.* London: SCM, 1965.

———. *The Trinitarian Faith: The Evangelical Theology of the Ancient Catholic Church.* Edinburgh: T. & T. Clark, 1988.

Turner, Victor. "The Sprit of Celebration." In *The Celebration of Society: Perspectives on Contemporary Cultural Performance*, edited by Frank Manning, 187–91. Bowling Green, OH: Bowling Green State University Press, 1983.

Tyrrell, George. *Christianity at the Cross-Roads.* London, UK: Longmans, Green, 1909.

Tyson, Esther. "The Church and the Nation." *Jamaica Gleaner*, January 3, 2010.

———. "Transportation Centre: Blessing or Curse?" *Jamaica Gleaner*, April, 5, 2009.

Unger, R. M. *Politics: A Work in Constructive Social Theory.* Cambridge: Cambridge University Press, 1987.
Vanhoozer, Kevin J. "'One Rule to Rule Them All?' Theological Method in an Era of World Christianity." In *Globalizing Theology: Belief and Practice in an Era of World Christianity,* edited by Craig Ott and Harold A. Netland, 85–126. Grand Rapids: Baker Academic, 2006.
Vassel, Samuel Carl W. "Understanding and Addressing Male Absence from the Jamaican Church." DMin diss., Columbia Theological Seminary/United Theological College, 1997.
Vlastos, Gregory. "Justice and Equality." In *Social Justice,* edited by Richard B. Brandt, 31–72. Englewood Cliffs, NJ: Prentice-Hall, 1962.
Vos, Geerhardus. *The Kingdom of God and the Church.* Phillipsburg, NJ: Presbyterian & Reformed, 1979.
Walker, Karyl. "False Gospel: Pastor Scolds Preachers of Prosperity Doctrine." *Jamaica Observer,* February 1, 2010. Online: http://www.jamaicaobserver.com/news/prosperity-gospel_7377441#ixzz1DM6Rt4Mn.
Wallis, Jim. *God's Politics: Why the Right Gets it Wrong and the Left Doesn't Get it.* San Francisco: HarperSanFrancisco, 2005.
Watty, William. "The Creator of the Young Culture." Sermon in Watty, *From Shore to Shore: Soundings in Caribbean Theology.* Barbados: Cedar, 1981.
Weir, Emmette J. "Towards a Caribbean Liberation Theology." *Caribbean Journal of Religious Studies* 12/1 (1991) 41–53.
Wells, David. *No Place for Truth, or Whatever Happened to Evangelical Theology?* Grand Rapids: Eerdmans, 1993.
West, Cornell. "Nelson Mandela: Great Exemplar of the Grand Democratic Tradition." In *The Meaning of Mandela: A Literary and Intellectual Celebration,* edited by Xolela Mangcu, 13–23. Cape Town: HSRC, 2006.
West, Gerald. "The Bible and the Poor: A New Way of Doing Theology." In *The Cambridge Companion to Liberation Theology,* edited by Christopher Rowland, 129–52. Cambridge Companions to Religion. Cambridge: Cambridge University Press, 1999.
Westermann, Claus. *Blessing in the Bible and in the Life of the Church.* Translated by Keith R. Crim. Overtures to Biblical Theology. Philadelphia: Fortress, 1978.
———. *What Does the Old Testament Say About God?* Edited by Friedemann W. Golka. Atlanta: John Knox, 1979.
Williams, Lewin L. *Caribbean Theology.* Research in Religion and Family: Black Perspectives 2. New York: Lang, 1994.
———. "Editorial." *Caribbean Journal of Religious Studies* 20 (1999) 2.
———. "The Indigenization of Theology in the Caribbean." PhD diss., Union Theological Seminary, 1989.
———. "What, Why, and Wherefore of Caribbean Theology." *Caribbean Journal of Religious Studies* 12/1 (1991) 29–40.
Wilson, Nadine. "Portmore Missionary Impacts Community with Social Outreach." *Jamaica Observer,* December 13, 2009. Online: http://www.jamaicaobserver.com/news/Portmore-Missionary-impacts/.
Winer, Lise, editor. *Dictionary of the English/Creole of Trinidad and Tobago.* Montreal, Québec: McGill-Queen's University Press, 2009.

Bibliography

Witvliet, Theo. *A Place in the Sun: An Introduction to Liberation Theology in the Third World*. London: SCM, 1985.

Wolters, A. M. "The Foundational Command: 'Subdue the Earth!'" In *Year of Jubilee; Cultural Mandate; Worldview*, edited by B. van der Walt, 27–32. Study Pamphlet 382. Potchefstroom, South Africa: Institute for Reformational Studies, 1999.

Wright, G. Ernst. "How Did Early Israel Differ from Her Neighbors?" *Biblical Archeologist* 6 (1943) 1–21.

———. *The Old Testament against Its Environment*. Studies in Biblical Theology 2. London: SCM, 1950.

Wright, N. T. *The Challenge of Jesus: Rediscovering Who Jesus Was and Is*. Downers Grove, IL: InterVarsity, 1999.

———. *Jesus and the Victory of God*. Christian Origins and the Question of God 2. Minneapolis: Fortress, 1996.

———. *The Lord and His Prayer*. Grand Rapids: Eerdmans, 1996.

———. *The Resurrection of the Son of God*. Christian Origins and the Question of God 3. Minneapolis: Fortress, 2003.

———. *Simply Christian: Why Christianity Makes Sense*. New York: HarperCollins, 2006.

Wüst, Ruth. "The Trinidad Carnival: A Medium of Social Change." In *Alternative Cultures in the Caribbean: First International Conference of the Society of Caribbean Research, Berlin, 1988*, edited by Thomas Bremer and Ulrich Fleischmann, 149–60. Frankfurt: Vervuert, 1993.

———. "The Trinidad Carnival from Canboulay to Pretty Mass." MA thesis, Berlin, 1987.

Wuthnow, Robert, et al. *Cultural Analysis: The Work of Peter L. Berger, Mary Douglas, Michel Foucault, and Jürgen Habermas*. London: Routledge, 1984.

Yeung, Hing Kau. *Being and Knowing: An Examination of T. F. Torrance's Christological Science*. Jian Dao Dissertation Series 3; Theology and Culture 1. Hong Kong: Alliance Bible Seminary, 1996.

Yorke, Gosnell L. "Bible Translation in Africa: An Afrocentric Perspective." *Bible Translator* 50/1 (2000) 114–23.

———. "Bible Translation in Anglophone Africa and Her Diaspora: A Postcolonialist Agenda." *Black Theology* 2 (2004) 153–66.

———. "Haiti's Rescue: Apparent or Real?" *Jamaica Gleaner*, January 28, 2010. Online: http://www.jamaicagleaner.com/gleaner/20100128/cleisure/cleisure2.html.

www.ingramcontent.com/pod-product-compliance
Lightning Source LLC
Chambersburg PA
CBHW051637230426
43669CB00013B/2345